SOMEBODY'S
GOT TO DO IT

SELECTED WRITINGS BY PAVEL BÜCHLER SINCE 1987

SOMEBODY'S GOT TO DO IT

SELECTED WRITINGS BY PAVEL BÜCHLER SINCE 1987

EDITED BY
NICK THURSTON

RIDINGHOUSE

FOREWORD

Planning for this book took seed in 2012 and editorial work began soon after. Between then and now – as might be deduced from the long bibliography at the back of this book – much effort has been made to filter and organise a selection that is both manageable and thematically comprehensive, albeit not exhaustive. As a writer and cultural activist, Pavel Büchler was a participant in Prague's samizdat communities before he left Czechoslovakia for England, via Paris, in 1981. He could speak and read very little English when he arrived. Although he began to write press releases and exhibition leaflets in 1985, it was another two years before his language proficiency allowed him to begin publishing regularly if unconfidently in a context where he feels, to this day, other to the mother tongue, hence this book's subtitle and start date.

Chronology alone seemed an inadequate principle for arranging 30 years of commentary, criticism and interventions given the stretch of interests and experiences Büchler talks from and to as an outsider on the inside. Accordingly, the selections that follow are pooled in three parent sections, each running from the oldest to newest by date of authorship not publication, and which together cover seven thematic areas. Section One includes a sample of his exhibition and book reviews and a spread of his more systematic writings on analogue media and their afterlives in our digital age. Section Two gathers articles and lecture scripts on the topic of teaching art and design and what I would call cultural theory with a small 't'. Section Three presents a selection of more discursive, formally playful contributions to catalogues and artist's pages – only including those that could be reproduced in plain text – as well as an extensive new interview prepared during winter 2014–15 for this book.

I am hugely grateful to the Ridinghouse team for indulging my focus on the abstract, macro and poetic aspects of Büchler's relationship to writing in both that interview and my introductory essay, where the problematic so central to his thinking and making – the 'question of work' as it is asked by and of art – is used to contextualise rather than explain what follows. This book extends over a decade of collaborations between Büchler and I, and it has unfolded, like those previous projects, as a kind of long conversation between two artists. Collecting this material would not have been possible without his willingness to talk, question and share, for all of which I am sincerely grateful. Equally, the generous assistance of both the Henry Moore

Foundation and the Paul Mellon Centre for Studies in British Art, as well as the support of annex14, Tanya Leighton and Tommy Simoens, have all been invaluable. Of course there are too many people who deserve our thanks than readers should have to endure reading about, but this first edition would not have been possible without the support of Louise Clarke, the Laurent Fiévet collection, Francis Gruwez, Sylvia Furrer Hoffmann & Holger Hoffmann, Claes Nordenhake, Herald Spengler, Peter Stämpfli, Simon Starling, Jobst Wagner and Melanie Wagner. I hope that what follows will repay the kindness of everyone involved.

WORK FROM NOUN TO VERB TO NOUN TO VERB ETC.

For poetry makes nothing happen: it survives
In the valley of its making where executives
Would never want to tamper, flows on south
From ranches of isolation and the busy griefs,
Raw towns that we believe and die in; it survives,
A way of happening, a mouth.
– WH Auden, 1939

At the end of an interview – one of many recorded in preparation for this book – I asked Pavel Büchler how it felt to look back at the range of English-language texts he had written about art during the last 30 years. His reply, parenthesised between long drags on a cigarette, expressed something closer to trauma than I had expected. In skimming floppy discs, remote servers and print archives to help me compile this collection, he had been reminded over and again of the contradictions in his own thinking, of the tortuousness he associates with writing anything for publication, of the disciplining effects of writing to word count for money, of the extent of his dyslexia, and of the blunt though layered shocks of migrating in 1981 to a language and West that he had known less about than he expected. Though part charming self-deprecation, Büchler's answer gives private reasons for the generally short length, meditative mode of analysis and playful rhetorics of the texts that follow, which range from magazine reviews, to essays, to lecture transcripts, to catalogue notes. However, locked though each of these texts is in its own complicated triangle between form, content and original context, what they all address are the limits and/or consequences of mediation – be that by the lens of a camera, or the words of a language, or the curriculums of an academy – for the phenomenal and epistemological status of the thing-in-itself, for the subject-status of those being mediated by or for the cultural and educational industries, and for our collective ability to communicate, miscommunicate or excommunicate certain aspects of life through the doing of doing art. These limits and/or consequences are worth writing about, he reminds us in turns directly then elliptically, because they are shared or public problems that constitute important aspects of our sociality, not least what art can allow people to think and to do.

The contents of this book do not *explain* Büchler's art work – an interpretative trap he has always avoided as a matter of principle, out of respect for both the object and viewer – but they do contextualise in three other ways what I would call his praxis, as a teacher, occasional critic and curator and foremost as an artist. This book organises Büchler's published writings since 1987 into three sections, each of which is chronologised. Between each of those sections I offer discrete readings, labelled Editor's Notes, each of which focuses on the poetic status of language in the foreground of one of Büchler's recent gallery works, to loop attention back to the interplay between what he writes about art and what he writes in his art. But to begin with, by way of a key rather than spoiler, I want to draw attention to the importance of the concept of work, as a practical and conceptual anchor, or polysemic false anchor, to anyone wanting to read Büchler's work.

The back and forth between making and critical reflection, between doing and thinking, which was collapsed for artists and viewers into the doing of thinking by strongly Conceptual art of the late 1960s, changed the artistic licence for all those who have practised since, not least by further complicating what we mean by 'work' when we talk about art work (pp.126–29).[i] In the context of art, 'work' always refers to a thing and an action through the form of a thing (being) done; and that oscillatory value complicates every approach we can make to exploring, let alone analysing or teaching, what art working can do *or* how art can work in what Büchler calls its 'social destinations'.[ii] Büchler works with this rhythm by elaborating the oscillation, from noun to verb, that constitutes every effort we can make to represent art work. In doing so he subtly continues a tradition of critical artistry that negates the idea of making as *merely* practical – as if making were isolated from thinking – in the synthesis of praxis. The Marxist notion of praxis describes the productive combination of practical and theoretical work as the *mode* of man's *being* freely creative, which can take positive or negative forms depending on how each action relates to the conditions of alienation (of the self and the we).[iii] It is the plural horizons of artistic praxes and their complicated embeddedness in the whole of life, posed by artists and their work as something we might call 'the question of work', that seems to reflexively underwrite Büchler's mode of praxis.[iv]

The titles of Büchler's first two museum retrospectives, *Absentminded-windowgazing* at Kunsthalle Bern (2006) and Van Abbemuseum (2007) and *Labour in Vain* at DOX Centre for Contemporary Art (2010), couch their contents in this question of work. In turn their contents, including *The List*

(2003, pp.82–84), *Limitation* (2007, pp.166–68) and *Il Castello* (2007, pp.228–30), direct that question back at their audience through specific acts of labour, reproduction, quotation, irrelation, excessive attention and *désoeuvrement* (unworking). Those cross-references stage the exhibits atop the platform of critical modernism, nodding knowingly to Karl Marx, Louis Althusser, Walter Benjamin, Samuel Beckett and Maurice Merleau-Ponty, and Maurice Blanchot and Jean-Luc Nancy respectively. What the writings in this volume reveal more clearly is that the precedent he always brings back – forward, or up, in an untimely sense, on to the platform of contemporary art's stage[v] – is Theodor Adorno's idea of art's purposeful uselessness.

Adorno famously proposes this idea in *Aesthetic Theory* (1970) as the philosophical means to distinguish critical modernist art from other life practices that design outcomes, in the context of the West where everything useful is complicit in capitalism's expansion. His idea is premised on a conviction that the modern work of art is characterised by a necessarily illusory autonomy.[vi] For Adorno, modern art is authentic in so far as it presents the necessary illusion of its own autonomy from the rest of life by its objects being useless. The 'self-'critical awareness that its autonomy is both necessary and illusory, or necessarily illusory, gives the work of modern art representative purpose as a social monad, a term he filters from Gottfried Leibniz via GWF Hegel thus: 'Artworks are closed to one another, blind, and yet in their hermeticism they represent what is external. […] The interpretation of an artwork as an immanent, crystallized process at a standstill approximates the concept of a monad'.[vii]

Büchler was raised in a Jewish-Catholic household in Communist Prague. As he recounted in a 1998 conference paper, the first barrier to artistic freedom that his generation faced was the oppressive state regime, which he had watched roll into Czechoslovakia with Soviet tanks in spring 1968. In the long shadow of the Iron Curtain the vinyl records of rock'n'roll music and black-and-white magazine reproductions of anti-object Conceptual art could only ever misrepresent the liberalism of the West (pp.215–17). These mistranslations amplified, or maybe grounded, the cultural shocks I alluded to above, when in 1981 he emigrated alone under force of expulsion to Cambridge, England, via three months in Paris.

In a 2008 interview with Neville Wakefield, Büchler describes how for the first five years in England he was so unsettled by the sheer volume (in the sense of both amplitude and extent) of Western visual culture that he could not answer the question, 'why add to this?':

> When I crossed the Western border for the first time in my life, I had this moment of absolute shock: I was astonished by how visually aggressive Western culture was. And for a moment – well, for a moment that lasted about five years – I felt that there was nothing I could do as an artist. I mean that in a positive way, though. Back in Czechoslovakia, many artists of my generation made the kind of work they did out of a sense of necessity, as though they felt obliged to keep things going until one day it may become possible to think more clearly again. When I came to the West, there just didn't seem to be any need for making art and adding to this visual pollution.[viii]

Whereas art's counterproductive value as subversive self-expression had made practical and political sense when, for example, he founded the action-theatre group KQN (an initialist decoy that did not refer back to any words, nor sensibly could it in Czech) as a student or collaborated in the samizdat movement through the late 1970s, this new uselessness – the peculiar functionlessness of late-modern art in Western high capitalism – seemed overwhelmingly purposeless too.

A feeling of being simultaneously overwhelmed by stuff and underwhelmed by its meaninglessness was at first paralysing. But in the model of what we might retrospectively call Adornean post-Conceptualism, by which the work of art is a social monad that is mediated by and against the field of contemporary art, Büchler realised the potential of inverting those two conditions. By the late 1980s he was (re)using otherwise underwhelming stuff to create the conditions for encounters that could be overwhelmingly meaningful. This economy of means has characterised his gallery work ever since and was first 'worked out', we might say, in parallel with the photography programme he curated as co-director of the influential Darkroom Gallery in Cambridge from 1983–87, which aimed to bridge the gap between art photography and emerging contemporary practice, yet inadvertently set a trend for exhibiting everything but photographs. Paying attention to other artists who also offer the artwork as a site of work, often against the overdetermined bombast of the fading New York and emerging Young British Artists scenes, had by the early 1990s become the focus of his book reviews (Gabriel Orozco and Joachim Schmid monographs, for example) and exhibition reviews (Roni Horn and Rebecca Horn, for example), as Sections One and Three of this book attest.

Section Two of this book is devoted to Büchler's writings about art and design pedagogy and cultural studies. For both, he uses subjective opinion based on personal experience as a scaffolding with which to build critiques that evince generalisable findings for specific contexts, and so might be described as theories with a small 't' (pp.90–96). That the resultant partial theories of culture and education – always built and aimed like site-specific responses, and 'partial' in the double sense of not whole and partisan – are profoundly entwined should by now come as no surprise. My claim above was that the work of making art, the work performed by the work of art and the work of reading art nominate the question of work as a key or conceptual nexus for all of the dimensions Büchler's praxis. Teaching became an important part of that praxis in 1988 when he began to work as a visiting tutor on the now famous MA Media Art programme at the Slade School of Fine Art in London, alongside founding course leader Stuart Brisley (pp.217–18). What and how the learning happened there contrasted with the technical training Büchler had experienced in Prague, first as a print student at the School of Graphic Arts (1970–72) then as a typography student at the Institute of Applied Arts (1973–76). In the post-studio, post-medium context of contemporary art education, Büchler came to see the paradoxical value of art's purposeful uselessness as the burden shared by all those who learn, teach and research fine art – those who share the responsibility of reimagining the future agency of artists and resisting instrumentalisation: 'we [artist-teachers] should remind ourselves every now and then that, after all, the most "relevant output" of whatever we might do remains the future of our students' (2001, p.141). Furthermore, as he summarises in the title essay of this book (2002, pp.142–48), given that 'art is a job that no one has asked you to do', the complicated inefficacy of this kind of work – its odd, maybe incommunicable ability to unwork – makes it more socially important than its products:

> The modern society undoubtedly needs creativity, critical imagination and resistance more than it needs works of art. It needs artists with their ways of doing things more than it needs the things that they make. It needs them for what they *are*, rather than for what they *do* – and if it needs them for what they do, then it is in the sense that artists are producers of culture rather than of discrete artefacts which characterise that culture. [… It] is the work of art, the actions and consequences of art, rather than works of art, that is the active ingredient of culture.[x]

Like all academic disciplines, fine art has subject-specific qualities that give contours to its disciplinary formation; unlike some subjects, even other arts and humanities subjects, the qualities that fine art emphasises make it unusually incompatible with the techno-scientific methodologies of the university industry (pp.133–41). Given this incompatibility or clash – between the modes of art work and the methodical logics of scientific research – with papers like 'Built-in Obsolescence' (2000, pp.126–32) Büchler stakes a string of sadly prophetic wagers about art education that deserve to be read rather than paraphrased. If clustered together in Section Two they seem repetitive, I think it important to bear in mind that the selections included are condensed from talks, journal articles, book chapters and journalism, all originally intended for different people in different times and places. Taken as such, as irregular interventions into a disjointed debate that has been skewed by the unprecedented commercialisation of education post-1992, these texts reveal a critical sympathy that could only be fostered from a certain vantage point within the establishment *and* a playful systematicity that is peculiar to much good art writing:

> Students have never been poorer; schools and colleges have never had to operate in a more restrictive economical and political climate; never before have the programmes of institutions been to such an extent controlled by bureaucrats ill equipped to pass academic judgement; and never before has so much administrative work been left to academics with no qualifications to handle any but the most rudimentary clerical tasks. Management has become the site of 'creative thinking'; the artist-teachers have been charged to 'deliver' the educational 'product'. The pessimist says, 'It can't possibly get worse'; the optimist says, 'Oh yes, it can'.[xi]

Büchler's vantage point changed unexpectedly when he was appointed to his first full-time job, as Head of Fine Art at the Glasgow School of Art in 1992. The swelling reputation of the school was due in large to the success of alumni from the Environmental Art department founded by David Harding in 1985. In 1996 former student Douglas Gordon won the Turner Prize (the first of five Glasgow-trained winners since) and thereabouts Hans-Ulrich Obrist coined the caricature 'the Glasgow miracle'. Büchler's tenure was short – indeed cut short by his acrimonious departure in 1996 – but his contribution significant. On the ground, for example, he began the Friday Talk lecture and book series with Nikos Papastergiadis, and invited departments to argue about the differing relevance of certain teaching methods to certain media. But behind the scenes, as the essay 'Bureauphilia: A Lost Case' (2000, pp.130–32) unpacks, he confronted the institution's conservative management by taking, rather than shirking (as so many other artist-teachers of his generation sadly did), responsibility for the administrative machinery that determines the superstructure of such places.

During the extensive new interview included in this book, 'Words Mean Nothing' (pp.198–226), Büchler and I revisited his opinions about what made the visual art scene in 1990s Glasgow so interesting, including under-discussed issues like the upshots of Scottish provincialism (pp.99–100), but also, more pertinently, the peer-to-peer collectivism amongst the younger artists involved. Talking about collectivity with Büchler sheds light on at least two important traits of the texts in this volume: Firstly, that his model of macro culture, within which 'the actions and consequences of art' are 'an active ingredient', is based on something very like conversation. And secondly, as my oxymoronic description suggests, the 'playful systematicity' of his writings *styles* their engagement with the subculture of art, via its discourses, as if art itself (signified by the mass noun) were a kind of long conversation.

Büchler's model of cultural engagement as conversational always presumes more than two participants and never presumes any equality of to-and-fro. This is not the *Öffentlichkeit* culture romanticised by Jürgen Habermas.[xii] Nor is the model strictly dialectical, in that subsumption is precisely what the conversation's indefatigability – what Blanchot would call its infinitude[xiii] – resists. It is, however, quite close to what is normally called, by default within aesthetics, collaboration. Conversation as a model of collaboration seems to describe how Büchler uses writing to productively extend the socio-historical dispute about how, why and where art works. For example, in 2003 he invited artists about whose work he had previously written to write anything they liked in response to his work and had i3 Publications publish it under the title *Conversation Pieces* instead of a monographic catalogue.[xiv]

In a similar spirit, Büchler's side of lots of conversations echo around in this book and in so doing they suggest a rhythm that I have tried not to control. For instance, the immersive code projections of his friend Charles Sandison provide a neat opportunity to meditate on the unreliability of language in 'Here's How It Works' (2002, pp.182–85), which is a theme he returns to a decade later when musing on the annotations that complicate Evangelia Spiliopoulou's quasi-diagrammtic drawings in 'Of Time And' (2013, pp.192–94). Accordingly, the taxonomy of sections that I have used to structure this collection should be approached as signposts rather than walls – they are there to help the reader navigate an *oeuvre* not to block the movement of ideas. And anyway, as the best writing in this genre often reminds me, an essay like 'Stalin's Shoes (Smashed to Pieces)' (1997, pp.107–16) constellates too much too well for me to surely regulate what it is *not* about.

Above I said that all of the texts in this collection address the limits and/or consequences of mediation. In the *Dictionary of Untranslatables: A Philosophical Lexicon* (2014), Ben Kafka starts his entry for 'Medium' philologically:

> The Latin adjective *medius* has roots in the Sanskrit *madhya* and the Greek *mesos*, all three terms meaning something like 'in the midst' or 'in the middle'. One could be in the midst or middle of any number of things, some quite concrete – the distance from here to there – and others more abstract. [...] 'Medium' approaches a recognizably modern sense when, in addition to being a place where ideas or affects can be brought forth, it becomes a way of bringing them forth.[xv]

He concludes the entry with a quote from Jean-Luc Nancy's essay 'Of Being Singular Plural'[xvi], first written in 1995 and published the following year:

> For the moment, it is less important to respond to the question of the meaning of Being (if it is a question, and if we do not already basically respond every day and each time [...]) than it is to pay attention to the fact of its exhibition. If 'communication' is for us, today, such an affair – in every sense of the word [...] – if its theories are flourishing, if its technologies are being proliferated, if the 'mediatization' of the 'media' brings along with it an autocommunicational vertigo, if one plays around with the theme of the indistinctness between the 'message' and the 'medium' out of either a disenchanted or jubilant fascination, then it is because something is exposed or laid bare.[xvii]

For Ben Kafka, Nancy's attention is symptomatic of the urgency, or immediate relevance, of 'medium' and 'media', and their cognates 'like "multimedia", "remediation", and "mediality"', to the globalised and untimely contemporary world we share.[xviii] Now that new media are ever-present and no longer new in the sense that theoretically sustained the category distinctions of Old and New Media, our theories of media are being rethought as something more like a question – what Geert Lovink calls 'the Media Question'.[xix] Alongside the European philosophers who readied the ground for our doing so, including Friedrich Kittler and Bernard Stiegler, is Vilém Flusser.

Flusser's influence on his compatriot Büchler is based on their shared fascination with photography, and surfaces repeatedly in Sections One and Two of this book. In 1983 Flusser proclaimed the 'invention of technical images' that we are living through to be the second 'fundamental turning point' in 'human culture since its inception'.[xx] As Büchler glosses in a review (2000, pp.46–49) of the 1995 translation of *Towards a Philosophy of Photography*:

> According to Flusser, we live in a world dominated by apparatuses – such as the photographic camera or the computer, or the agencies of the State or the market – which are the expressions of the hidden interests of those who control their inputs and outputs. But since these apparatuses have been designed to operate 'automatically', those who control their external functions are, in effect, controlled by their pre-programmed possibilities.

'For Flusser', as Büchler continues in the 2010 essay 'Live View' (pp.69–72), 'the possibilities of (photographic) situations cannot be found in the world but are "programmed" within the functions of the camera'. This reflective *mediatisation* of photography, Büchler had already claimed in the 2002 essay 'Delirium of Doubt', dictates that 'what appears in photographs are the structural conditions of photography rather than the object being photographed'.[xxi] This understanding correlates with the shift in approach made by conceptualist photographers to their medium since the 1960s, which Büchler interprets to be signified by the shifting keywords different generations use to describe their work. For Conceptual artists photography was an 'investigation'; for Neo-conceptual artists it was an 'inquiry'; and now for contemporary artists it is a 'questioning'. Issue 65 of *Source Photographic*

Review pitched a question as its title, 'What to Photograph?' (2010, pp.73), in direct response to which Büchler told the magazine's readers:

> Photographers should focus their lens on nothing – not merely because, as Susan Sontag says, we need an 'ecology of images', but above all because nothing is the natural state of the image. [...] What could be a greater challenge for the photographer than to demonstrate this paradox?

Büchler began working with photographs in 1970s Prague where anything made by underground artists needed to be impermanent or somehow transferable (pp.73), which gave photographic documentation the kind of double identity that, at the time, only performance art in the West needed to depend on. Büchler's earliest writings in English – a near-complete record of which are included in this book's bibliography (pp.231–37) – were reviews of photography shows commissioned by *Creative Camera*, for whom he served as design consultant from 1985–91, and catalogue texts for the Darkroom Gallery, beginning with the 1985 show *Re-visions: Fringe interference in British Photography in the 1980s*. His reputation garnered an invite to curate *Jiří Kolář: The End of Words* at London's ICA in 1990, which was the first of many projects he has guest-curated since, including *Whatever Happened to Social Democracy?* in 2005 at the Rooseum Center for Contemporary Art in Malmö with then-director Charles Esche. Curating, like writing, is another strand in his praxis – another way of engaging in the conversation of art – but unlike writing, became more occasional during his tenure as research professor at Manchester Metropolitan University from 1997–2016.

The trajectory of his profile as an artist since the millennium gives this collection, as a document, other art-historical significances. Just as his gallery work has changed, so too has what he writes about. However, for Büchler, three aspects of photography seem still to privilege it as the ensign of analogue media. Firstly, the extraordinary temporality of film photography and the afterlife of film as a metaphorical timeliness and substrate in the history and techniques of digital image-making (pp.97–98). Secondly, the materiality of the shadows or photographs captured on film and how they differ from the abstractions of the world made virtually real by digital image-making (pp.69–72). And thirdly, how photographers relate to their world qua their cameras' possibilities – what one takes when taking a photo – and how that has changed with the technology (pp.30–34). The texts that progress away from photography, those texts concerned with other kinds of image-making altogether, and those few texts that hint at his passions for music, typography and books, like 'Tenuous Notes' (2011, pp.74–76), lever this collection and the issue of analogue media into the general discourse of visual culture. What is literally and literarily made more apparent by his gallery work, and was spelt out in a 2010 interview with Patrick Van Rossem, is a reader's obsession with the materiality of language and an 'incompetent electrician's' (pp.201–203) obsession with misusing media to allow words to perform:

> 'Doing something with' words is different from writing. Writing is a way of giving words things to do. What I am trying to do is less active, more like taking a ride with the words and watching them as they do what they do. More like reading from a distance, perhaps, and machines can help with that.[xxii]

An introduction is only ever a kind of premature or false start and I have no intention of offering a false conclusion as well. Instead, I want to loop you, as Büchler so often does, back to the start of my false start and start as I mean to finish with the second movement in WH Auden's famous poem 'In Memory of WB Yeats' (1939).[xxiii] Büchler's writings turn our attention to the studio work of other artists – some well known, many not, and others anonymously represented by shared identities like 'art student'. Yet the concerns he projects as a reader of art are the same as those he brings to his studio, because, 'What feeds my interest in art is art, of course. And I say completely unashamedly that a lot of my work is realised, polished, and resolved through recognising the potential link to art history, to the works of artists that interest me'.[xxiv] As Patrick Greaney has argued, quotational art practices that evoke modernism challenge our philosophies of time by 'repeating the future'.[xxv] Be it Franz Kafka (pp.85–89) or Marcel Broodthaers (pp.186–87), or the pencil ends left behind by builders (pp.228–230), Büchler's writing and art are based on 'watching [things] as they do what they do'. Büchler distils the paradoxes of purposeful uselessness and unworking that give his praxis a radical coherence by trying to 'make nothing happen' (pp.198–99). In doing so he recasts Auden's anti-Romantic sentiment with a different kind of *poesis*. The praxis of art for Büchler, like poetry for Auden, is 'A way of happening, a mouth' in the conversation of culture.

i Peter Osborne, *Anywhere or Not at All: Philosophy of Contemporary Art*, Verso, London, 2013, pp.13–14.

ii See, for example, Büchler's 2010 interview by John Reardon, in David Molin and John Reardon (eds), *Ch-ch-ch-changes: Artists Talk About Teaching*, Ridinghouse, London, 2009, pp.76–85. The controversial nineteenth-century philosopher Pierre-Joseph Proudhon was the first to coin the phrase 'the social destinations of art'. See, for example, his 1875 book *Du principe de l'art* (The Principles of Art).

iii See, for example, Tom Bottomore, Laurence Harris, VG Kiernan and Ralph Miliband (eds), *A Dictionary of Marxist Thought* (2nd ed), Blackwell Publishing, Oxford, 1991, pp.435–40.

iv See, for example, the essay 'War of Words' (1999, pp.117–125) or his interview with Hester Reeve, revised 2010: 'as art only makes sense as an activity out in the world, in its social destination, it doesn't make sense "in the studio". But that applies to everything [...] Culture is a collective activity; it's not an individual activity.'

v The curious temporality, or untimeliness, of the concept of contemporaneity that we call forth when we talk about 'contemporary art' has been the subject of much recent philosophy. See, for example, Giorgio Agamben, *"What is an Apparatus?" and Other Essays*, trans. David Kishik and Stefan Pedatella, Stanford University Press, Redwood, 2009; 'Questionnaire on "the Contemporary"', *October*, no.130, fall 2009; and Osborne, *op.cit.*, pp.37–42.

vi *Ästhetische Theorie* was first published in 1970, one year after Adorno had died, based on drafts written between 1961–69 edited together by his wife, Gretel Adorno. All quotations: *Aesthetic Theory*, trans. Robert Hullot-Kentor, Continuum, London, 2004.

vii *Ibid.*, pp.237.

viii Interview by Neville Wakefield, in *Frieze Art Fair Yearbook 2008–9: Frieze Projects*, London, 2008, n.p.

ix See, for example, 'A Snapshot from Bohemia' (1991, pp.85–89); or for a broader discussion of these issues see, Pavlína Morganová, *Czech Action Art: Happenings, Actions, Events, Land Art, Body Art and Performance Art Behind the Iron Curtain*, Karolinum Press, Prague, 2014.

x 'Somebody's got to do it' (2002, pp.142–48).

xi 'No More '80s!' (1994, pp.90–96).

xii Jürgen Habermas, *The Structural Transformation of the Public Sphere* (1962), trans. Thomas Burger, MIT Press, Cambridge, MA, 1991.

xiii Maurice Blanchot, *The Infinite Conversation* (1969), trans. Susan Hanson, University of Minnesota Press, Minneapolis, 1993.

xiv Pavel Büchler (ed), *Conversation Pieces*, i3 Publications, Manchester, 2003.

xv Ben Kafka, 'Medium', in Barbara Cassin (ed), *Dictionary of Untranslatables: A Philosophical Lexicon*, trans. Emily Apter, Jacques Lezra and Michael Wood, Princeton University Press, New Jersey, 2014, pp.626.

xvi Jean-Luc Nancy's foreword stresses the significance of *when* he is writing. See, *Being Singular Plural* (1996), trans. Robert Richardson and Anne O'Byrne, Stanford University Press, Redwood, 2000, p.xii.

xvii *Ibid.*, p.28.

xviii B Kafka, *op.cit.*, pp.626–29.

xix Geert Lovink, 'Hermes on the Hudson: Notes on Media Theory after Snowden', in *e-flux journal*, no.54, April 2014, http://www.e-flux.com/journal/hermes-on-the-hudson-notes-on-media-theory-after-snowden, accessed 24 April 2014.

xx Vilém Flusser, *Towards a Philosophy of Photography* (1983), trans. Martin Chalmers, Reaktion Books, London, 1995, p.7.

xxi 'The Blind Train-spotter: A Delirium of Doubt', in David Green (ed), *Where Is the Photograph?*, Photoworks/Photoforum, Brighton, 2003, pp.81–91.

xxii Interview by Patrick Van Rossem, in *Labour in Vain*, DOX Centre of Contemporary Art, Prague, 2010, p.99.

xxiii Auden wrote the elegy in 1939 soon after hearing news of its dedicatee's death. It was first published in *Another Time*, Faber and Faber, London, 1940.

xxiv Van Rossem, *op.cit.*, p.96.

xxv Patrick Greaney, *Quotational Practices: Repeating the Future*, University of Minnesota Press, Minneapolis, 2014.

SECTION ONE

FROM PROMISES OF AN IMAGE TO ABSTRACTIONS OF THE WORLD

VAINLY I HAD SOUGHT TO BORROW
FROM MY BOOKS AAAABCCCDDDD
EEEEEEFFGHIIIJJJKKLLLLLMMNPPP
QQRRRSSSSTTTTUUUUUVVVWWW
XXYZZ NLY THIS AND NTHING MRE

Nothing More, 2012, letterpress on paper, 34 x 50 cm

Five lines of capital letters from a condensed grotesque font manufactured by Stephenson Blake in the early twentieth century fill the paper, letterpress printed against any economy of scale in an edition of just one. In the middle, a central block of graphemes form an unbroken and imperfect alphabetised lump, A–Z. They are unmistakably a type case synopsis print – a test of all the capital letters in the case. These three lines are the conceptual and literal centre of this work, *Nothing More* and nothing less. Either side of this central block, before the 'A's stutter and after the 'Z's finish, the rest of the letters from this case have been set into two phrases from Edgar Allan Poe's famous 1845 poem, 'The Raven'.

The first citation perfectly repeats a clause that bridges lines three and four in Poe's second stanza, even maintaining its line break:

> Eagerly I wished the morrow;—vainly I had sought to borrow
> From my books surcease of sorrow—sorrow for the lost Lenore—

Whereas Poe's character turns to his bookcase for distraction and advice, Büchler borrows what all English-language writers working with modern type do (including Poe): the 26-letter alphabet. Our commonly held assumption that we can infinitely reuse any letter because the alphabet is an iterable code can only ever be imperfectly mimicked when printing with moveable type, for which only limited numbers of each letter are made. The imperfection of Büchler's synopsis (the central block, the *centre* of this work) as a language act is obviously linguistic – these are letters but not words; and in a phonemic language like English these written letters are only graphemic units, not linguistically meaningful units. But is also numerical – there are only 25 letters.

After the six 'O's in the opening citation have exhausted the fount, an entire vowel is 'nevermore', missing from the rest of the print. The second citation closes the first stanza in Poe's poem:

> "'Tis some visitor," I muttered, "tapping at my chamber door—
> Only this and nothing more."

Poe's narrator is monologuing to reassure himself that the phenomenal 'this' is only what he declares it to be. Büchler's print repeats a 22-letter section but only has 19 of the letters it would need to do so verbatim. Yet, no substitutes or spaces have been introduced to mark the absence of the 'O's, reminding us that printed language has literal limits that literature can exceed by implication or repetition. The conceptual and material terms set for this print (which echo high modernist language exercises we canonically associate with experimental writers, from members of Oulipo to cryptographers like Poe) declare that there is only 'this' case of type 'and nothing more'.

With the advents of phototypesetting and then digital typesetting, the idea that compositors have a limited stock of characters to print from was made obsolete. Indeed, the idea that a printed instance of an 'O' is actually the impression or commitment of an 'O' in particular, which is still somewhere in the world as a lump of wood or lead with its uniquely imperfect surface, seems wholly alien to our idea (epitomised by the internet) that all public language is now hyper-situated – impermanent, infinitely replicable, and always moving or moveable. 'I like the idea that you can squeeze the last drop of meaning from technologies, materials or processes that have been outdated', Büchler said in a 2010 interview with Patrick Van Rossem. '"Doing something with" words is different from writing. Writing is a way of giving words things to do. What I am trying to do is less active, more like taking a ride with them and watching them as they do what they do. More like reading from a distance.' *Nothing More* strains analogue language to the cusp of illegibility by over-emphasising the message of the media it implicates: bookcases and typecases, the histories we organise within them, and indeed the languages that we could not organise without them.

BLACK (AND WHITE) MAGIC

In some cultures, where the black-and-white magic of photography is feared more than death, people do not let themselves be photographed – their image captured by the camera, never to be returned; their being split in two, the image behind the photographic surface and the imageless body in front of it. They fear being forever trapped in a body, which, without its image, can no longer be the mortal body of the living but is already a corpse. Nothing that even death would take.

In our 'enlightened' world, where death defies all magic and the living and the dead are part of the same closed system of the image, our very existence is confirmed through being photographed – as if this surgical operation could make us more 'lifelike', as if only through it do we assume our identity and gain a place in a reality that looks increasingly like a photograph. With the shadow of photography permanently attached to our feet, we don't think of photographs as part of our corporeal integrity, rather we see in them manifestations of our existence as living images. Yet, somehow, we also know that the body in our photographs is really a trace of us.

Being photographed, when we are conscious of it, can be a strange sensation – part suspense, part vertigo. The magical attraction that the camera has for many when it is displayed in a shop window can turn into a sense of distinct discomfort or panic when a photographer aims the lens at us. One moment it was an inanimate piece of technology; now, suddenly, it has become a part of another person – and not just a supplementary part (a tool or a weapon) but a kind of artificial organ, a completing part of a body, which, until now, appeared to be much like our own. (Some manufacturers actually advertise cameras as 'part of you'.) This body is armed not with vision – the camera does not need to be put to the eye – but with the power to reach out. As the camera is pointing at us, we are engaged in an intimate contact with the body of the photographer. Our smile, our self-conscious pose, are expressions of our simultaneous submission and resistance to the invisible touch. We are about to be seized ('taken', in the language of photography) by the hand with the camera, pulled in, coupled. It is not our image that we stand to lose; it is the privacy of our body, under threat of penetration (a theme often exploited in pornography) that makes us feel vulnerable and *exposed*.

In the photograph, the direct human interaction of the moment of photographing is replaced by the mediated experience of the image, physical intimacy reduced to a second-order simulation. But the photographic image still bears a trace of that ritual communion with the body of the other – united, for a fraction of a second, in the photographic act.

The main constituent function of any ritual is a unification of otherwise separate forces and identities. In the *ritual of photographing*, which is both social and private, it is the unity of 'subject and object' (or the unity of the body and the image) that is momentarily reached – a moment when imaginary and real existence are the same. The resulting photograph is present (albeit latently) already in the act: it is conceived in it ('born' afterwards from the 'body' of the camera). As it truly belongs to the fleeting moment of exposure, having taken on a life of its own, it can be seen as the moment's sole survivor – and where there is a survivor there must have been a close contact with death. And it is precisely the cycle of death-birth-rebirth – photographing is a *reproductive* process – which is at the centre of all rituals.

The body of the photographer also leaves its trace in the photograph – not as an imprint but as an absence of a body of which nothing is left but an image from its eye's retina. This 'active' absence is what forces us to look at the photograph (we say we are 'looking through the photographer's eyes') and confirms that this photographer was as much 'exposed' as the one whose body was registered on the film. Indeed, it is because of this double exposing that we might say that the body in front of the lens is posing *with* rather than *for* the photographer.

This is also why the word 'model' is so unsatisfactory when it comes to photography. It is true that where photography draws upon primarily visual concerns and ideals inherited from painting (think of the 'Nude' – and of the entire history of 'Creative Photography') the body is celebrated as *a* model: universal, belonging to nobody and all, asensual, asexual, timeless and immortal. But in their desire for an idealised reference, these practices only underline that there is no such thing as 'the universal' for photography. A photograph *of* a model (as in fashion, for example), regardless of all its possible intentions, is always an image of modelling, that is, a trace of a ritual staged around a communicative response between a camera and a particular person. The strenuous denial of the subjective specificity of the photographic encounter, by the institutions of the marketplace, including the photographic industry, as much as by many of their critics and commentators, is above all an attempt to impose on our bodies the categories and 'models' of the visual. This insistence on the autonomy of the image, the dominant mode of the photographic culture, serves to sanitise our self-perceptions, to banish the imperceptible and prevent the contamination of fantasy by the anxiety of absence, which lurks beyond the threshold of the photograph. It is the transformation of the body into the image, its disappearance, that marks the authenticity of the photograph. But it is only the intangible trace of our participation in the photographic act that can ever authenticate that (magical) transformation.

In a world in which, in the domain of photographic images, our mortal existence has been drained of so much meaning, and where photography has had such a dehumanising effect by making its subject both a thing and a ghost (the 'spectral mode' of our coexistence with photographs), it may well be that, in some sense, it is the human body rather than its image that has been trapped behind the 'mirror of the photograph'. The ritual of photographing is perhaps the closest we can get to the return of the magical, or – and this is a strange thing to say – to activating the conditions of a sense of existential affinity with the world denied to us by photography. (And this is where we must begin to speak about art.)

Draft for catalogue essay to accompany *Figures*, Cambridge Darkroom, Cambridge, 1987; in *Ghost Stories: Stray Thoughts on Photography and Film*, Proboscis, London, 1999, pp.32–34.

ANGLED MIRRORS

Roland Barthes's investigations into the *speciality* of photography began with his doubts as to photography's very existence.[1] In looking for the 'evidence of photography, that thing which is seen by anyone looking at a photograph and which distinguishes it in his eyes from any other image', he found that the essence of photography – its nature or genius – lies in the superimposition of reality and the past: 'that-has-been'.

This *condition* of photography 'without which there would be no photograph', its singular strength and its limitation, concerns a disposition of things in time, an event. Each such event, however brief or distant, comprising any number of elements, is always unrepeatable, always unique, always different. The only common denominator of all such events is the involvement of the photographic apparatus. The 'that-has-been' is a situation of openness to the participation or intervention of photography, a situation of *exposure*. The event must be *processed* and *developed* into a photograph, *fixed*. It must be extracted from a continuum of events, isolated, marked, branded – what Barthes was looking for was the *stigma* of photography – before we can speak of a photograph.

One of the first photographs, a heliotype by Niépce made around 1826, shows a table laid for a dinner complete with a loaf of bread and a bottle of wine. The choice and the arrangements of the objects, the overall composition of the picture, are strongly reminiscent of certain paintings of the period. Unlike any painting, however, this is not an 'ideal' image of 'ideal' bread: this bread is real, a loaf of bread that we know existed. In this picture (on this table – like Lautréamont's umbrella and sewing machine – a chance encounter that takes place once in a millennium) the object met the image and gave birth to a new kind of reality. In the photograph, we have before us not a reminder of a past existence of the loaf of bread and the bottle of wine, not their blurred shadows, but their direct descendant, a continuation of their physicality in another *object*, which is as real as they once were. A materialised view, an intangible *thing*, a bizarre contradiction, a 'mutant' to quote Barthes again, a 'new being'.

The table in the photograph is laid for one person. It is inviting, seen from the perspective of someone approaching it (and the approach is clear – there is not even a chair standing in the way). Yet *this* table, real as it is, will never be sat at, the bread will never be eaten, the wine never drunk. Not even by the person who was once standing behind the camera, the photographer, whose privilege of access seems to be stated in the image. Like a mirage, it will forever remain at a distance. This meal, then, is not a real meal after all. It is a photographic event, a kind of a spiritistic seance perhaps, in which the table is used as a focus for an encounter with the past. It is a ritual meal: the Last Supper of the Image which began at the very advent of photography, and in the course of which, as if by magic, one reality is being turned into another (water into wine) and multiplied (a loaf of bread that will feed thousands) *ad infinitum*...

In the 1980s world of mega-visual communication, it could appear that the reality of photographic images/objects is almost the only reality that there is. By now, the world is to a large extent *made* of photographs. As if we lived in a multitude of parallel realities, time frames, separated only by the *medium* – through which there speaks the spectre, the ghost – of photography. Like in a hall of mirrors, this is a world in which objects and images are becoming interchangeable.

Photography, the apparatus and the process, has profoundly changed the texture of this world. In its various capacities photography has penetrated all of this world's corners and affected almost every aspect of our lives. It changed the way we see the world as well as the way we resist its changing image. This 'luminous writing' has lead to a proliferation of testimonies – some of which in turn 'illuminate', to extend the metaphor, the stigma of photography. But in itself it neither says nor represents anything other than itself. In other words, it is photography that makes something 'apparent' but it is photographs that make something real: we see photography but we perceive, study, handle and live with photographs. And it is the exact way in which each photograph slides between the 'real things' – the way the 'that-has-been' relates to 'that which really is' – that makes the world what it is.

This world is made of photographs, not of photography. It is not photography, not even *the* photograph (and certainly not *the* image – a generic term, it seems, from the realm of occult sciences), but photograph*s* that make a claim on our reality. *The* photograph in this respect is always only the *first* one, whichever one that might have been, the celebrated moment, the point at which photography began to break down into photographs. *The* photograph is the First Event, the birth not of photography but of the First Object, the first in a multitude of material facts, a kind of Big Bang really. Since then what matters is not the unifying 'magic' of photography but only individual images, objects, events, the individuality of each of those *things* and their difference-in-repetition, even their 'sameness'. They may all belong to the same heterogeneous order, all the most distant relations considered, but they don't simply sprout by themselves from a family tree of photography, nor do they emerge fully grown from the subject matter with the photographic apparatus acting as a kind of midwife. They are made and used, each one separately, one by one.

In this world where our everyday participation has turned the photographic ritual into the most banal of routines, and where the omnipresent clicking of cameras has replaced a continuity of experience by the chaos of 'information blips', it is not possible to locate photography. There is no one large mirror as it might have appeared to Niépce when he realised that he was looking at his own reflection – the image of picture-taking. Instead, there are only fragments of a broken mirror, a mirror that is continuously breaking, never diminishing, without ever having been whole. Angled mirrors, like those built into the so called 'reflex' cameras to enable you to frame and see the image as it will appear in print, their precise positioning, the specific way in which they reflect the world (the memory attributed to them by the contemporaries of Daguerre is of the selective kind) is what informs and confuses our notions of reality.

It has been said often enough that to take a photograph implies an act of appropriation: a spiritual appropriation of the seen together with the actual possession of the physical traces, the photograph. 'Taking pictures' certainly has more than one meaning. It can also be understood as 'taking a stance', an attitude, a bid for control, maintaining a distance, but at any rate positioning oneself within a photographic event. By extension, this means taking a stance in relation to each specific incidence. There is a plurality of positions: each time a picture is taken, someone assumes a *particular* attitude to a concrete situation that is taking place in the world of real things. Each time something is 'captured', trapped by the camera (by opening and closing the 'shutter'), someone marks a point from which a photograph is subsequently 'released'.

'Taking a picture' also implies taking a stance in relation to the living culture to which photographs belong: photographs are suspended events, but they are not suspended in a void. And it is precisely this positioning of oneself, a point of view, this attitude, that determines the way the photograph reflects back on the world of which it already is a part.

It goes without saying that such a stance can never be an academic one: we don't innocently observe photographs as they happen; we make them through complicity with a process of manipulation, with specific purposes and intentions. The most prevalent attitude is, of course, the vis-à-vis of a family album snapshot, an attitude that reflects directly back on the event, a pure 'that-has-been' or 'that-has-been-me'.[2] It says nothing else. Even so, it is an active engagement, always *within*, which acknowledges the specificity of the method and the material properties of photography, but which must be ultimately concerned with the reality of the world *outside* the photograph. If the mirror of a photograph is to reflect the world in any meaningful way, it cannot be confined to reflecting simply photography as a subject in itself. It is not a question of various 'attitudes towards photography'[3] in terms of vocational preoccupations or professional interests, since this is no more than strategic manoeuvring within the abstract confines of the tradition of the 'photographic culture', an ideological construct, a kind of shadowy underworld of worshippers of The Medium. Neither is it a matter of theoretical questioning that reduces its object to a mere specimen, for 'demystification' addresses the dogma but not the experience. (A photograph, a photographic event, is not something that is easily unsaid or undone.) Finally, nor is it any rhetorical position. It is photography that is wrapped in words, whereas photographs begin with silence.

Photographs are generators of stories, indeed 'incitements to reveries' (as Susan Sontag remarked), but, in themselves, they do not 'make sense': the story is both inside *and* outside the frame presented to the viewer. To address the world meaningfully through a photograph requires a rejection of the self-referential 'language of photography' in favour of a radical position, in the true sense of the word, which creatively displaces itself: with every subsequent fascination it severs its roots to confront anew.

Photographs are reflections of the world coexistent with its reality. To be of consequence, the 'superimposition of reality and the past' must be invested with meaning. This cannot be done by striving for new ways of representing the same (pointing a finger at that which already is), but only by creating something that would have not otherwise existed, not through photography but through the singularity of a photograph. And if we want to make sense of photographs, and through them make sense of the world we live in, we must resist the *non*-sense of photography.

1. See *Camera Lucida*, Richard Howard (trans), Jonathan Cape, London, 1982.
2. 'This is my dog' or 'This is my house' in a family album snapshot should in fact always be read as 'This is me with my dog' or 'This is me in front of my house', which is exactly what makes family albums so exclusive.

3. *Attitudes Towards Photography* was the title of a highly publicised exhibition mounted in the late 1980s by (I think) The Photographers' Gallery in London, which foregrounded some of the then fashionable themes, such as 'demystification', alluded to in this paragraph.

Creative Camera, no.8/9, August/September 1989, pp.9–11.

THE FREEZE

There is no better illustration of a photograph's unconditional attachment to a particular moment than the stock-in-trade shorthand used by filmmakers: the freeze. This somewhat tautological device capitalises on the photographic pedigree of the 'motion picture' as it demonstrates that film is a sequence of photographs in their raw state, shown as taken at $^{1}/_{32}$ of a second. Easy to double-bluff the disbelieving eye: one moment, the fusion of images and afterimages, rapid dis/appearances, leaves the impression of continuous motion; next, a succession of a few identical frames flicking away in front of our eyes with exactly the same impatience suggests a still 'photograph', *as if* it were pointed out to us by the director's finger stuck in a flip book. (With the freeze, the cause seems to be the effect.)

A painting or a drawing cannot be so naturally 'revealed' in film. The black bars of unexposed photographic material excepted, film conceals nothing but photographs. All those *other* still pictures have to enter the cinema screen, in a creepy kind of way, from somewhere outside photography. The slow dissolve is the appropriate trick here: a view from a window of an artist's studio slowly turns into a watercolour sketch or a map dissolves into an aerial view of a landscape. A similar treatment can even be used when it comes to showing a photographic *print*: an image gradually emerging from the red glow of the darkroom safety light on the surface of a *piece of paper* submerged in a tray of developer. But the photograph *as a photograph* is invariably portrayed as a sudden disruption. In Antonioni's *Blow Up*, which features some of the most notorious and ecstatic examples of the cinematic licence ever applied to photography, the distinction between the photograph and the photographic print is precisely stated by the use of the two clichés. The 'photograph', always a picture-in-the-taking, is expressed by a brief suspension of animation, sometimes of colour, that is, by the suspension of film. And while it cannot be denied that the 'show goes on', that the film is 'still there', it is quite apparent that it has skipped a heartbeat, as it were.

Superficially, especially where it is accompanied by a flash of light or the sound of the camera shutter, or where a crescendo of 'shots' appears in a rapid succession, the frozen (or is it *freezed*?) 'photograph' seems to belong to the same dramatic vocabulary or cinematic punctuation as gunfire. It shows the photograph's complicity in the dramatic action. (To paraphrase Robert De Niro in *The Untouchables*, it comes 'from a neighbourhood where they say you can achieve more with a kind word and a photographic camera than just with a kind word'.) But on a deeper level, the shooting of the photograph is cinema's true fatality. It betrays the impossibility of accommodating in a 'movie' the rigor mortis of photographic stillness. (Worth noting that the only alternative purpose for which the freeze appears to be fit is the very last shot of most films, 'The End'.) The freeze is cinema undone.

The suspended still image is an isolated incident, a parenthesis, both absorbed into and extracted from the passage of time. It issues from the action, from its logic and from its flow, but it never returns to it. No matter that after the incident the action resumes – a body caught mid-fall by the fictitious photographer hits the ground, for example, or colour returns to a black-and-white still picture of a landscape – the story is never the same. A permanent transformation has taken place while, for a fraction of a second, we were not *watching* (quite literally – with our eyes on the screen, we were *looking at* a 'photograph'). The chronology of events had split in two parallel but asynchronous tracks and the story 'jumped' from one onto the other.

For the photograph, there is no 'after'. It belongs exclusively to a single moment, always in the past, always gone even before it becomes visible ('developed', 'fixed' – the real time of a photograph in the technical terms of film is the single frame, which the eye never sees). During the freeze, 'time stands still' as if waiting, in vain, for the photograph to *retrieve itself*. But in the 'still time' no 'past' can be located. This is why the sudden motionless apparition on the screen is not, in fact, a photograph but an image of its absence – like a hole in the chronological gap.

(Of course, there is also another way of looking at this: the freeze is a simple role change. For an instant, we are privileged to look through the camera – as though we hadn't been looking through it all the time – and see the the film crew making a pause for a pose.)

Written in 1991; first published in *Ghost Stories: Stray Thoughts on Photography and Film*, Proboscis, London, 1999, pp.61–63.

A 'BATTLE FOR THE SOUL OF ART'

Roland Miller in his 'polemic' *Art and Socialism – don't mix* (*Alba*, vol.1, no.1) doesn't offer us much of a clear position or a coherent argument. What he does offer us instead is a vivid manifestation of the severe lack of understanding of the socio-political realities of post-1968 Czechoslovakia, and the lack of insight into the position of professional elites in Czechoslovak society, which marks the majority of current Western comment. It is not simply that Miller's 'portrait of an artist as a suffering man' is painted from a long-range perspective of a Scottish observer, but rather that it is presented without any regard for the differences of context – which I understand to be the relationship between public art and a ruling bureaucracy in Slovakia and in Scotland – that renders his 'conclusions' quite useless.

Even the opening remark regarding the backgrounds of the leading dissidents in Prague, associated professionally with theatre and literature, and their Slovak counterparts, associated with the visual arts, is both misled and misleading. It is misled because it uncritically accepts the image of the Eastern European dissident as an 'intellectual', something which may have been the case in the late 1960s, when indeed it was a 'dissent' at a conference of the Czechoslovak Writers' Union that triggered changes in the country's political establishment, but which by the late 1980s was not much more than an optical illusion caused by the international exposure granted by the Western media to several dissident writers. By 1989, the majority of oppositional activists in Czechoslovakia were being recruited from a younger generation which, in the aftermath of 1968, failed to comply with the requirements of political 'normalisation' and consequently to achieve professional qualifications and status. Civic Forum in its early days, for example, represented a very broad spectrum socially and professionally, comprising at least as many unskilled labourers as professional writers or actors. In any case, it was the 'high moral ground' rather than the trade affiliations of its leaders that held the movement together and earned it popular support – for how many of the hundreds of thousands of Václav Havel's followers had ever seen a Václav Havel play?

The remark is also misleading because it ignores the problems of the comparison between artists and theatre practitioners or writers in the context of Czechoslovak society and fails to take into account the broader differences between the dissident movements in the respective parts of the Czechoslovak federation. It is not an accident that in Bratislava artists are 'part of the new political establishment', while in Prague the establishment has formed itself around 'the playwright'. The reason for this is likely to lie in the 'battle for language' that has recently developed in Slovakia (and whose one result so far has been the hyphenated neologism, *Czecho-Slovakia*, that Miller uses to name the country). It is obvious that the oppositional group 'Verejnost' proti násiliu', aligned to the policies and ideals of the Prague-centred 'Charter 77' should find more supporters among visual artists, especially of the 1968 generation, than among writers more inclined to support the present-day opposition, a nationalistic tendency based on an autonomy of the Slovak language. Perhaps Miller sees Slovakia as the Scotland of Czechoslovakia and draws his inspiration from the current ambitions and difficulties of the Slovak nationalist movement. But then it would have been appropriate if he had acknowledged the nature of the political relationship between Czechs and Slovaks and the differences between their respective goals.

Yet more important here is the relationship between writing and theatre and the visual arts in terms of the positions of the practitioners in the conditions of the centralised 'bureaucratic capitalism'. Compared to writers or actors, visual artists in communist Czechoslovakia were on the whole considered politically harmless. This came partly from the traditional belief in the 'might of the word', the manipulative power of language, common to much of our Western culture, and partly from the object-oriented 'physical' nature of the artist's work. The censorship and the bureaucratic control of the visual arts, for instance, was delegated to the Union of Artists, who oversaw the programming of galleries and museums, commissioning of work for public display, allocation of studios and the distribution of specialised artists' materials. The responsibilities for censorship of literature, theatre and 'the word' in general, in contrast, were never vested in the respective professional unions but resided, much closer to the centre, with the Central Bureau for Press and Information. The clearest evidence, if such is needed, for the relatively oblivious attitude of the establishment towards the work of visual artists can be seen in the fact that while most practising artists where able to show their work openly (albeit not always 'officially'), the critical response to such work could only be 'published' clandestinely. The restrictions under which art theory and criticism (an 'art of language') had to operate were so much harsher than those imposed on the visual arts that they eventually led to an almost complete disappearance of the critical practice. It is also worth noting that while the Marxist-Leninist doctrine still provided a compulsory base and framework for any public discussion on the theory of art, the very same doctrine (as manifest in Socialist Realism) had long been *officially* abandoned in artistic production itself. In fact, the only (if numerous) examples of political censorship of visual work of the period, equal to that to which writing was summarily subjected, could be found in an area 'on the edge of language' – the art of the political cartoon!

The destruction of (commissioned) artwork on public display, as described by Miller in his article, can hardly be seen as a direct equivalent of the sustained campaign against literature and writing (which often included the destruction of manuscripts and even typewriters). I suggest that the former should be seen as an expression of the state vandalism of which the artists' work was as much a victim as any other product or object, whereas the latter should be seen as a manifestation of the state terrorism aimed specifically at positions formulated in language. It is true that all arts, all culture and all social life were subjected to the malice of censorship and were operating under conditions of severe political control, just as did any form of political and cultural expression and even the conscience of the individual. But it is quite wrong to perpetuate the impression, as Miller does, that the persecution and injustice that so many had suffered had much to do with the character of their work as artists.

Of the particular artists in his article, Miller writes that, expelled from the Union, 'officially they could not work as artists'. Such situations however should properly be interpreted as a case of 'denial of a privilege' rather than as an instance of 'punishment'. The broad practice of visual arts, centred as it is around object-making, had until recently been nearly the only 'officially' recognised category of self-employment and free enterprise – a condition which neither theatre practitioners, musicians nor the majority of writers enjoyed, having to be employed by state-run institutions, theatres, orchestras, magazines and the media. Furthermore, the economic circumstances of the enterprise were rather advantageous in that the principles of 'social commission' in the subsidised economy virtually freed the artist from the pressures and risks associated with private enterprise elsewhere. At the same time, the small number of practitioners meant it was unnecessary for the regime to regulate the matters of taxation, social benefits, etc. It was an aberration from which the material well-being of the artist could only benefit. This situation gave, in time, rise to a powerful economic elite. The artist gained a significant operative advantage – sheltered and protected by the system, yet respected and envied (there is only a small difference between the two) by the common man who, far from having been reformed by the ideology of socialism, looks up towards those who 'have done well for themselves'. An average Czechoslovak reader would feel a degree of sympathy towards anyone who had ever appeared on the 'black list' of the old regime – be it an artist, playwright or a factory worker. But such a reader would probably find it hard to digest the image of suffering and struggle, suggested by Miller, when reading about someone who had been lucky enough to even contemplate building (privately) an extension to his (private) studio in his (private) garden in the middle of 1970s ('communist') Bratislava.

What Miller 'uncovers' in his story – and what he, I suspect unwittingly, partakes in – is a tale of personal quarrels among members of an elite, complete with naming the 'informers'. Miller clearly feels for those whose political and artistic attitudes prevented them from 'getting rich' (whatever that might mean) on the subsidies of the state. This puts into a strange perspective his complaint about the situation of artists in Scotland, where he seems to advocate a degree of local political control as part of 'artistic freedoms'.

Indeed, 'the problems of Scottish artists are nothing compared to those of their Slovakian colleagues'. Yet this is not because of a freedom from fear of officialdom, but because the economic, social and political position of most artists in capitalist society is so marginal (and marginalised) as to put them beyond the interest of the establishment. Many of the great problems facing artists in Slovakia today probably revolve around the need to deal with the possibility of their own future marginality and insignificance in a society where Roger Scruton inspires the philosophers of the free market *and* where Roland Miller (so he tells me) advises the decision-makers in the domain of art. Any such society is bound to have some serious problems besides a 'battle for the soul of art'. It is only to be hoped that his advice to the arts bureaucracy in Slovakia is of a firmer foundation than the views on art and socialism that he has offered to the readers of *Alba*.

Alba, vol.1, no.3, June/July 1991, pp.18–19.

BUSTER'S BEDROOM
REBECCA HORN

There could hardly be a better way of starting a series of screenings of artists' films than with a homage to one of the greatest actors of performance cinema, Buster Keaton, made by one of the great artists of this precarious historical moment (i.e. the end of the mechanical era), Rebecca Horn. Keaton and Horn stand at the opposite ends of a period during which, in performance and cinema, the body and the machine have swapped sides, as it were – or, in art, the moving image has undergone a kind of alchemical transformation from illusion to a new order of reality. Or else, we could see them as being positioned side by side, ahistorically, at a point at which the circular developments of film, as the mechanical counterpart of performance, and performance, as the bodily aspect of the cinema, close up on themselves.

Either way, the work of Keaton and that of Horn are milestones in this crucially important strand of modern art – or perhaps the only true art of modernity – which keeps alive the tension between the human body and the machine, between the body as a machine and the machine as persona. And it is precisely the concern with the machine-like conditions of the modern body and the lifelike operations of the modern machine that makes film so relevant to artists, and that marks, at least to a degree, all the best work of artist-filmmakers.

Keaton, born 101 years ago, made his classic films in the 1920s: *The Navigator* in 1924, the year of André Breton's *First Manifesto of Surrealism*; and *The General* in 1928, around the time when Marcel Duchamp's *The Large Glass* (1915–23) famously cracked while in transport on the back of a lorry on a bumpy road somewhere in Connecticut. As with early Surrealism and its near-obsession with automatic processes and the 'mechanics' of the unconscious, and as with the symbolic 'language engine' and the conceptual 'engineering genius' that drive Duchamp's work, Keaton's films are not just a product of the machine aesthetics of their time. Rather, they are visionary speculations on the possibilities of creative freedom in the regime of mechanical perfection, explorations of precision for perfectly anarchic and transgressive ends.

The word to describe Keaton's artistic attitude is, perhaps, *animation* – in the literal sense of 'giving soul'. In Western art, the soul had gone out of fashion with Romanticism. With modernism, it also had to leave the human body. It was dislocated from its living form. (Why else would anyone come up with the idiotic term 'figurative art', if it were not for the difficulty in locating the soul within the form of the body?) In fact, the banishment of the soul from the body in modernist art has been so complete that even now we utter the word soul only with utmost trepidation. Yet the soul is not something that would easily go away or curl up and die. If it can no longer reside in the body, some other place must be found for it. And what better place can there be than a machine – something entirely made of imagination – which can provide the surrogate body in which the soul can be reclaimed in a kind of man–machine partnership.

In Horn's work since around 1970, the human body and the machine coexist in close proximity. In her early sculptural pieces and performances, the body acquires, or is equipped with, all kinds of extensions and appendages strapped to the performer's head, fingers, arms or legs, which make the body reach further while simultaneously constraining it. Later on, in the 1980s, she made strange mechanical automata, powered by motors, which endlessly perform and repeat the same simple actions, seemingly erratic but in fact always very precise: two metal hammers suddenly wake up from their dormancy, swing with evident force against each other and stop just a millimetre short of hitting one another, for example, or a very long metal rod suspended from the ceiling swings violently, in a jittery fashion, just a fraction of an inch above an egg placed on the floor.

There seems to be a constant 'ornithological' theme or leitmotif in Horn's work: feathers and plumage, quills and wings. She has made feather masks and body extensions for her performers; motorised feather wheels; several versions of the *Peacock Machine* (1981–), which spreads a set of long metal 'feelers' into the space like a peacock tail; and machines whose movements seem to be best described by words like 'flapping' or 'pecking'.

There is indeed a whole art form that combines and unites this kind of imagery: a certain kind of formal dance, flamenco and particularly tango – inspired by the spontaneity of the courting dances of birds, it requires the bodies of the dancers to move with machine-like precision and coordination. For Horn, the tango is a key image in her first two feature films, *The Dancing Cavalier* (1978), and *La Ferdinanda* (1981); for Keaton, the grace of formal dance is always present as an aspiration and latent reference.

In Christian iconography, birds and dancing belong to the symbolism of the soul (think of the dancing angels). In the history of technology, this imagery belongs to the 'dream of flying' – and flying, as we know from the myth of Icarus, has little to do with the practicalities of transportation, but is all about the heroism of transgression, about overcoming the earthbound condition of our existence in which our imperfectly designed bodies present such severe limitations. As though it was some kind of a perverse joke of the gods to give us the bodies that we have, while also giving us the imagination to go so far beyond what our bodies can actually do.

The mechanical era of modernity came up with two different strategies for realising the 'dream of flying'. The first is of course aviation, the flying machine, in which the body can literally rise above the earth (like in an extended leap or jump in a dance). The second strategy is the cinema.

It is not just a coincidence that so many early films include the image of the human body in flight, suspended in the air, or falling through space. And it is also no coincidence that aerial photography was one of the first revolutionary developments following the invention of the cinema. Almost as soon as the image could move, it could also fly.

In Keaton's classic period, the 1920s, it was still possible to 'dream of flying'. Both aviation and the cinema were in their pioneering infancy, both required a considerable investment of human physical energy, skill and courage to make the body and the imagination fly. The human body was still chasing its soul in the machine. By the 1970s and '80s, the time of supersonic flying, Technicolor cinema and global satellite TV transmission, flying in that ambitious sense of early modernity had become all but impossible. As technology took over from the body, rather than being an extension of it, it lost its human scale and also lost that link of animating partnership through which the soul could be reclaimed in the machine. It is now technology, rather than the person, that flies. In this sense, our flying is once again only a dream.

In a short text of 1983 dedicated to Keaton, Horn writes:

> His films begin in the daily routine of events, in the streets, backyards, stairways, in scenes of sudden abandonment where railway trains race panic-stricken through the streets, trees are torn up by their roots, houses fly through the air, where the mechanics of human civilisation confront nature, challenge it. In the course of the plot, events escalate to chaotic, threatening signs. He alone through his inventive intelligence can, like a dream-dancer, master the dangers with daredevil precision [...]
>
> Gradually he begins to test himself against the energies in short lessons, like bungled acrobatic exercises. [...] He develops magical powers, which enable him to overcome all obstacles, as unperturbed as a fallen angel. His escape schemes are a ballet

> in defence of gentle violence. The helpless young man turns into a person who with the help of his mania for inventions is able to tame the elemental forces. Help doesn't come from the animate worlds; rather, he breathes soul into the machines: they become his allies and partners, whom he can trust to aid him in warding off the unleashed energies.[1]

And after mentioning the destructive phase of Keaton's life, his 'falling into silence', brought about by changes in film production methods and the failure of his marriage, Horn concludes:

> In his office at MGM he builds a huge nutcracker where various devilish mechanisms pick up a walnut, toss it through the air, rattle it, shake it to the point of fainting, and finally at the outlet of this monstrous machine crack the walnut. The machine stands for the hierarchical structure of the MGM film company to which he is still bound by contracts and in which he desperately tries to assert himself. He himself has become the little walnut, a parody of his own reality.
>
> He is unable to find the way back to the spiral movements that were able to hurl him into infinity.
>
> He can no longer undo the knots of the strait-jacket. The circle of the earthbound holds him captive, reintegrates him.
>
> Keaton, once elated by the dance of weightlessness, returns for a measured span of time, now cloaked in silence, to the world of the blind.

It must be that metaphorical possibility of flying – what Horn calls being 'elated by the dance of weightlessness', lost somewhere in that span of time between 1920s silent cinematography and the high technology culture of the last couple of decades – that makes film so attractive a medium to artists. Unlike video, and unlike the new media of digital image-realities, film with its mechanistic foundation still allows us to make analogies with the animating principles of our existence. In a way, every artist's film is a prototype of a machine that contains the promises of freedom for the lost souls of modernity, of flight and escape. But how does this machine do it? Or, as someone wrote of Duchamp's imaginary 'machine': 'Where does it take us? To answer these questions, the best we can do is to make it run.'[2]

1. Rebecca Horn, 'The Inner Straight-Jacket within the Outer', in *Rebecca Horn* (exhibition catalogue), Kunsthaus Zürich, Zurich, 1983.
2. This (together with some other borrowings throughout the text) comes from Jean Suquet, whose question about the *Large Glass*-as-a-machine goes on: 'if it has a meaning, it is in its running. But how are we supposed to make it work since it appears inexorably stopped?' Jean Suquet, 'Possible', in Thierry de Duve (ed), *The Definitively Unfinished Marcel Duchamp*, MIT Press, Cambridge, MA, 1991.

Buster: Tramline no.4, Tramway and Glasgow School of Fine Art, Glasgow, 1996, pp.1–116.

READING VILÉM FLUSSER (BACK TO FRONT)

The editorial blurb on the handsomely designed cover of the present edition announces that, in his first book, 'Vilém Flusser proposes a revolutionary new way of thinking about photography.' Written in the early 1980s, the last line of Flusser's text acknowledges that his way of thinking is revolutionary by a double necessity: the philosophy for which he strives to build the foundations is 'necessary because it is the only form of revolution left open to us'.

According to Flusser, we live in a world dominated by apparatuses – such as the photographic camera or the computer, or the agencies of the state or the market – which are the expressions of the hidden interests of those who control their inputs and outputs. But since these apparatuses have been designed to operate 'automatically', those who control their external functions are, in effect, controlled by their preprogrammed possibilities. Human involvement with the apparatus is then reduced to an absurd contest of chance and necessity where the players 'control a game over which they have no competence, the world of Kafka, in fact'.

Taking photography as both a symptom and the most familiar manifestation of the multiple crises of the post-industrial social existence, Flusser identifies and builds up a case for a certain kind of 'informative' or 'experimental' photography, which deconstructs the techno-scientific 'apparatus' and its political and economic programming so that it may succeed in exploring the possibilities of the hardware and software in directions not yet predetermined by the photographic culture and industry. The job of the photographer is to 'place, within the image, information that is not predicted within the programme of the camera', to produce 'improbable' images which will generate equally improbable responses on the part of the audience. This experimentation is, however, not confined to the aesthetic realm (as in the practices of avant garde art), but covers also the cognitive and ethical aspects of photography and the respective scientific and political 'channels of distribution'. Indeed, it is the often unintentional slippage among these channels, arising from a positive confrontation between the intentions of photographers and the agendas (or 'programme') of the distribution media, that 'makes photographs into dramatic images'.

The task of the philosopher is, then, to make the photographer conscious of the general consequences of photographic practice. Photography, as a critical probe into the problems of the 'programming and distribution of information' in the post-industrial context, provides a model for coming to terms with 'the fact that there is no place for freedom within the area of automated, programmed and programming apparatuses'. It is left to philosophy to show that it is 'nevertheless possible to open up a space for freedom', and that there is a way in which, 'despite everything, it is possible for human beings to give significance to their lives in face of the chance necessity of death'.

No wonder, given the urgency of his mission, that Flusser has no time for the amateur photographer whose camera clubs are 'post-industrial opium dens [...] places where one gets high on the structural complexities of cameras'. Nor does he care for the documentarist who is merely 'interested in continually shooting new scenes from the same old perspectives'. They both produce photographic mementoes rather than information, 'and the better they do it, the more they prove the victory of the camera over the human being'. Likewise, in his efforts to equip photographic practice with a philosophical consciousness, the philosopher displays little patience for 'standard photography criticism' which fails to decode the complex relationships between the concepts programmed into the camera and the intentions of the photographer – just as much as it generally fails to expose the struggle between those and the 'distribution media'. This 'uncritical reception' gives photographs a critical carte blanche to programme our responses, as if by magic, for the ultimate benefit of the apparatus. With a latent assistance from the critic, the camera once again wins.

These and some other generalisations ('standard' never means very much) seem to be signs of the philosopher's all-too-human weaknesses, minor intellectual prejudices without which no critical text is worth reading, rather than flaws in a brilliantly argued philosophical case. More surprisingly though, Flusser attacks, in passing, the cultural criticism of the Frankfurt School – 'a second-order paganism' – whose ideologically biased lack of recognition for the mindless arbitrariness of cultural programming he sees as a function of the programme itself: 'A thoroughly disconcerting process in which, behind the ghosts that have been exorcised, more and more new ones are summed up.' Yet it is to the Frankfurt School, and specifically to Adorno, that Flusser seems to owe at least a small debt, as much for the ethical foundation of his critical commitments, as for his philosophical method. He rejects the humanistic line of criticism with its invocations of human responsibility and its omission to acknowledge that in the world of apparatuses 'the human being would be ruled out'. Yet he seems to dispense with human agency primarily as a matter of tactics, even expediency. In his plea for a critical solution to the paradox of having to uncover 'the terrible fact of this unintentional, rigid and uncontrollable functionality of apparatuses in order to get a hold over them', Flusser aims to prompt the critical mind into action by framing the definition of the photograph clearly outside the humanistic agenda. He proposes, instead, a quartet of key interactive concepts, 'image – apparatus – programme – information', and 'such further concepts that are logically contained within these'. Although he volunteers no answers himself, he declares defiantly that:

> This definition has the particular advantage for philosophy of not being acceptable. One is challenged to prove it wrong since it rules out the human being as a free agent. It provokes one into contradiction, and contradiction – dialectics – is one of the spurs of philosophy.

There is a sense of melancholy in Flusser's vision of 'the universe of technical images', which 'represents the fulfilment of the ages', the deterioration of value and meaning into information that can no longer be resolved historically. This melancholy, and the ethical imperative for putting the apparatus of the technical image on trial, may have been informed by Flusser's life experience of groundlessness and displacement. As a Jewish refugee from the German occupation of Prague, he is compelled to question, throughout his writing, the purpose of freedom 'when freedom is achieved ... freedom for what?' The sense of arbitrariness is inescapable.

Yet if philosophy is able to recover a sense of direction on the journey to nowhere, its promise is finally grounded, in Flusser's work, not in a moral authority of existential reflection but in the supremely insightful theoretical diagnosis. This, performed with an exemplary precision and economy, makes his argument for the necessity of a conceptual revolution overwhelmingly convincing. The text is a lesson in the logic of theoretical reasoning. It progresses through a rigorous application of a sequence of speculative propositions towards establishing the terms of the argument rather than predicting its outcome. And on the way, the clarity of Flusser's observations guides your inquisitiveness constantly beyond the ostensible themes of the text in the best tradition of European philosophical essayism.

As a work of intellectual craftsmanship alone, *Towards a Philosophy of Photography* deserves to become a classic. With this new edition and an excellent translation bringing it out of the obscurity of its original 1983 publication, the temptation to recommend that the book should be placed at the top of every art school reading list can only be resisted by the command of experience. This teaches that, in the practice of art education, reading lists are places where bodies of literature languish in an air of irrelevance and that it might be more productive to rely, in Fusser's term, on the 'chance necessity' of reading.

Review of Vilém Flusser, *Towards a Philosophy of Photography*, Reaktion Books, London, 1996; in *Dpict*, no.5, December 2000, pp.46–47.

THEORY TAKES A HOLIDAY

ANNE ZAHALKA

> Australia is the driest land on earth and spans three time zones [...] More than a third of the country is classified as desert [...] The service sector accounts for almost three quarters of GNP [...] There is a strong agricultural base which contributes 40% of export earnings.

The introduction to *Journeys in the Dreamland*, a recent exhibition featuring the work of Anne Zahalka at Ffotogallery in Cardiff, begins with a few paragraphs that must have been copied from a geography textbook. How relevant is it to know such *realia* of the work's place of origin? And why do geopolitical considerations of its antipodean provenance so often greet contemporary art from Australia in Europe and guide its critical reception? Or more to the point, is 'Australia' where Zahalka's work originates? Is it where it belongs? Why should I not, for instance, try to find a central European gene in her photographs, hidden perhaps in what seems a loose allusion to her Czech father's name in *Leisureland* (1998–2001)?[1]

In 1985, Zahalka exhibited a set of photographic tableaux with a title borrowed from an article in a critical journal, *The Tourist as Theorist* (1985). They present a cast of characters from travel brochures and holiday snapshots, in T-shirts and sunglasses, suitcase in hand, camera at the ready, in front of sights from 'elsewhere'. There is the Louvre, the Eiffel Tower and the London Underground, Florence, Venice, New York and Hollywood, and yes, there is also the Old Town Square in Prague. The *mise-en-scène* is obviously a back-projected image. These are souvenirs from the artist's travels in the hyper-reality of the photographic studio: 'theory takes a holiday', the subtitle announces in parentheses, in the photographic practice. The trip to the studio is a journey into a foreign land where the artist, disguised as a native, is herself a stranger. She travels alone, or in the intimate company of her models, sometimes plotting her outings from the map charted by art history, sometimes following the itinerary of pure curiosity. The 'artistic licence' is her passport; 'theory' is perhaps her Baedeker; her pictures are postcards sent back home to show what is 'there' to see.

In *Leisureland,* her most recent project, Zahalka ventures into the territory of visual display, an environment in which images are actively produced, and indeed whole worlds and cultures are invented, rather than viewed with detachment. A miniature railway passes a whitewashed mission church before crossing a bridge over a deep mountain gorge. A few crudely painted clouds hover at a discrete distance above a woodland landscape in the background, and the blue of the sky spills over onto the breeze-block wall behind. There are some spare landscape parts and landmarks in a polystyrene box tucked away in a cave-like opening in the bowels of the papier-mâché geology. In the Star City Casino, the scenario is reversed. A mountain formation is jammed underneath the ceiling of a cavernous subterranean gambling hall. The picture is taken from high above, from where security cameras survey the whirlpools of the roulette tables. It is like the view from a Scenic Skyway cable car suspended, it seems, from the horizon that separates the real Blue Mountains forest from the real Blue Mountains sky. Except that in this photograph the sky could be a watercolour sketch, the forest in the valley has the texture of the green sponge used by model makers, and the old-fashioned yellow carriage, level with the camera, looks as though it has just been taken out of a toy box and put in this place to turn land into a scenery for the benefit of the photographic memento.

'Display' is an etymological cousin of 'diaspora'. The *scattering,* dispersion, cultural displacement of *things* are the diasporic conditions of display – things unsettled by conflicts of perception and interpretation, uprooted from their familiar relationships by never-ending symbolic violence and chaos. In the culture of visual display, any image is always only provisional. As soon as it is formed, it is absorbed into the flux of complex transactions between appearances and symbols governed as much by the rules of economic and social exchange as by the principles of an indiscriminate cultural import of the old, traditional, rural or ethnic into the new, modern, urban and cosmopolitan, history into heritage, and even of the futuristic (as another traditional category) into the technological. Or better still, this unstable image is formed on the move, as it were, always between places.

Zahalka's photographs are often staged and always constructed with a great deliberation, rather than 'taken' in an unpremeditated instant. She uses photography in its optical capacity, as an instrument of perspective. Her pictures offer a point of view, rather than a 'slice of time'. Like tourist attractions, they deal in the illusions of immediacy and authenticity compromised by photography's own aspirations; like the environments of organised leisure and like leisure pursuits, they are engaged in a reconfiguration of identities and relationships on the threshold of fantasy; and like theories, they are speculative rather than evidential. They show, indeed, what there is to see – as long as the 'there' is not a place but a proposition by the artist intended to make us look. And there we see it, arrested in its transience, in its interminable flow. But what is it?

Zahalka's pictures do not direct us towards 'Australia' or the 'Australian' (except in that banal metaphorical sense in which a stroll down the underwater glass walkway of a marine aquarium in Oceanworld is a trip 'down under'), not least because the logic of display permits no exemptions. Rather, they prompt us to disbelieve any itinerary of departures and destinations.

The slim catalogue that accompanied Zahalka's exhibition *Fortresses and Frontiers* in 1993 may hide a clue. It is made as a conventional spiral-bound picture-postcard set. The standard postcard design on the back of each card indicates that these are intended for use. But in the bottom-left corner, where the addressee's eye turns to verify the sender's location, it will encounter the word 'untitled' under the name of the photographer. This withdrawal of information frustrates the attempt to identify topographic facts and places. For while 'untitled' refers us to the visible, it always contains a warning that things may not be what they seem. Either the pictures are open scenarios, which gain their currency as they unfold, or they defy those terms by which connections between appearances and places are established and confirmed. 'Untitled' is not a toponymic category. No place is untitled, but if there is an untitled place without a name, without a nominal identity, then it must be a mirror image of the no-place with a name. Or the name without a place, Utopia.

Untitled No.11 shows a desolate excavation site, a vacant lot in the centre of a city, with a rim of temporary structures and prefabricated cabins. This large hole in the ground, partly flooded with water, looks like a reflection of the rust-brown facade crowned with green copper cupolas of the building on its far side. Once a grandiose piece of Eurocentric colonial architecture, it is now besieged by modern tower blocks. A steel-blue skyscraper at the top and an abandoned red haulage container at the bottom of the frame provide a central axis, which, at once, joins the foreground with the background and splits the image in half. This visual symmetry, hierarchy and multiple framing within the frame correspond to the symbolic asymmetries between high-rise luxury and temporary hostel living, the token of bulk transportation of produce and merchandise and the citadel of corporate business, demolition and construction, monumentality and the banality of debris, inducing simultaneously the sense of claustrophobia and vertigo. A small detail adds to the confusion. Almost trimmed off the edge of the picture, there is a steep metal staircase. A sign on the top of the stairs reads: 'No vacancies'.

But all these careful arrangements orchestrated by the artist for our critical pleasure are thrown into disarray by what there is to see. In the original light box version of the work, the image is saturated with improbable light. The sky is cold blue, the windows of the tower block glow orange, the water is an impossibly bright green. It seems to emit light like a pool of poisoned potion from a mystic tale, or like some luminous matter from fantasy UFOs and alien landings – a treacherous, spellbound image, not from this world but definitely in it.

We are left transfixed in front of the picture, where we belong and where geography no longer matters.

1. In Czech, *zahálka* means 'idleness'.

Review of *Journeys in the Dreamland*, Ffotogallery, Cardiff, 2000; in *Portfolio*, no.31, June 2000, pp.12–16.

MAPPING A PLACE IN TIME

We are contemporary only for the time being.
– Günter Grass, *The Flounder*, 1977

El Lisszitsky, perhaps the best known of the early avant-garde experimenters with the possibilities of the print media, wrote in 1923 that 'the printed page transcends space and time'. Interestingly, in the writing on more recent artists' experiments with the magazine page, temporality (a defining dimension of periodical publications) and the implications this may have for the production and reception of art, seems to have given way to the specificity of the page as a 'site' or the magazine as a vehicle within the 'territory' of culture.

The cartographic metaphor in the subtitle of this conference ('mapping the cultural periodicals of photography') is quite indicative of the dominant critical perceptions, preoccupations and problems in (for the sake of another spatial metaphor) the 'field'. The notion of mapping implies demarcation, boundaries and limits, and is wrought with the uncertainties of identification and definition, orientation and hierarchy. The well-rehearsed arguments for and about the magazine page as an alternative art space (or 'the third space'), which have been heard up and down the art world fringe for over a quarter of a century, have always suffered such difficulties as they struggled to contain a far too diverse range of works, attitudes and approaches, and to reconcile too many competing claims. The recent history of this debate is one of a proliferation of stylistic and conceptual categories devised by critics, publishers, librarians, collectors and artists themselves to accommodate virtually any primary artwork conceived for publication or reproduction, and to reflect the variety of available publishing methods and technologies. Even on the smaller scale of the conditions and alternatives that the magazine page offers specifically to photographic or lens-based artwork, these problems are evident and, indeed, it seems that every attempt to resolve them only adds to the confusion. Yet if the ongoing efforts to chart this metaphorical 'space' have so far failed to outline a consistent geography, there seems to be enough agreement about its underlying ideological coordinates.

In general, artists' experiments with, or uses of, the magazine page have been seen as both a gesture of appropriation of the means which dominate the dissemination and interpretation of modern culture and art –

hence the possessive 'artists' pages' – and as a form of a direct confrontation between art and its broader interpretative context – hence the term 'interventions'. This too has been often understood and expressed through spatial or territorial metaphors. At least since the mid-1970s, the exploration of the means of printed communication by artists has been largely construed as a transposition of creative practice from the aesthetic to the social or political arena. The majority of critical opinion and comment has focused on the questions of distribution and dissemination of ideas, access and reach, with their more or less obvious economical and political ramifications – an embodiment of 'the idea to move the product in large numbers', as the American art critic Edit deAk saw it; a trend 'toward making work available cheaply to as many people as possible', in the words of Jon Hendricks, curator of the Silverman Fluxus Collection. Almost equally prominent has been the discussion of the semiological or structural conditions of the page and their transformations. This has been most commonly exemplified by the comparisons drawn between the page and the gallery wall (as on the present occasion), or between typography and layout, their rules and traditions, and architecture – but also by the perceived analogies between the consciously linguistic regime of visual/textual juxtapositions characteristic of the contemporary magazine and the regulatory systems and power relations governing our political and social topography. For many critical promoters of artists' publications, such as Lucy Lippard, it was precisely this that, in the 1970s, promised 'the easiest way out of the art world and into the heart of the broader public'.

In the deeper background of the 'alternative', even 'subversive', image (and self-image) of the 'genre' lies the modernist and particularly avant-garde relationship with the media and the critical evaluation of art they facilitate, and the tendency of both to equate the means and ends, form and content, the medium and the message.

The concept of 'artists' pages' emerged in the aftermath of the epoch of the historic avant gardes which (for the sake of mapping) begun in Paris with the publication of Marinetti's 'Futurist Manifesto' on the front page of *Le Figaro* in 1909 and ended 60 years later in the same city with the last issue of *Internationale Situationniste.* From a variety of individual positions and political creeds, the avant-garde artists ventured into print with the conviction that art had to embrace all social life and that tradition and conventions that had confined its social performance had to give way to a history-in-the-making. The desire to transform both art and the social world called for vigorous experimentation with the semantic and visual unity and illusory coherence of the languages that supported conventional views, norms and beliefs so as to manipulate and change the way people saw, read and thought. Newspapers, magazines and pamphlets became the front lines of the battles. Nowhere more than on the magazine page – in its layout and typography as much as in its editorial tactics – have the futurist, dadaist, constructivist, surrealist or situationist attacks on tradition left their mark. And almost nowhere else. Together with the syntax of newspaper headlines, and the characteristic juxtaposition of dissonant items of content, the Italian and Russian Futurists initially adopted multi-column newspaper layout for their publications, promoted visual and semantic contrast and, later on, the integration of photographic reproductions and words on the page. Soon, however, the dynamic and asymmetric innovations of Futurist and Constructivist typography and the techniques of Surrealist montage and collage became the standard of all but the most conservative periodical publications. Mainstream magazines, such as, the American *Time*, *Life* or *Fortune*, which began to emerge in the 1920s and '30s, were quick to absorb the radical impulses into a new tradition of a lifestyle media culture – a culture which since then has assimilated and reprogrammed *en masse* the effects of multiple artistic revolutions as a core part of its self-identical message.

The 'dematerialisation' of the art object – separation of the 'art' from the 'object' – and its reduction to a material pretext for questioning the nature of art itself by some of the neo- or post-avant-garde generation of artists in the late 1960s and early '70s was, first and foremost, an attempt to transcend the autonomous artwork so as to recover the conceptual essence of art. By abandoning the autonomous object, artistic production was to be freed from the specific concerns, formal restrictions and aesthetic unity of a given medium, such as painting or photography, free to adopt any available means and forms. As a strategy of a dispassionate investigation of the conditions of art and its reception and interpretation, Conceptual art saw itself symbiotically attached to the production of culture in general and, paradoxically, as a mode of theorising about art, functionally detached from any of the culture's specific effects and manifestations. The critical discourse and its subject become interchangeable but neither reducible to criticism nor to an individual art form. To some extent, this also meant the abandoning of the avant garde's militant rhetoric and a retreat from their utopian idealism. The 'page' became an almost iconic constituent in the process – particularly in the work of North American and British artists, most literally exemplified by such purist works as Dan Graham's *Schema* (1966), an ontological description of a magazine page, first published as an 'artist's page' in the journal *Aspen* in 1967.

It was inevitable that the very insistence of Conceptual art on having no definitive formal or stylistic conventions of its own would produce, in contact with the printed media, a characteristic 'look' by default. Alongside the widespread use of photography in its instrumental capacity as visual evidence, it is worth noting that virtually all early Conceptual art publications retracted stylistically to a typographic traditionalism or conservatism, mistakenly considered to be 'neutral'. Until now, informed by the ambiguous approaches of Conceptual art, artistic interventions in the press media often seem to be consciously complicit, albeit perhaps as a gesture of a critical engagement, with the operating conditions and context of their setting. But equally often they display an ostensive ambivalence towards the form of their presentation, while at the same time the structural (and nominal) separation of 'artists' pages' from the body of the magazine still serves partly to preserve an unmediated sense of primary artwork and to protect the artwork from the contamination by, and the interference of, typographic design or editorial style.

From the magazine page, art faces its own condition 'in the age of mechanical reproducibility' when all art has become in some sense 'art as photography', hailed by Walter Benjamin in the 1930s as a radical means for the democratisation of culture, but denounced by Carl Andre four decades later as 'a kind of pornography of art'. Having lost the aura of unique value, the work of art has become the product of a branch of the culture industry. Freed from its 'parasitical dependence on ritual', it has found itself at the mercy of the homogenising principle of media culture and its levelling of values. Lippard believed that 'in an era of proposed projects, photo-text and artists' books, the periodical could be the ideal vehicle for art itself rather than merely reproduction, commentary or promotion'. But a 'rebellion against the increasing elitism of the art world and its planned obsolescence', which she identified in 1976 as a point of departure for artists' adaptations of printed matter – a 'declaration of independence by artists bypassing the system', as she added in 1983 – is not the same as the 'revolutionary criticism of traditional concepts of art' that Benjamin demanded as a minimum compensation for the demise of art's aura. The magazine page, which for Benjamin was one of the means by which the work of art would 'leave its locale to be received in the studio of a lover of art', has become itself the work's final destination: a location of a different sort of 'parasitical dependence', a critique of 'the system' from within, one which relies on that system for its effectiveness and even its material support – and above all for its ability to claim not just a place but a place in time, its 'contemporaneity'.

In my mother tongue, Czech, 'magazine' is *časopis*, literally 'the script of time' or 'time-script' (as in the German *Zeitschrift*). The expression resonates with chronology (writing about time), and chronography (writing by time); with the sense of the passage of time (as in the word 'journal'), and with the sense of 'the times' as the momentary state of culture. Time and the times, as recorded and reflected by the magazine, 'the script of time', are then the denominators of the discussions that shape our sense of 'where we stand' as participants in culture.

This does not mean, of course, that magazines and other periodical media in their plurality reflect, register and record 'our' collective time as something like a common standard in a given culture. Quite the contrary, with their diverse allegiances, constituencies, agendas and interests, magazines play a major part in our perceptions of time as fragmented, uncertain and volatile, and somehow always unsynchronised with reality. Each magazine turns the simultaneity of events and cultural phenomena into individual 'issues' and 'topics', releases them into or places them in time, according to its own editorial, political and commercial priorities. Even within a single field and a narrow geography, such as contemporary Western art (or independent photography, for that matter), the sense of time that magazines reflect collectively is held together by nothing more substantial than the continuity of advertising or the chronology of exhibition listings, but collapses into diverse strata the moment we consider the relationship between an individual magazine's content and coverage and its respective claims to temporary relevance, expressed not only in its overt point of view but also, more obliquely, in its editorial style, design and production values, or its distribution.

In his series of 'timeless political' cartoons, which appeared fortnightly in 1946–47 in the liberal New York magazine *PM*, and continued sporadically in various publications until 1961, Ad Reinhardt proposes the question of a critical reception of art as a political issue in the broadest sense. The most frequent title of the cartoons, 'How to Look at…', parodies the simplifications to which art is exposed in the populist media interpretation; their style is a pastiche of ('low art') collage techniques, a caricature of the Dadaists' and Surrealists' preoccupation with vernacular images and expressions. By extension, this serves as an ironic self-reflection of artists' excursions into the popular press for the purpose of 'cultivating the public'. A key motif, reappearing throughout the series as a signature or a trademark, is the confrontation between a viewer and an abstract painting, where the viewer's bemused incomprehension ('HA HA WHAT DOES THIS REPRESENT?') solicits an angry objection from the painting, concerning the viewer's socio-political credentials ('WHAT DO YOU REPRESENT?'). While the questions persist unanswered, the painting in the cartoon undergoes a number of changes – from a Cubist composition to cuneiform script, a spiral and, finally to the $ sign – and on occasions the whole mini-cartoon becomes an object/picture. This change-in-repetition might be an allusion to the essential timelessness of art – yet it also indicates the political currency of the questions that art should ceaselessly ask of itself by putting its own history and conditions on trial in its own time.

The political is of course never timeless but historical and temporal. Reinhardt, for whom art was 'art as art' and 'art as art [was] art and everything else [was] everything else', understood the challenge that the time-bound space of the magazine page poses to art. Magazines are not only 'spaces' – storehouses for ideas or containers of ammunition for critical battles – they are also, and much more importantly, the means by which our culture reflects our feeble attempts to keep apace with its rapidly disintegrating time and to postpone an immediate collapse of our times into history. And this is perhaps the most important 'alternative' that the magazine page can offer to the work of art: a realignment of the timeless with the temporal, a synchronicity with the world – and with everything else.

Unpublished, 2004; with material from 'A Double-Page Spread', *Creative Camera*, no.321, April/May 1993 and 'Studio Irrational', *Variant*, vol.2, no.6, 1998.

THE AUTHOR SCAVENGER
JOACHIM SCHMID

On the flyleaf of the book *Joachim Schmid: Photoworks 1982–2007*, a pretty, dark-haired stewardess, from the pre-safety obsessed, pre-guilt-ridden, pre-bargain-priced days when flying was still glamorous, offers a welcoming smile to the reader. The photograph – a souvenir perhaps of a trans-Pacific love affair that had faded with time like the cheap Kodak print – was rescued by Joachim Schmid from underneath the pedestrians' feet on a San Francisco sidewalk in March 1994. This may seem like a chivalrous gesture, were it not for the fact that Schmid is something of an indiscriminating scavenger who has lived off such photographic detritus since at least 1982. Plus, it is sediment rather than sentiment that seems to concern him. Indiscriminate, that is, in so far as he includes in his open-ended sequence of pictures from the street (*Bilder von der Strasse*, 1982–) every scrap of a lost photograph he ever finds, yet is discerning enough to select the perfect one from the hoard of nearly 900 when the occasion demands.

Or so it would appear from the careful presentation of his works in this lavishly produced monograph, complete with installation shots and even reproductions of selected pages from the small publications that sometimes accompany his exhibitions. What is less apparent, at least to most of the commentators assembled here, is how obviously Schmid is, above all, a skilled user-manipulator of photographs, how he puts them to work and what he makes them do. His creed echoes Susan Sontag's call for an 'ecology of images', demanding emphatically, 'No new photographs until the old ones have been used up!' His methods and strategies may be 'hands-off', but his enterprise is founded in production rather than restraint.

The nature of his prolific endeavours, and the identification of Schmid himself as a collector, critic, editor, archivist, lay visual anthropologist, sometime photographer and a conceptual artist – to name but a few of his roles – are the dominant, intertwined and overlapping topics throughout the book. Almost in unison, the contributors declare an open verdict on the matter. Yet if Schmid emerges from their writing as an elusive, enigmatic figure – 'Who is Joachim Schmid anyway?' Stephen Bull rhetorically demands to know on everyone's behalf – it is at least partly because the texts focus on his source material before they discuss how he makes it his own. Unsurprisingly then, half of the contributors are preoccupied by the question of 'authorship'. For Jan-Erik Lundström, for instance, 'there are few other projects in the history of cultural production that as radically [...] reject the *auteur* principle' (save for Pierre Menard, a character whose existence alas must be unambiguously credited to no less an author than Jorge Luis Borges). In their ponderings on what may seem a rather generic question, these authors repeatedly call on the authority of Schmid's own statements and quote one another prolifically, almost to the point of mutual embarrassment. Far from presenting a united front, however, the frequent circular cross-referencing leaves the core arguments of the book somewhat entangled in all manner of minor contradictions. At times, this makes the reading experience feel close to being stuck in a traffic jam. The two notable exceptions are the essays by Val Williams, who avoids stepping on anyone's toes by citing exclusively her curatorial self, and Joan Fontcuberta whose references shoot off, bravely and unexpectedly, in all directions at once – from Schmid's near namesake Michael Schmidt to (for no apparent reason) the Chapman brothers; from Plato to Santayana by way of Nietzsche; and from architecture to cybernetics. His energetic prose prompts you to read on – 'memory should not be a cemetery' is a gem of an impatient phrase – while some of his tangential observations reward you with the sense that the reading is not in vain and that there will be more to discover in Schmid's work than he himself, or his advocates on his behalf, would lead you to see.

This is not to say that such discoveries should be made entirely unaided. The running commentary to the reproduced extracts from Schmid's major projects provided by John S Weber is indeed helpful in locating the artist's points of departure and indicating the distance his random samples of demotic photography have travelled on their way to the gallery wall. It perhaps also helps Schmid to make good on his promise as the founder of 'The Institute for Reprocessing Used Photographs', a public campaign to entice donations of source material, to give 'old photographs [...] a new and useful purpose'. But despite Weber's best efforts, this informed and informative account still largely obstructs the view of Schmid's achievement by constantly pushing into your face the undeniable interest of the source photographs.

In the end – or, if you will, from the start – the smiling stewardess may be a more reliable guide. She may usher you past such obstructions into a truly intriguing world where, much for the better, the artist has the upper hand; where the performance of the images varies from one project to the next; and where questions arise not from the anonymity of old photographs but from the conceptual rigour and the formal inventiveness with which the works are constructed. Schmid obviously thrives among the abundance of photographic 'trash' that once worried and disgusted Aldous Huxley, but, equally, he obviously does more than claim a respectable place for it in the broader visual culture. He looks not just at but beyond what is already there. Why is it then, you may wonder, that the moment he lifts his eyes from the pavement to the sky to photograph helicopters hovering overhead, his advocates raise their alarmed critical voices (albeit with their tongues in their cheeks)? 'Has he forgotten "No more photos, please!"?' cries Stephen Bull; 'The fact that the artist himself has taken these photographs remains the single remaining [sic] possible "objection" to this piece', adds John S Weber.

For my part, I have no objections. Well done, Herr Schmid!

Review of *Joachim Schmid: Photoworks 1982–2007*, Photoworks, Brighton; Steidl, Göttingen and Tang Museum, Saragota Srings, 2007; in *Source*, no.52, autumn 2007, pp.76–77.

THIS MORNING THERE WAS NO NEW IDEA

MAEVE RENDLE

In the appreciation of a work of art, any familiarity with the artist's intentions seldom proves helpful. With Maeve Rendle, it becomes an outright hindrance. No matter how I try to engage on my own critical terms with what she makes, I cannot forget that what she makes is, for Rendle, not the work. So, what is it? And how do I reconcile my understanding of the artist's argument with the experience of – why not use the term – 'the work'?

The argument goes like this: the artist undertakes a mundane task, which usually involves a physical manipulation of something readily available in her surroundings. The task has no predetermined objective nor are there any criteria for its execution. The activity creates, in her words, a 'thinking environment' in which 'the work begins to emerge'. The intention is not to produce a new reality – hence there cannot be a work as such – but to put the idea of 'the work' to work in the reality of thinking. She acts as if the work already had an identity and the sole purpose of her actions was to demonstrate its potential.

There is a result, of course, or a residue: a sequence of snapshots taken in the process. Photographically, they are both unremarkable (badly exposed, often blurred) and rather intriguing. They seem like random photographic accidents, without a subject, purpose or logic, and without any sense of singularity. Even where Rendle's photographs may repeatedly focus on a discrete object, they display no particular interest in it and there is no evident effort on the part of the photographer to convey information. And yet, arranged next to one another, they present a compelling account of photography's power to incite curiosity. Their very ambivalence becomes a source of wonder and the frustrating question of intentionality (why would anyone take pictures like these?), reveals quite a fascinating challenge to classification: what do I mean by 'pictures like these'?

In so far as Rendle's photographs are recordings of a studio activity, they belong to the tradition of performance for the camera pioneered in the 1970s by Vito Acconci or Bruce Nauman. But while they share with such conceptual antecedents an ostensive disregard for the visual aesthetics of the photographic art, they are decidedly not a dispassionate 'documentation' of immaterial performative 'works'. They seem to testify to the possibilities and limitations of their own photographic condition, rather than providing a factual account of an external creative act. Nor do these strange pictures comfortably fit the developing fashions of the 'post-critical' artistic explorations of the arbitrary. For that, they are far too much like documents after all. But documents of what?

For her project *Mount Purgatory*, Rendle committed herself to a quixotically ambitious task. Over a period of a week 'in residence' in the domestic setting of Manchester's Apartment – a one-bedroom council flat-cum-artist space – she stripped the place bare, packed away the owner's belongings, dismantled fixtures and fittings, unhinged the doors and took down the shelves, only to return everything to its former place by the time the owner-gallerist returned back from his self-imposed exile on a neighbour's sofa. Somehow, between filling cardboard boxes with kitchen utensils, books and socks, deciding where to put a five-litre tub of emulsion paint and wrapping the washing machine in plastic sheeting, she found the time every day for a tea break with *The Guardian*. In the series of about 90 photographs she took of the growing mayhem in the living room, the newspaper features almost from the start. It appears, sporadically at first, sometimes almost out of sight, on a coffee table next to a small old-fashioned chandelier and something that looks like a loose caster wheel that had fallen off a piece of furniture – exactly the sort of things that you never know where to put when you are packing to move. As the series progresses, the growing stack of newspapers moves from the periphery of the viewfinder centre stage, until, quite abruptly, a detail of a newspaper page fills the frame. In each of the next few frames, a word or two are highlighted on the printed page, gradually articulating the sentence 'this morning there was no new idea'. Then, the camera moves back again, as if contemplating a job half-done, before the sequence concludes with a step-by-step account of the newspapers being neatly wrapped in brown parcel paper, almost in the manner of an illustrated DIY manual.

For the presentation of – let me call it – 'the work' a month or so later, Rendle once again emptied the apartment's living room and mounted her pictures, edge to edge, in a continuous line high up on the walls. In this somewhat uncomfortable viewing arrangement, the photographs explicitly become a configuration of objects, what Vilém Flusser called, in a term borrowed from Wittgenstein, 'states of things': both documents of what took place and new material facts. This, in turn, puts an emphasis on the complicated relational bond in photography between the recording and transformation of the world, the 'state of affairs' in which the photograph originates and to which it returns. What emerges through Rendle's efforts is, then, not so much the abstract work, as an unexpected state of the world that gives the work its meaning. As a meditation on the potential of 'the work', it is as defeatist as it is defiant. And it works.

Review of *Maeve Rendle: Mount Purgatory*, Apartment, Manchester, 2007; in *Source*, no.51, summer 2007, p.40.

DEAD OWL AKA DEAD OWL
RONI HORN

Halfway through the exhibition, there is a pair of identical photographs of a snowy owl. The side-by-side correspondence of the pictures makes you wonder what the result of one + one might be. Is *Dead Owl* (1997) two dead owls or an owl twice dead – a taxidermied bird and an image – or two asymmetric halves of an incalculable whole? And what of the gap that separates one from its double, the delay between one and the next? Just as it is said to be impossible to step twice into the same river, it is evidently not possible to see the same photograph twice. The duplication of the same without repetition heightens the unsteadiness of the singular. These are photographs as well as a photograph. They are (it is) really a semantic trap, which the artist had set already at the entrance to the suite of galleries, where her enlarged signature transferred onto the wall introduces 'Roni Horn aka Roni Horn'.

The dead owl aka *Dead Owl* is almost the essence of photography, but the 'photographic' is not the essence of Horn's photographic projects. Horn works with materials. Like the pigment, varnish and graphite in her drawings, or the metal or glass in her sculptures, a photograph seems to be a substance rather than an image for Horn. It has a clarity, concreteness and integrity, yet its place in a larger composition is determined by a visual syntax rather than the photograph's capacity to gather and convey information. There is a sense of measured precision, construction, rhythm and pace which owes as much to poetry as it does to abstract visual concerns, and a kind of cinematic continuity of time and space that images alone cannot sustain.

The 12 large photographs of the surface of the River Thames, with their delicate colour evoking toned black-and-white prints, resemble the liquid-like surfaces of Horn's sculptures cast from molten glass, while the constellations of tiny white numbers scattered across each print make a conceptual connection with Horn's method of collaging drawings out of the segments of several separately drawn images. They are like the annotations on a cutting pattern or the configuration of clues in a puzzle. Searching for the numerical sequence among shadows and reflections, small undulations, swirls and ripples, brings to mind the eye movement experiments of Alfred Yarbus. It restores the sense of motion to the still photograph, as much as it demonstrates that the transient play of light recorded in the image is also a fiction to deceive the eye and an invitation perhaps to look outside the frame towards the view of the river behind the gallery window.

The numbers cross reference details of the image with footnotes printed below. Some of these are anecdotal observations or speculative comments, statements and propositions, others are citations of literary sources or works of popular culture. Some are addressed to the viewer. 'What are you thinking about?', 'Are you paying attention?', Horn asks with an almost impertinent intimacy which suddenly makes you interpret her ostensible references to further reading – 'see poetry', 'see gelatine' – as actual appeals to vision and, by extension, as allusions to the depth below the surface inaccessible to sight but open to imagination.

In *You are the Weather* (1994–95), a composite portrait made of 100 photographs of a young woman bathing in the steaming waters of Iceland's volcanic pools, seeing and looking are brought into a confrontation. The photographs are life-size, closely cropped, focused on the model's eyes and arranged around the room at an eye level. The expression on the woman's pale, wet face subtly varies from a self-possessed calm to restrained discomfort and sensual pleasure. The changes had been provoked by the inclement sub-Arctic climate but her direct stare is enough to make you feel that your presence is the true subject of the work and the cause of its disturbingly erotic effect. Neither the remote echoes of classical themes nor the allegory suggested in the understated purity of the images offer much reassurance as you feel yourself becoming a somewhat out-of-place catalyst for what you see.

The portraits are grouped into several short sequences of shots taken at separate times in separate locations. Formally distinct, some in colour, others black and white, counting five, six or seven frames, these nevertheless seem to be equivalents, like alternate takes in the making of a film or an entry from a thesaurus, or perhaps better, like a chord in a piece of music. Horn achieves something similar by different means in a work titled *Pi* (1998) – from π, the ratio between the diameter of a circle and its circumference. The project began as a series of books but installed in a continuous line high on the wall, the pictures tell a story from the daily life of an elderly couple in rural Iceland without any concession to narrative logic. There is drama but no plot, a flow but no hierarchy of events, duration but no beginning or end. Close-ups of people's faces, birds, live and stuffed animals, sparse Icelandic vegetation, rugged landscape, grainy stills from an American soap opera: each motif repeatedly engages another in multiple echoes, exchanges and flashbacks. Here and there, the horizon line, exactly in the middle of the frame, connects two images like a hyphen or separates them like the minus sign. The work becomes a text but never a sentence, an equation but not a formula. It seems to change, like the weather, every time you look. The only constant seems to be the one in the title. It may also become, if you will, a photographic essay or even an essay on photography. But why categorise what is so self-evidently itself?

Review of *Roni Horn aka Roni Horn*, Tate Modern, London, 2009; in *Source*, no.69, summer 2009, p.46.

LIVE VIEW

A recent technological innovation, 'real-time live view', which enables us to preview the image on the display screen of a digital camera with 'zero image latency', throws into further confusion our already fragile beliefs in photography's fundamental correspondence to the perceptual reality. It may function, give or take, like an old-fashioned optical viewfinder, but it poses a new challenge to how we understand the tension that photography creates between the world and 'the world as image', and exemplifies the psychological shift, if not reversal, from 'vision' to a pure illusion that digital technology seems to propagate, promote and facilitate.

The view through the viewfinder is always a promise of the picture to come. It is less a confrontation with the present than a moment of anticipation, in which the conventional criteria of looking and observation are suspended for the benefit of a hypothesis and what is seen is no longer the world 'out there', as it would appear to the 'naked eye', but a tacit image. It presents a potential 'state of things', in the limited sense in which Vilém Flusser coined the term to denote photographic images, not the existing 'state of affairs', the actual existence of 'a configuration of objects' as 'facts', whose total sum makes up the world according to Ludwig Wittgenstein.

For Wittgenstein, 'a picture is a model of reality'. It 'contains the possibility of the situation that it represents'. Picturing, the making of a picture, is a way of 'looking outside': thinking about reality, imagining and grasping its structure. This is as true of an immaterial mental image (which is what Wittgenstein had in mind) or a language construction as it is of a photograph, or indeed any picture, but in the technological domain of photography the relational bond between the model and the situation is complicated by the technical functions and capacities of the camera which seem to unite the two, briefly, in the moment of exposure.

It does take time, albeit generally a short amount, for the light passing through the lens of the camera to register on the sensitive surface of the film or the image sensor. But psychologically, we associate photography with instantaneity rather than duration and we experience the moment of exposure as an almost dimensionless temporal contraction in the endless flow of observable events, a sharp demarcation between 'before' and 'after', the seen and the as yet unseen. This is not only because modern photographic equipment can record images at speeds which cannot be accounted for by our sense of transience and lived time but also because of the completeness and irrevocability of the recorded image. Witness, for instance, the distinct echo of both instantaneity and finality in the vocabulary we use ('capturing', 'shooting', 'snapping') or in the click of the shutter to whose speed and precision photography owes much of its authority (and which for that very reason has survived electronically reproduced in our compact digital cameras). In this respect, Henri Cartier-Bresson, who 'craved to seize the whole essence [...] of some situation that was in the process of unrolling itself before [his] eyes', rightly spoke of 'the decisive moment'.

In the moment of exposure 'the possibility of the situation' is decided, realised, and in some manner exhausted, as a latent image. There is, strictly speaking, no gap between reality and representation or a clear distinction between existence and non-existence. There is nothing, or 'no-thing', an interim 'state' (stasis) of an object not yet 'displaced' by the action of the camera (in photography things lose their place) but no longer simply 'out there' either. The possibility of the situation as it had appeared to the observing eye has been realised but is as yet without a consequence. The 'no-thing' is really a paradox: a theoretical construct, in the literal meaning of θεωρία (observation, a looking at), which is at once unproven and fully resolved. Or to put it differently, this is where Wittgenstein's 'state of affairs' precisely overlaps with Flusser's 'state of things'. But this is also where, at another level, they split apart.

For Flusser, the possibilities of (photographic) situations cannot be found in the world but are 'programmed' within the functions of the camera. This 'programme' is designed in such a way as to help us make sense of something 'out there', by enabling us to make images that reach out to reality, but only within the programme's own predetermined parameters and norms and their possible permutations. A photograph is not, then, a slice of the real or its frozen fragment but merely 'a realisation of one of the possibilities contained within the programme of the camera.' It restructures reality according to an image scenario derived from techno-scientific theoretical concepts. It produces a new 'state of things, a situation never seen before', by transcoding 'a theory of optics into an image'. Its material sources and all its references are always external but their effects are theoretically predicted and emerge from within the functions built into the recording technology.

The exploration of what the camera can do, Flusser argues, is the sole preoccupation of photographers. They 'look through the camera out into the world' but 'their interest is concentrated on the camera; for them, the world is purely a pretext for the realisation of camera possibilities'. These possibilities are practically endless and determine not only how the picture is taken, by providing a range of spatial and temporal categories (focal length, shutter speed etc.), but also, indirectly, what can be photographed: the possible situations or 'states of things'. To realise any one of the possibilities of the camera, photographers proceed through a series of provisional choices before arriving at 'the final decision taken in the act of photography: pressing the shutter release'. In Flusser's interpretation, there is no ultimate decisive moment and the apparent singularity of the image is but the cumulative result of a decision-making process.

In any case, a photograph is a record of observation. It is a summary of looking concluded and condensed in a picture at the exact moment the picture is taken. It is inscribed at a single stroke, as it were, like a full stop at the end of a sentence. And it is also all that there is. To some extent, this is so even with some fully automated forms of recording (traffic speed cameras, for example), but it is certainly so where it confirms the observation as a self-conscious search for the picture. The decision to press the shutter is, if not 'decisive', then perhaps 'critical'. It plays a 'critical' role in deciding that this is how things should be seen. It involves an analysis and evaluation of the given situation, discernment (as to what is included and what is left out) and a value judgement. It is also 'critical' in the sense that its urgency or arbitrariness is the critical message of photographs, as well as in the sense in which the term implies a quantitative threshold and the need to act. In short, and rather obviously, without the 'critical' decision to press the shutter release being acted upon, there is no photograph.

In the 'critical' moment of exposure, we sense that we already hold onto something. Not yet a photograph but more than merely raw data: we possess information. But as much seems to be taken away as is gained and we also sense a loss: the information that we now possess is something that is no more, the recorded event has passed, the 'state of things' has lost its contingency, its random suggestiveness as a tacit image, which is exactly what we had been looking for from the start. Precisely because we have decided to take the picture, we have lost the picture promised to us.

The notion of immediate verification of the result runs counter to this psychology. In our practical experience of picture-taking, we may not be conscious that the latent image captured on film is different from one recorded and stored digitally, but the difference seems to have nevertheless a bearing on our expectations. It may not be in the foreground of our photographic thinking that digital cameras do not retain traces of the chemical action of light but transform light continuously into electromagnetic impulses and transcribe those as instantly retrievable binary data, but the difference nevertheless affects our imagination. The information that is waiting to 'come out' on the film in the darkness of the camera is, figuratively speaking, like dark matter whose presence can only be inferred from visible reality. Our instinctive anticipation of this prompts the eye pressed to the viewfinder to keep the 'outside' in view. Even as we concentrate on what the camera can do, we imagine that it will preserve the 'critical' parameters of a special moment 'out there'.

The instantly processed digital image is more like a found object, something that we come across without knowing what we are looking for. It encourages as to 'take' the world as it is displayed to us: a readymade image. The instant availability and therefore disposability of the image creates the impression that we can manipulate time in the still image as we do with video and that our decision to isolate one moment from the continuum preserves the readymade picture without any slippage, loss or any promise. But as the uninterrupted flow of information on the 'live' preview screen blocks the view of the moment 'out there', it highlights the imperative of thinking critically whenever we press the shutter release.

Philosophy of Photography, vol.1, no.1, 2010, pp.14–17.

WHAT TO PHOTOGRAPH?

Photographers should focus their lens on nothing – not merely because, as Susan Sontag says, we need an 'ecology of images', but above all because nothing is the natural state of the image. For an image to exist, there has to be a corresponding something in front of the camera. Yet every time the camera shutter exposes the sensitive surface of film to light, the recorded object or situation ceases to exist in some sense. In the moment of exposure, there is, strictly speaking, no gap between reality and representation or a clear distinction between existence and non-existence. There is nothing, or 'no-thing': a latent image, an interim state of something not yet taken out of the world by the action of the camera (in photography things are displaced), but no longer out there either. The potential of the situation to generate an image has been realised but it is yet without a consequence. What could be a greater challenge for the photographer than to demonstrate this paradox?

Source, no.65, winter 2010, pp.28–29.

TENUOUS NOTES

JEREMY MILLAR

Preparations, getting ready… for what? In his 'Lecture on Nothing' (1949), John Cage describes the composition of the text 'like an empty glass', the purpose of which is its readiness to receive what comes along. Cage's lecture is conceived as an organised 'space of time' open to anticipation or one that 'will keep us in a state of not knowing the answers', as Cage says elsewhere. The printed form of the text, first published in 1959, is structured like a score for a piece of music, divided into parts and those into regular units of 12 lines, each made of four rhythmic measures or bars. One large section consists entirely of what a musicologist might call discursive repetitions; others begin in mid-sentence or even start with a run-over full stop, as if to mark a rest on the first beat of a musical phrase; and the typography and layout of the page systematically indicate patterns of sound and silence for the reading voice.

Punctuation and hyphenation play a prominent part in the arrangement of the text as a graphic score. Words are hyphenated in the middle of the line, parentheses are detached from the phrases they enclose and commas, periods, colons and semicolons are generously spaced away from the words. These indicators of phrasing follow the invisible typographic grid rather than the conventions of grammar or the logic of syntax and act as small obstructions placed within the text, almost in the manner in which the composer had been known to insert small objects between the strings of a piano to change its sound. For the score of his *Sonatas and Interludes* (1946–48) for prepared piano a decade earlier, Cage devised a precise assortment of such 'mutes', consisting of nuts, bolts, screws, pieces of plastic and rubber, measured their relative distances from the instrument's bridge and the dampers, and provided notes on how they should be used. The table of the preparations published with the score reads like a shopping list for a trip to the hardware store: 10 gauge, 3/4 inch long, flat head iron wood screw; 13 gauge, 1 1/4 inch long, washer head furniture screw; 10/24 × 1 inch round head iron stove bolts. The inventory ends with an item that Cage might have used to revise his early sketches of the piece, an American Pencil Co. #346 eraser. I would like to think that the pedantic identification of a particular make and model of this indispensable 'mute' from the writing desk drawer may be a little joke by the artist who spoke of 'contradictions in which we have the room to live', who prolifically used chance operations as a compositional tool and whose name has become synonymous with everything that is unpredictable. It could be even a light-hearted rebuke to those who might take his instructions too literally or try and prepare themselves for the experience of the music by a careful scrutiny of the artist's intentions. It says to me, erase all that and it sets me adrift.

In Jeremy Millar's film, preparations are an end in themselves, not an *a priori* act but all that there is. There is nothing to follow nor is there anything to tell me that the process is complete and its purpose, if any, has been attained. The film shows the interior of a grand piano, the strings, hammers and dampers with the various objects prescribed by Cage placed here and there. An invisible hand taps the piano keys, a large bolt vibrates and gently rocks, an oversize nut threaded loosely on the shaft of an old wood screw bounces up and down and a well-used eraser tensions apart three strings. Its provenance is indeterminable but it seems just right for the job. The sound is beautiful. There are no chords or any musical figures, just single slightly off-key notes at irregular intervals and some faint background noises. Like in Cage's music, silence and intentionally produced sounds seem to play equal parts. There is a sense of duration but no narrative or development in the sequence of evenly composed static close-up shots edited without transitions. After some 12 mesmerising minutes the film abruptly ends, leaving me adrift once again.

The piano had been prepared by John Tilbury, a virtuoso interpreter of the music of Morton Feldman and a biographer of Cornelius Cardew, whose 1975 recording of *Sonatas and Interludes* did a great deal to introduce 'Mr John Cage' to the record collections of my generation of enthusiasts for music strange and weird. Tilbury does not appear on the screen, yet the film is as much his portrait as it is an indirect tribute to the progressive spirit of the latter part of the 1960s and the 1970s, when the commitments of musicians and artists to formal experimentation offered radically new ways of thinking about meaning and strived to renew the transformative and aspirational role of art in the world of perception and social experience. A framed poster on the wall above the Steinway in the opening silent shot of the film attests to Tilbury's credentials as a free improviser, a movement spanning several musical traditions, which emerged out of the collapse of the utopian idealism of the interwar avant garde. In its rigorous forms, free improvisation was one of a host of diverse artistic strategies of resistance to resignation and the ideological indifference of high modernist art and, at times, even a part of a self-consciously revolutionary cultural praxis. Rather than merely calling for criticism and refusal, such strategies engendered small-scale models of social organisation, emancipation and a productive confrontation of authority. The demands of spontaneous creative exchange, where the results and power relations were not prescribed, gave social and political dimension to aesthetic practices and inspired and kept alive a sense of possibility.

The tampering with the received qualities and characteristics of the instrument in this experimental spirit is less an assertion of individual preferences than it is a self-imposed limitation, if not a complete abdication of control. In a conceptual sense it proposes a more ambitious understanding of freedom and its conditions than the (literally) exclusive freedoms granted to artistic vision or sensibility in the liberal-democratic order as an exemption from norm. The determination to let go and control less has implications beyond the search for new sounds or new artistic forms. It may be the most challenging creative response to a world where 'choice' is increasingly an illusion promoted by the ever-growing standardisation penetrating every sphere of life and where, in an ugly contemporary term, 'customisation' is the false promise of technology apparently designed to homogenise all of humanity into customers whose needs and desires are pieced together from a catalogue of predetermined options.

The film that has prompted this thought, perhaps against its maker's intentions, is a work of art. It should be experienced, rather than merely seen, projected on the wall of the gallery where the scale, light and ambience of the space are all brought into play.

I missed that chance. As I watch it now again and again on the computer screen, I cannot help but notice that the few adhesive labels with hand-scribbled letters E, F, G, B provisionally stuck to the piano bridge, resemble closely the shape and size of the keys at my fingertips. For a few moments, the strings run from the bottom of my screen to under the bridge at its top and the row of felt-padded hammers is lined up in front of me as if it were this keyboard, the one on which I type this text, that operated the instrument. As the film runs, the hammers move seemingly of their own will, no matter what my fingers do. In the hammers' disobedience I see a glimmer of hope – a hope that somewhere, in the narrow difference between anticipation and not knowing the answers, there is still an imprecisely outlined space in which we have the room to live. It may be opened wide by the most modest of means.

In his reflections on playing Feldman, Tilbury concludes with an old Taoist wisdom: 'The greatest music has the most tenuous notes.'

Exhibitions 2010, Highland Institute for Contemporary Art, Inverness, 2011, pp.9–13.

A REBELLION WITHOUT CLUES

DIANE BIELIK

The Hungarian Club in Bradford is no more. For a half a century it was a place out of place, a token of a home left behind by a generation. Founded by refugees from the failed 1956 anti-communist uprising in Hungary, it had outlasted the end of its era, the Cold War and 'Eastern Europe', serving a shrinking expatriate community to maintain a sense of belonging to something that could have been had its time not passed even before it came. The Club had kept alive a collective memory of an ideal, a past inscribed into the present not as a history but as an ever-elusive promise.

One of the most enduring and eloquent images from 1956 – the year of the Suez Crisis, outset of the Cuban Revolution, the Melbourne Olympics and 'Heartbreak Hotel' – is a Hungarian flag with the insignia of the communist state cut out. At once a confrontation of a symbol of oppression and a violent gesture of revolutionary contingency, the flag with a hole became the emblem of the popular revolt against Stalinist political hegemony, Soviet military presence and 'foreign' cultural and ideological imposition. The void left in the middle of the flag instantly and dramatically reclaimed the iconography of resistance and struggle for the imagery of Hungarian national sovereignty and pride born out of the defeats, betrayals and retributions of the mid-nineteenth century war of independence and the military humiliation and territorial disintegration following the collapse of the Austro-Hungarian union, and fuelled by ethnic isolation and historic grievances against geographic neighbours.

In one of Diane Bielik's photographs from the soon-to-be decommissioned club, a few small Hungarian flags adorn an empty display cabinet as if it were a building decorated for Independence Day. The arrangement has all the metaphorical efficiency of the revolutionary flag but none of its drama, defiance and patriotic pathos. The living-room scale, the shelves left bare after the ornaments and trophies had been packed away, the dead surface sheen of the fake veneer, even the snug fit of the cabinet into the niche next to the chimney breast, all evoke values and sentiments at odds with the resolute battle calls of Sándor Petőfi and Lajos Kossuth and their twentieth-century successors. The modest aspirations of this 'makeshift monument' undermine the very essence of the monumental. It doesn't rise above the quotidian; it commemorates nothing but fading memories.

In another picture, a large flag on a wooden pole appears to be flying triumphantly in the wind – but this is only because the image is rotated 90 degrees and presented to us provisionally turned on its side. Such impromptu adjustments to the habitual ways of looking may not be enough to resolve the conflicts between the historical terms of reference, fatally contaminated by nostalgia, and the need to contest the significance of their symbolic currency in today's global 'post-national' reality. They may be not much more than temporary diversions. But a diversion may be exactly what Bielik had in mind when she staged her last-minute photographic intervention into the symbolic deficit of the outmoded furnishings, utensils and decorations in the club's deserted rooms. In her improvised scenarios the cultural displacement of the everyday objects and folkloric motifs is unsettled once again by the manner of their display. The mildly bizarre configurations suggest a purpose but offer no clues and the more Bielik overtly tries to give these leftovers-of-meaning one last chance, the more they drift into ambiguity. It is as if every attempt to hold onto the affective ties to tradition and heritage were also a small rebellion against their persistence… for the time being.

Review of *Diane Bielik: Makeshift Monuments*, Hungarian Cultural and Social Centre, Bradford, 2011; in *Source*, no.26, spring 2011, p.37.

LOVE AND DEATH
THOMAS SAUVIN

'Smoking kills'. The 'voice of the nanny state' proclaims the danger of indulgence from every cigarette packet. Long gone are the days when Gauloises Bleues were the trademark of emancipation, freedom and resistance: 'Liberté toujours!' But then again, so may be the days when love was forever and the matrimonial bond was meant to hold a lifetime – or, for that matter, the days when your wedding party snaps were printed by a high street chemist from 35 mm negatives. Today, the silver salts that can be extracted from used film seem more precious than happy memories.

Some half a million such negatives were salvaged by the French photographer Thomas Sauvin from a recycling plant on the outskirts of Beijing. Dusted off, scanned and classified, they have become a collective self-portrait of the nascent Chinese middle class. From this archive, Sauvin has selected 50 pictures documenting wedding party games and customs from the end of the last century, those ridiculous and sometimes humiliating rituals that nevertheless we perform with joy to mark special occasions. On the evidence of the images, cigarettes, with their erotic symbolism, were as indispensible as 'silly string' spray streamers and bananas.

The pictures are of and by people enjoying themselves, having a good time, unsuspecting of the upheaval that the mass-produced anxieties of risk-averse correctness will bring into the uneasy relations between tradition and regulation. A generation later, Sauvin's homage to a vanishing 'tradition in which love and death walk hand in hand' inevitably imposes on the subject a more contemporary spirit of harmless fun. His little photo book is itself something of a party joke. It is presented as a perfect lookalike of a packet of Double Happiness, a popular cigarette brand in China, produced with the deceptive fidelity of a counterfeit Rolex. The only indication that you may not get that much fun with it is the conspicuous absence of a health warning.

Review of Thomas Sauvin, *Until Death Do Us Part*, Jiazazhi Press, Beijing, 2015; in *Source*, no.84, autumn 2015, p.64.

SECTION TWO

THERE IS A DIFFERENCE BETWEEN KNOWLEDGE AND KNOW-HOW

September 2003

Dear Penny Smith,

Your name has been removed from the list.

Yours

The List, 2003, inkjet and pencil on paper, 242 sheets, 29.7 x 21 cm each

From October 2001 to September 2003, Büchler took it upon himself to send a stock reply on unheaded paper to the named sender of every template promotional letter he was sent in the mail. The typed reply read:

> [date]
> Dear [addressee's name],
> Your name has been added to the list.
> Yours,
> [PB's signature]

Below this message, the digitally scanned signature of the original named sender was reprinted in the same place on the paper where it appeared on the original letter, like a palimpsestic trace. Every such signature was reprinted, in its place, on every future letter in the series, such that 'the list' visibly grew with every reply Büchler sent, like an asemic constellation. By sending their artificial autography to someone willing to take it too literally, each named sender inadvertently signs themself up to a list that is never explained because its identity is marked as definite and singular – as *the* list – as something that need not be explained.

Those 242 private replies began the project that became *The List*. By writing back to someone who has not asked to be contacted personally, Büchler is inverting the interpellation performed on him by the first letter's impersonally personal address. Database-driven marketing is an exemplary everyday form of mass customisation, which substitutes an individual's details for x-values within a template to feign a kind of sincerity-on-demand. Whilst database-driven models of direct marketing depend as much on the stuffy manners of formal letter writing – which have long governed socially accepted formulas of 'correct' phrasing as customs – such mass customisation has become more virtually real in our age of networked computing, which has made available interconnected databases, profiling techniques and processing power with previously unimaginable extents.

The List is exhibited as 242 A4 inkjet prints, individually framed and always hung in sequence according to date, but their content is a second round of correspondence that collectively perform a diminuendo or reprieve. They are duplicates of a second stock letter sent by Büchler to his list of recipients in reverse order, informing them:

[date]
Dear [addressee's name],
Your name has been removed from the list.
Yours,
[PB's signature]

Below this message, the addressee's name has been removed from the tangle of scanned signatures – literally and metaphorically, a deleted (Photoshop) layer – such that the list-as-line-drawing steadily disappears.

Just like the first round of correspondence, Büchler's second letter offers no explanation of why a reprieve has been granted, and nor does it offer any chance for consultation or challenge. The influence of Luis Camnitzer's seminal 1971 letter to President Pacheco Areco of Uruguay, sent under the quasi-corporate pseudonym Orders & Co. as a work of Conceptual art, which instructed him 'to do things he could not help doing, so as to expose the dictator to dictatorship' (Lippard, 1973), is clear but inflected by the folkloric spectre of Büchler's compatriot, Franz Kafka. In his trilogy of novels, in particular *The Trial* (1925), Kafka separates the law from any shared moral concept of justice and strands his protagonist K. 'before the law', as Jacques Derrida famously described it. *The List* reminds us that, now as then, in daily life a pressure to answer for an act that is never defined to an authority that is beyond definition can be created by any power with singular authority, be it a totalitarian state or the organons of everyday capitalism.

A SNAPSHOT FROM BOHEMIA

> I admire the attitude of combating invasion with folded arms.
> – Marcel Duchamp, 1915

There are some books on my shelf that I always look at with admiration bordering on envy. They are books on trends in music, jazz and rock'n'roll, which used to make the world revolve at 78 rpm; on -isms in art and thought that gather dust in libraries; on artists, actors and poets who in this day, age and country have long been surviving only in footnotes. Still, to me these books are precious. They were all published in Czechoslovakia, a decade or so ago, some semi-legally, some clandestinely, through enormous collective efforts, enthusiasm and energy. The contribution they made to the corporate knowledge of mankind was hardly indispensable. Yet they made a gesture of resistance and struggle to which I pay respect. Badly printed or mimeographed on fast yellowing paper, these books are monuments to a political attitude. They were published to challenge the neglect of the continuity of culture, which was brought about by a popular submission to the belief that culture is a historical convention. They were published out of necessity, out of a sense of urgency: not to 'break a silence' but to speak clearly in the prattle of so many obedient voices, to act, to participate, to continue…

One of these books presents Jindřich Štyrský's photographic work, the most convincing and consistent part of his output, which included surrealist painting, poetry and biographies of Rimbaud and the Marquis de Sade. It was published in 1982, at a time when Štyrský was seen by the then political establishment as an eccentric of a bygone era, a charming hero of the harmless lumpen petite bourgeoisie. His work (or at least selected fragments of it) was being exhibited and published in an 'appropriate historical context', his milieu promoted as a tourist attraction. Under the rubric of the 'avant garde', Štyrský even found his way into classrooms and lecture theatres. It would seem that there was not much point in an 'underground' publication, especially not one that brought out the least controversial part of the artist's work. Yet, for those who published it, 'made it public', and those for whom it was published, the book was an act of appropriation, indeed an acknowledgement of spiritual kinship.

Some of these photographs are from a series, published illegally in occupied Prague in 1941, a year before Štyrský's death and entitled, enigmatically, *On the Needles of These Days*. Disquieting words for disquieting times. To this day they resonate with some of what comes out of Prague.[1]

In the last 20 years, the ancestry of Štyrský and his peers has also been claimed for Czech art photography by its various professional commentators and 'overseers' – not in a singular gesture towards a specific audience, made at a particular moment from a declared position, but in the generalising terms of Tradition. These critics, curators, editors and such like describe a photographic culture of a 'multitude of individual approaches', a diversity paralleled only by the 'pluralism of the sources of its searching innovation'.[2] At the same time, the 'singular originality' claimed for the current work is attributed to a coherent and uninterrupted spiritual and stylistic continuity; never shaken by crisis, free from doubt. The diverse strands of the practice are said to always converge at the same point – the 'poetic' and 'humanistic' tradition of the Bohemian avant garde. Behind these contradictions and paradoxes lie urgent questions: How could it be that in a country which for decades knew little else than social and political upheavals, the art of photography – tied as it is to the reality of the external world – sustained such seamlessness? How can you have such an easy ride on the bumpy road of Czechoslovak history? Is it not likely that the true point of convergence is not the Czech surrealist experiment but rather a renewed interest in it in the 1960s by a generation that made claims to History while disowning its own past?

Surrealism was 'officially' born in Bohemia ten years after Breton's Manifesto of 1924. It was among the so-called 'second wave' and rooted in an earlier home-brewed petty liberal movement called Poetism – a peculiar blend of proto-surrealist and machinistic aesthetics. Occasionally, Prague Surrealism did reflect the experience of a society in crisis, but by the late 1940s, the beginning of communist rule, it had fully degenerated into academicism. For the artists of the period, the schism between the aesthetic commitments of their predecessors and the demands of culture shattered by the turmoil of war and the brutality of Stalinism was too great to negotiate, directly at least. The credo of Surrealism – 'defence of beauty against loss in contact with life' (Breton) – was of no use after Auschwitz and the bankruptcy of the culture of lyricism (as Adorno taught). Nor was it possible to call for the 'destruction of the old world' as the avant garde once did. The old world had already changed beyond recognition. The surrealist tradition, or what was left of it, was no more than a substitute for confrontation with the reality of life – and confrontations had to be faced. The requirements of artistic experimentation conflicting with the demands of unquestioning submission to the ideologue's decree, made such a confrontation inevitable. While the option of direct political participation in society was precluded, the artists' concern with the 'polity', and with their role in it, found its expression in a paradox: the politics of *anti*-political art.

By the end of the Stalinist era, however, a new generation of artists had begun to emerge. This generation had grown accustomed to the materialistic rationalisation of culture whose arbitrary absurdity was trapped in the seeming coherence of language and symbols in which it had shaped itself. They had learnt to ignore the crude ideology, which explained everything by forbidding doubt and reducing the itinerary of philosophical concepts that inform the complex relationship between art and society to a simple formula. They lost interest in Progress, which had stood still for 20 years facing a fossilised Future. By then, culture was largely left on its own – as long as it accepted and declared the vanity of its aims – as the bureaucracy shifted its demands from ideological zeal to silent compliance. Art had been designated a quiet corner in which to mind its own business. The events of 1968 and their aftermath then finally destroyed much of the remaining interest in the links between art and the world's socio-political realities. The consciously anti-political stance of many of the older generation of artists gave way to a plainly *a*political position.

In this context, more boring than cruel, Surrealism was being discovered again. It provided the most recent connection with the ideal of Modernity – and Modernity was seen as the paradigm of creative freedom. For some artists, this was a departure from the formalistic conventions of the officially permitted approaches. For others, it introduced an element of humour and of play. For most, it was a challenge.

Yet this inspirational rediscovery was steeped in nostalgia, a 'yearning for home', for a pure 'culture of art'. Surrealism, its origins and its inheritance, were idealised so as to become a shelter, a protected zone of an 'absolute autonomy of imagination'. The self-certainties of Surrealism (no less dogmatic than the prohibition of doubt in the political domain) offered a 'historical' continuum of 'artistic concerns', which seemed to confirm and justify the Surrealists' belief that 'art resides above all reality', outside all moral or practical preoccupations. A continuum that ignored the continuity of lived experience in a concrete culture and society.

This newly found genealogy presented a particular challenge for photography. It 'liberated' the artists from the considerations of their relationship to the political realities of the contemporary world, but it could not free photography from the burden of representation.

It was not only the 'magic' of the photographic process, the 'alchemy' of photography that made it a tool of the surrealist trade. It was also the perceived ability of photographs to signify the world without interpreting it – to be passive reflections, 'readymades'. But the photograph can be a projection of imagination only through the process of active intervention in the world. (There is no immaculate conception in photography, no innocence: the photograph is a *corpus delicti*.) To be of consequence, the photograph must then acknowledge the reality in which it intervenes. It must declare its complicity (not mere coincidence) with the external world. No interpretation can simply refer it back to an 'inner world' or to its 'spiritual origins' without turning the world that the photograph reflects into a reflection of fiction. In other words, to be of consequence, the photograph must acknowledge not only History but also the past; not only Humanity but also society; not only Freedom but also politics.

In June 1958 the authors of the first issue of *Internationale Situationniste* identified the problem: 'All those who attempt to situate themselves *after* Surrealism, once again discover questions which *predate* it'. In Czechoslovakia, the problem is yet to be faced. Among the artists of the post-1968 era, only a few have recognised the necessity to leave the securities of the academic History of Art. Even fewer have seen the need to participate through their art directly in the debate that shapes their society. Others have chosen their 'absolute autonomy of imagination' because they saw no choice (or did not like what they saw).

> 'I always wanted you to admire my fasting,' said the fasting showman. 'We do admire it,' said the overseer affably. 'But you shouldn't admire it,' said the fasting showman. 'Well, then we don't admire it,' said the overseer, 'but why shouldn't we?' 'Because I have to fast, I can't do anything else,' said the fasting showman. 'What a fellow you are,' said the overseer, 'and why can't you do anything else?' 'Because,' said the fasting showman lifting his head a little and speaking with his lips pursed, as if for a kiss, right into the overseer's ear, so that no syllable might be lost, 'because I couldn't find any food I liked. If I had found

any, believe me, I should have made no bones about it and stuffed myself like you or anyone else.'
– Franz Kafka, *A Hunger Artist*, 1922

1. The title has been appropriated by artists, writers and journalists on so many occasions that it has gained, on a local scale, something of the cultural ubiquity of *Casablanca* (1942). As with the film, the political commitment of the original work has been obliterated by nostalgia.
2. This short piece is dedicated to my friend Joska Skalník, an artist and organiser, whose selflessness and courage was largely responsible for the publications mentioned in the opening lines. If his achievements differ from the painfully tedious products of the many commentators whose vocabulary I borrowed from a random collection of texts published in Czech catalogues and magazines in the 1970s and '80s, it is perhaps because he was not afraid of 'the word politics, which makes most of our compatriots shit their pants'.

Creative Camera, no.310, June/July 1991, pp.34–35.

NO MORE '80S!

Like the rest of this 'paper',[1] the title comes from a low vantage point of everyday observations – the gents' loo in the basement of the student union building at the Glasgow School of Art. Here, a voice from the school's 'graffiti department' points out one of the main distinguishing features of our modern times: the chronic contamination of any present order by the failed prophecies, promises and priorities of the previous one.

In the routine senior common room self-flagellation, the 'critical evaluation' of the present miseries nearly always manifests itself as a nostalgic recollection of the old and invariably better days: an 'old days' fantasy through which every epoch underwrites its attempts to think up new ways of making things work. The golden age: always once removed from the immediate past… In a *New Yorker* cartoon published some ten years ago, one bespectacled academic armed with a pipe and a glass of port responds to another: 'Yes, the 1970s, that was the time when we used to talk about the 1960s.'

The irony of the cartoon – itself an aspect of the 1980s' self-identification as a time of reflection on the previous decade – could not be less of a joke in the debates raging in student toilets. Down in the basement, where actuality reigns supreme, there is no room for nostalgia and no time for going over old ground (the ground that separates 'today' from the 'old days'). There, 'NO MORE '80S!' is not just a rejection of a bankrupt 'old order' but a call for a conceptual purge: 'No more of the 1990s' talk of the '80s talking about the '70s, talking about the '60s…' and so on, back to the dark ages of modernity… ('No more 1848!', or 'No more 1789!', or 'No more 1640!')

While a similar slogan on the walls of the Sorbonne (or, closer to home, Hornsey or Guildford) in the 'old days' of May 1968 would have signified a desire for radical change at a time when progressive political transformation of society still seemed possible (indeed, when it seemed imminent), the cry of Glasgow's *enragé* in 1994 may well be demanding an end to the 'old' ideology of change at a time when a revolution seems no longer feasible. The once revolutionary sentiment has been displaced by profound scepticism.

Disillusionment is inevitable. The impatient radicalism of the *soixante-huitards* was inspired by the historicity of the modern impulse experienced as a tension between the 'old' and the 'new' – where the 'new' had always been latently present in the 'old' and the 'old' had always been an aspect of the 'new'. But the 'old' and the 'new' are no longer what they used to be. As Frederic Jameson argues (in a different context), the 'imagination of change', as an acceleration of the historical process, is only meaningful while (or where) the project of modernisation is still incomplete: 'the word *modern* loses its point and its meaning where modernisation has become the law rather than the exception [...] the new is experienced as the obsolescent'.[2]

Over the last 25 years, 'modernisation' has indeed lost its former progressive gloss and 'become the law'. As such, it is no longer a matter of creed, aspiration or faith, but of enforcement. The current regulatory power relations of the 'regime of modernisation' are summed up in the catchphrase of Thatcherism – 'market forces': not just a principle of economic management but the restless, invisible core of all social organisation.

On the ideological front, 'market forces' have gained the authority of natural laws. Impersonal and free from moral constraints, they vindicate the brutality of the capitalist revolution when it can no longer be justified as a historical necessity. Once the market rule of self-perpetuating change has become established and accepted, the tension between the 'old' and the 'new' collapses under the pressures of temporary objectives. There is no longer an 'old order' to be overthrown, yet the revolution driven by ever-shifting market priorities must go on.

The words of the all-too-soon thrown-out-with-the-bathwater German philosophers have lost none of their prophetic urgency in 150 years:

> Constant revolutionising of production, uninterrupted disturbance of all social conditions, everlasting uncertainty and agitation distinguish the bourgeois epoch from all earlier ones. All fixed, fast-frozen relations [...] are swept away, all new ones become antiquated before they can ossify. All that is solid melts into air [...][3]

The cultural transformations and shifts of the last quarter-century – in social institutions, in the arts and media, in the legal profession – have, above all, affected education, and higher education in particular. No sooner had the student protesters of the late 1960s and early '70s grown up and re-entered universities and polytechnics as teachers and academics committed to the transformation of progressive social and political ideals into 'good practice', than the colonisation of education by the market began to destabilise their early achievements. The apostles of the market – managers, business executives, consultants – began to penetrate the professional core of the institutions and take over the responsibility for 'innovation' and change. From bottom to top, as if aiming the first onslaught at the most vulnerable, the Thatcherite revolution turned education into an ideological battlefield. First, school-age children were taken hostage; then, secondary education was remodelled and disciplined according to the market gospel. Partly in self-defence, partly in self-delusion, tertiary education had already rearmed itself with the ammunition of Thatcherism (witness the language with which institutional positions are defined and framed) when, under the command of the current prime minister, 'market forces' struck again in the grey camouflage of a back-to-business-as-usual civility.[4]

Post-Thatcher educational policies remain controlled by the crudest of economical calculations. 'Efficiency' is now leading the campaign aimed at nothing more noble than the provision of a less educated (i.e. cheaper) labour force to assist the international competitiveness of British business. After all, in an economical system where retraining has become the accepted strategy for sustaining employment, education is bound to be seen as a short-term investment.

By what means, then, could a student from a generation that has never known anything *but* the 'perpetual uncertainty and turmoil' of change sustain a belief in the feasibility of a revolution if the ruthless logic of its nihilism allows no final victories? How could a student, who throughout his or her entire education has been subjected to relentless entrepreneurial 'innovation', have any faith in those who call for a 'change'? Why should a student who has witnessed at first hand and step-by-step the assimilation of radical rhetorics into the mumbo-jumbo of bureaucratic management speak differentiate at all between my or your 'progressive' ideals and the revolutionary zeal driven by 'market forces' alone? It almost seems that the current radical position must see the 'new' as the already corrupt.

We know, much as we would like to pretend otherwise, that every 'golden age' was always flawed. We also know that acceptance of that fact provides no alternative when the present system can no longer be 'modernised'. What kind of a model or a strategy can we advance to break this impasse?

I studied in Prague at the beginning of the 1970s (in the 'old days', if you will). Every morning at the same time, our professor, a small man with a big book of Holbein's drawings under his arm, walked into the studio to survey the progress of the life class. His critical observations and comments had the same reassuring monotony as his punctual arrivals. He would nod his head here and pause a little there, until he would reach the easel of one particular student whose dark charcoal drawings were the exact antithesis of the mandatory Holbein paradigm.

'It's too black, Johnny, far too black,' the professor would invariably declare in passing. On one occasion, Johnny had just repositioned his easel and pinned a new sheet of paper on his drawing board when the professor arrived.

'How many times do I have to tell you, Johnny? It's far too black again.' 'But, professor,' Johnny tried to defend himself, 'I haven't even started yet!'

'Never mind,' the reply went, 'it's *always* too black.'

A couple of years ago, a friend of mine found in my story a curious affinity with his own experience of an art school. Each time, he told me, as the end of the life drawing session was approaching, his tutor would clap her hands for attention and call at the top of her voice, 'It's a quarter to eleven, ladies and gentlemen, please start shading.'

This anecdote exemplifies two approaches to art education. In the former scenario, the emphasis is on the *process*, in the latter, on the *product*. 'Never mind what you are actually doing, it is that which you *always* do, your attitude, style, or the characteristics of your working method, that matters', versus, 'No matter where your way of working is taking you, it is where you get "at the end of the day" that counts.'

Art education is, of course, a precarious balancing act between the two – process and product. Their relationship and interdependence are intricate and complex, and, in practice, they can never be separated quite as crudely as in my metaphor. Any attempt to identify where the contemporary emphasis lies will not escape generalisations, and will be in danger of confirming certain common prejudices and over-simplifications. Yet, even at that cost, I must claim that the dominant approach in British art schools is increasingly product-driven. Further, I believe that this is not simply a matter of a tradition of making art as an activity resulting in the production of objects or artefacts, nor even an inevitable condition of the long-accepted 'professionalist' aims of education, but a consequence of the current ruling social and political ideology.

Under the cannon of 'assessments', 'audits', 'league tables' and 'performance indicators', process-led education is difficult to justify. It does not provide the convenience of measurable 'outputs' and does not lend itself easily to the self-regulating order of competition. Where the process is in the foreground of the teaching approach, the focus is on the student's experience, on 'you', relative to the experience of the teacher. As it prioritises the identification of individual needs, process-led education conforms, to some extent, to the privileged market model. But this is not necessarily the same as bowing to the freewheeling individualism of entrepreneurial culture: the 'exchange' taking place between the teacher and the student is activated by the 'social' context of learning and teaching. At its best, this approach is characterised by sharing responsibility for the formation of a practice which is sustained by 'making' rather than 'production', by 'discovery' rather than 'invention', or by 'participation' rather than by 'enterprise'. (And at its worst, as in my own case, it at least makes you aware that, as an artist, you are not in competition with Holbein but with yourself!)

Product-driven education is much more adaptable to, and much closer to the reality of the marketplace. Here too the emphasis is on the individual, but rather than the intangible 'experience', it is the demonstrable 'evidence of achievement' that is the focus: not 'you' but 'it'. The student–teacher relationship is mediated by 'results'. ('Solution-driven' would be another way of describing it.) As teaching and learning are finally consumed through a quantifiable 'outcome', the division of responsibility between the student and the teacher is more sharply defined along the lines of an essentially economic model of exchange. The 'value' of the student's work is negotiated on the basis of 'ownership' ('my work', 'my opinion', etc.) and competition (the criterion of 'originality' in the sense of 'newness'), and is relative to the equilibrium of demand and supply (an equivalent of 'price').

This does not mean that the process by which results are achieved plays no part in product-driven education, nor that 'products' are but an accidental residue where the process leads the educational approach. The distinction is above all a matter of philosophical and ideological positions: while process-led art education is primarily concerned with art and its social foundation or function, 'there is no art, only artists and their artworks' (to paraphrase Thatcher's notorious dictum) for the extremes of the product-driven approach.

The main difficulty with the dominance of the product-driven approach in British art education, from the perspective of my argument, is its relationship to the past – its concern with that which *has been* done (or *will have been* done). It operates in a reactive mode, where the results, achievements or solutions provide, in theory as much as in fact, the starting points for evaluation and exchange. Insofar as the solutions are almost invariably expected to be 'innovative', even that which precedes them, the idea or the brief, can be seen as already obsolete at the point of conception.

This seems to make the product-driven approach vulnerable to the pressures of the 'regime of modernisation'. No surprise that, in practice, the general and well-intentioned resistance to the imposition of the 'market model' on education has ended in constant tinkering with every detail of every part of every structure in a perpetual reformist urge. Or in other words, in adaptation and conformity.

An alternative is not easy to find. Changes *are* necessary and confrontations *are* inevitable. There is no point in trying to reverse the doctrines of the market model. That would only mean returning to the models and ideologies of the 'old' radicalism that failed to take account of the diversification of contemporary life and social conditions, and hence failed to contain the 'market revolution' in the first place. Nor is there, of course, any point in trying to overcome the damaging side effects of the market model by revolutionising the revolution.

A far-reaching debate is needed before we can even guess what an alternative regime or social conception might look like. Both art and educational practice are fields where this kind of discussion may be usefully conducted. But first, we must try to find tools and forms which are more resilient to contamination by 'markets' than our present practices. It seems to me that a methodical shift of emphasis from the product-driven to a process-led approach in art education might be one way of starting.[5] At the very least, it could lead to a renewal of faith in what can only be described by such difficult and worn terms as 'change' or 'future'.

The 'old days' were not 'better' – they merely had 'old' problems. After all, we now live the *future* of a past 'golden age'.

Students have never been poorer; schools and colleges have never had to operate in a more restrictive economical and political climate; never before have the programmes of institutions been to such an extent controlled by bureaucrats ill-equipped to pass academic judgement, and never before has so much administrative work been left to academics with no qualifications to handle any but the most rudimentary clerical tasks. The management has become the site of 'creative thinking'; the artist-teachers have been charged with 'delivering' the educational 'product'. The pessimist says, 'It can't possibly get worse'; the optimist says, 'Oh yes, it can.'

(There is an optimistic reading of that old joke. It identifies optimism with mental and spiritual readiness and, by extension, it identifies problems with opportunities.[6])

1. As the present text is compiled from hastily scribbled notes and from memory, with the intent to preserve some of the improvised manner of my conference contribution, the use of the term 'paper' deserves quotation marks.
2. Frederic Jameson, 'Postmodernism and Utopia', *Utopia Post Utopia*, Institute of Contemporary Art, Boston, MA, 1988.
3. Karl Marx and Friedrich Engels, *The Manifesto of the Communist Party*, 1848. They might have not lost their prophetic urgency but the collective and collectivist interests which drove the earlier stages of the revolution have been completely replaced by a fake and faceless 'egalitarianism' of individual needs. With thanks to Peter Sloterdijk for reminding us; see Peter Sloterdijk, 'World Markets and Secluded Spots' in Pavel Büchler and Nikos Papastergiadis (eds), *Random Access: On Crisis and its Metaphors*, Rivers Oram Press, London, forthcoming [1995].
4. 'Back to basics' – a notion whose potential consequences for art education are too grim to contemplate – is nothing but another twist in the perversely self-fulfilling revolution: a tactical retreat into the fundamentalism of the market aimed at undermining the positions and influence of 'new' professional elites.
5. Given that there seems to be a widespread agreement that such aspects of product-driven art education as, for example, marks and degree classifications might actually be harmful, it is somewhat surprising that the process-led approach has not been generally adopted already.
6. As I write, John Patten, Secretary of State for Education, has lost his Cabinet seat. Having just been exposed to the 'optimistic' assessment of today's reshuffle by a television commentator, I wonder whether my concluding remarks are quite appropriate.

'No More '80s!', *Drawing Fire*, vol.1, no.1, December 1994, pp.25–29.

VIRTUAL CONFUSION

With the arrival of 'virtual reality' the sell-by date of the future is no longer 2001. Flanked in the dictionary by 'virtu' and 'virtue', the term itself has caught the imagination of the visual arts community with a sudden sense of urgency. No matter how we see the world around and ahead of us, and no matter how used we have become to the perennial invasions of the 'new' (or how cynical we have grown about the unfulfilled promises of past 'innovations'), this greatest challenge to the mechanical principles we have lived by for centuries calls for an imminent, radical change in the way we think of *the image*. But as the essence of our visual culture threatens to become obsolete and we are trying to imagine the shape of an imaginary 'reality' beyond illusion, both indistinguishable from the 'real' one and totally different, our minds are experiencing serious confusion. Among those of us involved with the visual arts, not many seem to be sure about just what is so new about these 'new images'. Even fewer seem to be certain just how 'real' – or how 'virtual' – these 'images' really are. The concept of virtual reality does not merely pose questions to reality (such questioning is the mode of the image); it puts the imagination itself on trial.

We have learnt to assume that reality underlies all appearances, images and concepts; it is the 'real thing' of which the image is a double, a surrogate. Much as we (some of us) would like to believe that through their omnipresence and inflation in this techno-scientific world, images have lost all signifying connections with reality, we still know that it is 'reality' which gives substance to the image's loss of signification. Reality surrounds every image. Every image, even the purely 'abstract' one, has to negotiate its relationship to facts, phenomena, mechanisms and processes external to itself. For even 'negative representation', as Kant called it, is representation – the image still demonstrates ex*istence*.

The 'new (virtual) image', however, constitutes a complete world of its own. It submits happily to the authority of the natural order of cause and effect (hence it is not an illusion) but only inside its own self-perpetuating system. It doesn't seem to reflect or 'represent' anything outside itself. Is it then an image at all? It certainly is not a *trace-image*, an image-as-we-have-known-it, from cave paintings to photography and video, which bears witness to a particular physical event and comes into being through a direct contact with pre-existent reality, matter or energy. It is not an image *of* something, a duplication by recording. Rather it is a relative numerical simulation, a *matrix-image* – a mathematical model, a formula made visible. The constituent components of this 'image' are interdependent numerical quantities, infinitely modifiable relationships of values in constant flux. Thus, the 'virtual image' is a *liquid* image, a visual state of a language ruled by the principles of the calculus.

It is true that the language in which the matrix-image creates itself is a highly formalised system of abstract symbols, but it is a language all the same, a code. Yet, a strange paradox is at work here: this 'image', created as it is in a language, does not appear to form a *message* that could be received and decoded. Instead, it exists as a field of data in a kind of a dialogue with the viewer/participant. It is not received but *entered into* like conversation.

Things being what they appear to be in cyberspace, it would seem that the direct, non-sensory, interactive participation demanded by the virtual 'image' should be a purely interior adventure. The dialogue with the model does not require any consideration of the exterior world (just as it is of no direct consequence outside its own digital framework). For as long as the system is in operation there seems to be no distinction between the 'virtual' and the 'real'. Yet, any interlocution is an encounter of at least two identities (the kind of exchange from which images are born – one imprinted on the other). In the digital intercourse, the two identities are linked, becoming parts of the same system, but since the dialogue requires polarity they cannot merge into one. Presumably, this dialogic mode will always retain at the very least one external referent: the actual identity of the viewer/participant, complete with the norms, beliefs and uncertainties that determine our perceptions of the world. And so our interaction with the digital designer universe of 'virtuality', the techno-nature of our own making, will produce a *meta-image*: the reflection of our feeble attempts to make sense of the world we actually live in (and to formulate our reality in images).

Edited extract from *Words in their natural setting: Tramline no.1*, Tramway and Glasgow School of Art, Glasgow, 1994. First published in *Ghost Stories: Stray Thoughts on Photography and Film*, Proboscis, London, 1999, pp.90–92.

SCOTLAND V EUROPE, 0–0

This June, when the word Wembley featured more prominently in seasonal conversation then even Wimbledon, I found myself without a suitable denomination through which to channel my enthusiasm for the game. 'Czech Republic' is to my nostalgic mind not the same as 'Czechoslovakia', the team that I supported 20 years ago when they won the European title over 'West Germany' – which, in turn, is not the same as Germany, where a part of my ancestry lies. 'Scotland' is a name of the place where I live but so is 'Britain' or 'United Kingdom', where in Cambridge, England, I have had a home and studio for over a third of my life.

Even though there are few things more international than football – a 'national game', pretty much, wherever you go – and even though the game is played by the same rules everywhere, the unquestioning identification with the national strip seems non-transferable. It is as if only some kind of native sensibility could feel comfortable in that mythology, made up of reminiscence, betting-shop wisdom, edited highlights and slow-motion replays, which passes for collective inheritance and defies all divisions of club loyalty and rivalry. No matter where I feel at home, my sense of belonging is confirmed or tested in the symbolic dichotomy of 'home' and 'away'. And then, when the match is on and European history is in the making, the sense of belonging is carried along by the dynamics of expectation or hope (or, in the case of 'Scotland', by defiance), by a desire to be recognised by others as part of a collective entity among the competing 'nations'.

On cultural turf, identity is formed differently: not by contest but by a context that cannot be localised within the limited framework laid out by national boundaries and geopolitical forces. Rather, cultural identity must be conceived of as a creative articulation of the space between history and contemporaneity. In this culture, such a symbolic space can be described by the difficult term 'Europe'.

In Scotland, 'Europe' is a future notion – part of a political ambition of self-determination. But Europe as part of Scotland's cultural self-identification is hard to perceive from here just yet – at least when it comes to the role of art and its institutions.

Contemporary art, both as a tangible manifestation and a producer of culture, discovers and makes visible the complexity of influences and currents that have brought us where we are. But it often seems as if the challenges of this time, of the contemporary, do not quite matter in Scotland. The capitulation of critical debate to the popular press due to lack of support for independent publications is one example; the absence of contemporary art of international standing from Scottish public collections is another; the manifest confusion between tradition (through which the contemporary seeks its legitimation) and traditionalism in civic art politics, and even in art education, is a third… What is at risk is not our recognition in Europe but our recognition of Europe in us.

(As for Euro '96, I ended up, reluctantly, supporting the German team against my former compatriots, on the premise that young men who can't be bothered to have a shave and comb their hair for a final with record television ratings do not deserve to win.)

Circa, no.77, September 1996, pp.15–16.

A SHADOW OF THE CROWD

On the one hand, it is still possible to speak of the *presence* of sculpture in the contemporary city in the 'objective' terms of time and space; on the other, any discussion of the *role and function* of such material manifestations of creative or artistic interventions in the physical environment must, sooner or later, turn towards the question of the conceptual, technological and logistical conditions that determine their perception. Central to this will be the question of collective public interaction for which public sculpture, in a historical sense, provided both a possible focal point and a means of regulation (as an expression of legislative power or authority, as well as part of an overall spatial or environmental scheme).

It could be argued that with the advent of modern communication media, particularly photographic and digital image technologies, and the consequent necessary changes in the demarcation and self-perception of the 'public domain', the primary role of public sculpture may have become substitutive rather than communicative. (It *stands for,* rather than *says,* something.) Instead of being a physical 'marker' of collective interaction, it has become the last symbolic reminder of the absence of 'the crowd' from the conceptual 'space' of the contemporary metropolis.

1. The crowd is both a product and an active agent of the urban milieu. The notion of the crowd is virtually synonymous with the dynamics of the modern city, which facilitate circumstantial concentrations of collective activity and which are, in turn, affected by the constant necessity to regulate and absorb such activity.

Yet, it is possible that in the contemporary Western city the crowd can no longer be perceived as a distinct formation – that it is no longer distinguishable from the forces that it is ruled by – and that it has been diffused or dispersed throughout the demographic and social structures of the city.

2. The disappearance of the crowd, its dissolution, is a result of changes in communication and perception, which parallel the shifts in technology and economy by which post-industrial urban society sustains itself; from sequential modes of communication and exchange to the mode of

instantaneous contamination – or, seen from the perspective of the crowd, from a participation in a process to a random exposure to effects and products. Both the historical and the geographical coordinates of the crowd (its 'time' and its 'space') have been radically affected:

> The early modern city was steeped in an indirect conception of time, where time could only be derived from the experience of succession and simultaneity of phenomena in space. The contemporary metropolis, however, informed as it is by the irradiative model of instantaneous contamination of entire regions or populations, embodies a dramatic alteration in the conditions of perception. Space is now suddenly condensed, and time, rather than passing, exposes itself.[1]

3. The effect of these changes on the state of the crowd can best be seen if the crowd is considered not as a social configuration, governed by general socio-economical laws, but as a conductive field of interrelationships among individuals – a *medium of communication* – particular to the conditions of the temporal and spatial relationships which occur in the contemporary city.

4. The most visible feature of the crowd understood as a medium of communication is the ripple effect caused by the spreading of information from an individual to an individual through direct contact (like a rumour or a virus).

The crowd is, undoubtedly, a symptom of activity: a shape of an event. It is formed and held together by a response to external stimuli. Our everyday anthropomorphic vocabulary unites such a response into a single 'body' and one 'voice'. But the seemingly immediate reflexes of this 'body' only trigger off further complex reactions involving large numbers of individual relative operations. A round of applause is a typical example: it erupts (almost) instantaneously as a direct 'corporate' reply to an outside impulse but it develops, breaks up and eventually comes to an end through mutual interaction among the people in the crowd.

5. Information spreading throughout the crowd is, as in any system, subject to friction, entropy and absorption. But because it spreads through active contacts among *individuals*, through constant recoding and reformulation in a continuum of social exchange, the inevitable modulations and mutations of the initial impulse facilitate an awareness of collective

interdependence as they affect the very social bond on which the transmission depends: the flow of information is conditioned by a *mediation of immediacy*.

Thus the internal cohesion of the crowd and its existence as an active agent are determined by the individuals' experience of their participation in a collective transformation of information into knowledge. 'Being there', in a place and at a time, means sharing in the power to transmit, that is to say, the power to *transform*.

6. The crowd has no centre. There are no firm points (and no fixed hierarchy) in the crowd, only an external shifting focus, which becomes internalised and ultimately dissolved in a process of continuous mutation.[2] Information travels throughout the crowd from a more or less random point of entry in all directions, at once generating a wave of response and gradually affecting the overall state of the crowd.

However, a mode of transmission that can neither be regulated from a centre (because such a point cannot be isolated within the 'system') nor coordinated externally (because any external focus is always created only by the gaze of the crowd itself) is inevitably unpredictable and uncontrollable – and potentially disruptive to the 'normal' functioning of social mechanisms.

7. As a controlling measure modern society has therefore introduced a whole array of technologies and standards aimed at systematising, synchronising and simplifying the functioning of the basic components of the 'system', the relationships among individuals: from legal provisions governing the rights and social obligations of the individual, through health and safety systems, to the system of education and professional qualifications, urban planning and coordinated design, standardisation of working hours and leisure time, etc. While these measures do not eliminate the transformative powers of the crowd, they do nevertheless enable external agencies to control the spread of information, its radius and its influence, more efficiently by allowing them to predict and locate with some accuracy the moments and points at which the process of transmission can be interjected, polarised or disrupted. Indeed, these measures can effectively be used to turn the power of the crowd into the means of self-control.

8. Yet controlling the 'system' through selective regulation of the social contact among individuals is not only too slow but, importantly, it requires individual interpersonal links to be maintained. To be effective, the regulatory

principles must be integrated into the process of transmission itself in such a way that, for example, criteria of interpretation precede information, or readymade 'facts' strategically coincide with 'common knowledge'.

It is only when an external agency can reach every individual simultaneously that the active social interrelationships become redundant. The modern mass communication media provide the necessary conditions: a contraction of distance through ultra-rapid transmission, a massive scale of operations, and the anonymity of dehumanised technology.

9. A key role in harnessing (and utilising) the transformative power of the crowd is played by the camera technologies, from photography and film to television and video. In particular, the transition from symbolic representation to mechanical recording and to image processing, storage and manipulation (in both analogue and numerical formats) has, since the beginning of the twentieth century, produced a new order of information which, being neither true nor false, denies participation, resists transformation and generates instant polarisation of positions. The photographic or photo-based image is not merely an inert trace but an implosion of a 'photographic event'. As with a black hole, metaphorically speaking, nothing can escape from the image. Nothing can therefore be transformed in the process of communication. Instead, communication itself seems to be absorbed by/into the image.

10. This, however, is not to suggest that these images, moving or still, are in any way immutable. On the contrary, subsequent manipulation of the recorded image is in many respects intrinsic to photo-based media. (Its use dates back to the beginnings of photographic time and is not only a standard practice in all movie making, in advertising, propaganda, editorial illustration, architectural design and, of course, art, but it is also a necessary condition of image technology.) The manipulation of the image presents itself as an effect of (technological) reality, which cannot be reabsorbed into the immediate reality of direct social contacts. It seems to be precisely the technology's power to manipulate time and space, to collapse it into the image, that makes a claim on individual perceptions, consciousness and memory while it demobilises the collective powers of the crowd.

It abolishes the connections between space, time and experience by seamlessly fusing the present moment with the past in a perpetual appearance and disappearance of images which follows its own chronology of broadcast and publication schedules and which overthrows the order of geography by uniting all locations into one, on the same 'dimensionless' picture plane or screen.

11. The confusion that this creates is best illustrated by the example of our everyday diet of news media. In an older model in which the dissemination of information still involves human interaction (and the necessity of active participation), such as the purchase of the newspaper from a street vendor, a certain awareness of a chronology of events is maintained: we know that even the 'latest' news is already old news; or that, metaphorically speaking, there is no such a thing as 'today's paper'. With the more technologically advanced media, such as television, which combines 'live' elements with recorded and reconstructed information, it becomes very difficult to maintain a sense of correspondence between space, time and experience.

12. We are 'bombarded with images', as the cliché goes, in a kind of perpetual 'precision bombing' campaign (a notion which emerged at the time of the first 'television war', the American intervention in North Vietnam in the mid-1960s). The same technology that assists 'pinpoint accuracy' in disseminating death also creates a deadly isolation of each individual when it is aimed at the crowd.[3]

In the near future, the miniaturisation of equipment, electronic superhighways, interactive television, etc., will probably shatter even the last remains of collective public interaction by vastly multiplying image-realities and competing for the 'public domain' from a myriad of individual and corporate centres of influence.

13. Like an open-air cinema, where, at night, the projected collides with the reflected and 'architecture becomes the paradox of the show',[4] the contemporary city is a continuously reorganised image-space. Its walls and boundaries are not merely shifting, contracting and expanding with a flow of images – they are, in fact, only perceptible as 'afterimages' (retinal residue) always in the process of disappearing. The street, the agora, the forum, or the piazza, have dissolved in the limitless periphery of global satellite TV transmissions and mail-order shopping. The only space still reserved for 'public gatherings' is the self-defining space of close-circuit television – a space not of transformation but of passive transit.

Dublin, 1992 – Glasgow, 1995

1. Michael Feher and Stanford Kwinter, 'Foreword', in *Zone 1/2*, Zone Books, New York, NY, 1987; they refer to the article 'The Overexposed City' by Paul Virilio in the same publication.
2. Literary expressions such as 'at the centre of the crowd' or 'leading the crowd' really signify outside positions: 'surrounded by', 'followed by', etc.
3. Indeed, one could almost speak of the effects of these technologies in terms of organised violence, even media torture, insofar as torture and organised violence can be defined as 'an assault on the links and connections between people and the patterns of relationships through which [...] the individual develops further patterns of interaction and communication.' See RD Blackwell, *The Disruption and Reconstitution of Family, Network and Community Systems Following Torture, Organised Violence and Exile*, Medical Foundation for the Care of Victims of Torture, London, 1989.
4. For an illuminating discussion of the (con)fusion of urban and cinematic space see Nikos Georgiadis, 'Open Air Cinemas: The Imaginary by Night', *Architectural Design*, vol.64, no.11/12, London, 1994.

Coil, No. 4, February 1997, pp.10–15.

STALIN'S SHOES (SMASHED TO PIECES)

I've never yet seen a statue take a step.
– Ota Filip, *Café Slavia*, 1985

One of my earliest memories is of posing for a family album photograph on the toe of a granite shoe as big as a motorcar. The oversize footwear belonged to a giant statue of Joseph Vissarionovich Stalin, standing on top of a steep slope high above the river and the Jewish Quarter of Prague Old Town. It was a proud moment in which my five-year-old self enlisted Stalin as the great wonder of the world, and which continued to resonate years later in an indistinct mental image of the Colossus of Rhodes as a huge grey man in a military coat, with a moustache, Caucasian eyes and Asiatic cheekbones. My father, an engineer by education and a builder's hand by trade, praised the statue as an impressive achievement of both construction and the art of urban planning. It had taken 600 men almost two years to build the 30-metre-high, 14,000-tonne sculpture and its ziggurat-like pedestal surrounded by terraces, wide stairways and waterworks. There was something of collective pride in my father's voice as he explained that the hillside beneath Stalin's feet had to be reinforced by injections of concrete and a vast expanse of parkland re-landscaped.

The technical ambition of the project was in keeping with the symbolic convention by which Stalinism was a 'triumph over the past' and Stalin the Conqueror of the Future. The statue showed the *generalissimo* standing in a Napoleonic pose – one hand resting between two buttons of his double-breasted coat, the other holding a book – at the head of a small procession of workers, farmers and soldiers. It seemed that the company had just arrived under a large flag held by the first of them and, while Stalin was already putting his left foot forward to march ahead, the soldier at the rear of the group was still glancing back to where the last battle of the previous era had been fought. At any moment, Stalin would step off the plinth and follow the axis of his gaze on the city plan, across the bridge, right down the main boulevard of the Old Town, to the Jan Hus monument in the Old Town Square. He would extend his hand to the late-fourteenth-century reformist preacher, Hus, and embrace him in the sportsmanlike manner with which a champion shows respect for a loser.

Stalin never had much time for the past. As he saw it, the past that his propaganda troops had fought was not the past of neat categories regulated by the unidirectional 'laws of history', but something rather ambiguous, dismal and irritable that denied historicity. The past was the traces of an old age within the new epoch: 'the burden of the past, the habits and memories of the old life', the 'inertia and mental stagnation, [...] the philistine narrow-mindedness and routine' of the old, 'barbaric and savage', that which must be disposed of 'definitely and for good'.[1] The mission of Stalinist propaganda, and its doctrine of 'historical necessity', was the ideological homogenisation of diverse cultural heritage. There was something of a contradiction in the idea of building a monument to the defeat of the past as a quasi-historical event, but then 'the past' can only be defeated in the realm of historical representation, and besides, Stalin was rather fond of the word 'contradiction'.

The Old Town of Prague is a place where the past is an eclectic fusion of half-remembered legends and forgotten aspirations, and both are made of soft sandstone, stucco and bronze. Only resistance and resentment build their barricades and monuments of granite.

In his novel *Café Slavia* (1985), the Czech writer Ota Filip gives a fictional account of a conversation with the architect of Prague's Stalin monument. The architect is worried about his work's relationship to the plethora of statues of saints and historical heroes in the city. Some of them may have to be re-sited so that they don't block the view, or turned around so that they face the monument. 'The most important ones are turned away from Stalin, and those who have to bear Stalin's stony gaze from the side have for centuries had their faces turned heavenwards or else stare at the pavement.'[2]

One of the bronze saints who, according to the rumours reported by the novelist, may have to be 'removed because he is in the way' was the semi-legendary counter-reformation martyr St John of Nepomuk. The rise of his cult in the eighteenth century was closely associated with the growing ambitions of Bohemian patricians and clergy, who turned Prague into a city of architectural wonders. St John's statue on Charles Bridge was the first in the astounding baroque sculpture gallery in which, like in a diorama, the past seemed to unfold before the eyes of the granite onlooker towering on the hill above. But looking in the opposite direction, from Kampa Island just below the west end of the bridge, one could have imagined the Stalin monument, its scale and detail diminished by distance, as though it was just another of the bridge statues, right by St John's side and trapped in the same mythical past of the patron saints. (At that distance, even the giant wreaths, the size of tractor tyres, laid with great pomp on the steps of the monument on Victory Day would have appeared no more ostentatious than the modest floral tributes quietly left on the plinth of the Nepomuk statue every year, exactly one week later, on 16 May.)

At least one major figure from the panopticon of national mythology, however, was directly facing Stalin's gaze: the turn-of-the-century equestrian statue of St Wenceslas in Wenceslas Square. Ever since Czechoslovak independence was declared at the legendary hero's feet in 1918, St Wenceslas has been a public rallying point, a place where history has been lived. At Stalin's feet, the past was laid to rest. The distant eye contact between Stalin and St Wenceslas was, by ideological design, not only a confrontation of the hierarchy of monumental presence, or iconography of scale, but also a takeover of symbolic patronage.

Presided over by Stalin, Wenceslas would be able to retire from active duty as the guardian of the nation's emotional attachment to the symbolism of the past and become a kind of a godfather to a new era in which people are displaced by the 'masses', their past is disciplined into 'historical lessons', and monuments are built as goalposts for an ideologically predetermined future. But just as the majestic beauty of Charles Bridge could not be intimidated by the scale of the grim statue on the hill, so the history underwritten by moments of popular spontaneity remained oblivious to the symbolic cancellation of the past by the authors of the design brief for the Stalin monument.

The monument was commissioned by the new communist administration of the City of Prague in 1949. By the time it was unveiled in 1955, this emblem of 'triumph over the past' had already become a memorial to it. Stalin had been dead for two years; the first president of communist Czechoslovakia, Klement Gottwald, 'caught a chill' at Stalin's funeral and died of 'pneumonia' before even the foundation stone was laid; several workers lost their lives on the building site and the architect, Otakar Švec, shot himself some weeks before the work was finished.

Within a year, Stalin's successor, Nikita Khrushchev, denounced the despotism of Stalinism and the 'personality cult' which had grown around the dictator. Gottwald's protégé and political heir, President Antonín Zápotocký, died a year later and the new regime began to 'rectify the past deformations of socialism' by quietly consigning Stalin to history. The first task was to remove many of Stalin's effigies from public view. But the colossal statue in Prague could not be ushered away discreetly. It was built according to the protagonist's own advice to architects, 'to think on the scale of centuries', and the technical problems involved in its demolition equalled those of its construction. As an interim measure, the monument was shrouded in scaffolding (allegedly to prevent subsidence), imprisoning the group in a steel cage. Then in January 1962, a special government commission was set up to oversee the destruction of the statue. Stalin's head was removed from his shoulders while the commission contemplated alternative proposals for the remodelling of the statue, until the monument was finally demolished in a series of nighttime explosions over two weeks in October.

Over the next decade, the ceremonial chambers in the base of the monument, which had reputedly housed a secret air-raid shelter for the Party top brass, became a potato store. The pedestal was converted into a viewing platform and some of the terraces were reclaimed for trees and shrubs. After 1989, the iconoclastic time when parliamentarians joined art students in repainting a Soviet tank on a Second World War memorial pink, a brash kinetic sculpture symbolising a pendulum or a large metronome was hastily erected on the vacant pedestal and a club, 'The Bunker', opened in the catacombs underneath. And then a year ago, lest we forget what it was designed for, the platform provided a temporary site for an inflatable reincarnation of the statue in the likeness of Michael Jackson – Stalin-sized, a wonder of the post-communist world, in a military coat, with surgically reshaped eyes and Asiatic cheekbones.

In her autobiography *Lost in Translation* (1989), Eva Hoffman recalls how as a schoolgirl in Poland she heard the news of Stalin's death. 'This was both very abstract and near unbelievable. On the one hand, since Stalin wasn't really a mortal but a great granite monolith in the middle of our lives, he shouldn't have died. On the other, aside from surprise, one can't feel much about the death of a granite monolith.'[3]

'Abstract' and 'unbelievable' were also the sentiments that accompanied the spectacle of the Party's contorted attempts to regain credibility by the post-Stalinist strategy of 'normalisation'. The removal of Stalin's statue was meant to signal to the 'masses' the system's return to political viability. But in the imagination of people who had come to see the workings of politics as a natural disaster – self-perpetuating, cyclic and purposeless – the statue, a Titanic of public sculpture, survived its physical destruction. The ritual decapitation, the nighttime demolition of the statue, and the 'deconsecration' and gradual deterioration of its symbolic site, left an equally symbolic absence which has given the missing statue a lasting place in the psychological topography and vernacular toponymy of Prague. Where Stalin once stood with an entourage that reminded many of a 'funeral' or 'bread queue', there is now 'Stalin' bracketed in quotation marks – the wings of a mythological messenger – announcing the bankruptcy of a history written by 'normality'.

Like many other sites, buildings or institutions which remain known under their original denomination long after their function or purpose has changed, 'Stalin' is 'Stalin' with neither affection nor aversion, neither respect nor objection ('one can't feel much about a granite monolith') – as though 'Stalin' were simply a generic term like 'river' or 'castle'. Yet 'Stalin' is not just a physical location or structure but an aspect of Prague's *genius loci* and a symptom of the city's state of mind. The symbolic absence that bears Stalin's name has been absorbed into the sense of undifferentiated time, unaffected by change, which has haunted the city for the last half-century – a time which 'stood still' and even 'ceased to exist altogether' for at least two political generations following the end of Stalin's era.[4] And while 'time stood still', the 'past' and 'history' became indistinguishable. 'To this day', wrote the Italian Bohemist and poet Angelo Maria Ripellino in 1973, 'Stalin winks malevolently from his enormous monument.'[5]

What does it take to recover the past from history where dynamite is not enough?

Lawrence Weiner's text-work, *SMASHED TO PIECES (IN THE STILL OF THE NIGHT)* (1991), painted in large block letters on the top part of a Second World War anti-aircraft defence tower in Vienna, evokes the past while it revokes the symbolic licence that history holds on the present.

The 50-metre-tall concrete *Flakturm* – simultaneously a bunker and a gun tower – is one of six such structures (of two basic designs) built in Vienna in 1943–44. It was designed by the German architect Friedrich Tamms as part of the city's defence system at a time when the Eastern Front was already moving steadily westwards and German armies were experiencing heavy losses in Russia. But alongside its practical military function, it was also conceived as an arrogant monument-in-advance. It was to become, in Albert Speer's term, a 'sublime ruin', a permanent war memorial in the spirit of the *Totenburgen* built by the Nazis throughout Eastern Europe to immortalise the remains of the fallen. Placed, it seems, with perverse cynicism in Esterházypark, a small square in a densely populated residential district close to the city centre, this 'castle of the dead' retained its morbid presence long after it had ceased to be a potentially deadly military target. Some time after the war, the interior of the decommissioned structure became home to an aquarium and the surrounding area was turned into a communal garden with sandpits, park benches and a children's playground. There are now plans to install a climbing wall on one side of the tower and open a cafe on the raised platform which formerly housed the 5-inch anti-aircraft guns. This swords-into-toy-ploughs change of use is perhaps an attempt to reclaim the site for those who live and grow up in the (metaphorical) shadow of the tower and to confront the tension between the offensive symbolic purpose of the 'monument' and the defensive impotence of its former military function.

In this setting, Weiner's intervention is as delicate as it is contentious. His 'writing on the wall', in grey (the colour of SS uniforms) on white on the rough-cast concrete, seems to accept the authority of the mass and weight of the architecture, dictated by the combined demands of warfare and psychological security, and the pathological aesthetics of hard-as-steel Teutonic austerity – which measured so unfavourably against the cultured splendour of the imperial Ringstrasse, the cosmopolitan vitality of the Secession, or the filigree elegance of the Ferris wheel in the Prater. Yet it dominates the structure by the force of poetic suggestion, which brings to the fore the silent presence of the tower (and the ichthyological *Kunstkammer* of silence in it) as an embodiment of disruption, both actual and symbolic, material and temporal. The deliberate ambiguity of the text in relation to the specific connotations of the site provokes a reflection on the past articulated as a history, as much as it insists on the openness of its potential meanings. It demands that history is put on trial – yet it refuses to take the witness stand, and even less to pass a judgement.

Like the remnants of the Stalin monument in Prague, the defence towers in Vienna dominate their surroundings by their very redundancy. Yet, like 'Stalin', these bleak edifices owe much of their psychological impact on the life of the city to the symbolism of protection, of the watchful eye, metaphorical in the case of 'Stalin' but quite literal in respect of the former function of the *Flaktürme*, with their observation platforms rising above the levels of Vienna's roofs. And like 'Stalin', they are 'indestructible', or at least difficult to remove.

When in 1991 the Vienna Festival Committee chose the tower in Esterházypark to become a site for a public artwork, the first in a five-year public art programme, 'Topography: Relevant Information', it ostensibly aimed to mark the presence of the tower as part of the city. Topography is the anatomy of the city. It seeks to survey and describe the features and functions of the place, rather than to alter them. But as with all Weiner's work, his response to the place contains a proposition which invites the contemplation of the site it occupies as a temporary condition of the physical form of the architecture.[6] By extension, it confronts the original memorial purpose of the tower as a potential 'sublime ruin' inviting its own destruction.

The circumstance of the violent act, envisaged in the words 'smashed to pieces', is the 'still of the night', the 'peace' implied by the German word *Frieden*, which the tower symbolically both guards and disturbs.

The implementation of Weiner's proposition is discretionary and subject to individual interpretation. The work may or need not be materially realised. The tower – or indeed anything, anywhere, at any time – may or need not be 'smashed to pieces'; 'the night' – or any night – may or need not be violently disrupted. As Weiner stipulates in the formulation he had used consistently for almost 30 years, 'the decision as to the condition rests with the receiver upon the occasion of the receivership'.

This also includes the responsibility, on the part of 'the receiver', to locate the moment of perception, 'the occasion of receivership', as a relative vantage point in time. Each time a passerby looks to the top of the tower, the text offers itself as a report of a disruption which has become an event of the past through the act of reading. In this respect, it seems significant for the interpretation of the work within the inevitable historical connotations of the site (and the reliance of both on the representational capacity of language), that the physical form of Weiner's proposition is itself temporary. Weiner stipulated that the lettering was not to be maintained, or restored in future, but should be left to slowly fade away. The message may or need not be remembered and spoken of long after the text has disappeared, but it can be located in time by the act of reading only while the text remains visible.

Meaning does not remain attached to words for long. Language is unstable, it fades, words wear thin. How much of the sense of humiliation and defeat can still be found today in the popular neutralist term 'collapse' with which Austria summed up its self-perceptions in the aftermath of the Anschluss?

National histories have a strong tendency to disperse the totalitarian past within the broader frame of world events and to disown its symbolic manifestations as attributes of essentially foreign conflicts. As a consequence, the impact of the remnants of totalitarian symbolic language in monumental art and architecture in Eastern and Central Europe is all too often dismissed in geographical rather that cultural terms.[7]

In Austria, the brief period of denazification following the end of the Second World War soon gave way to a 'politics of silence', which still surrounds the complicity of Austrofascism and its bloody episodes. In the words of the Viennese writer and political activist Doron Rabinovici, the wartime past 'has simply been exported to Germany'.[8] The *Flaktürme* left behind became incomprehensible signs of a history estranged to itself.

In Prague, the transformations of the Stalin monument marked the Calvary of the centralist-bureaucratic idea and ideology (which has only just come to an end in the bizarre resurrection of Joseph Vissarionovich as Jacko). The purge of Stalinist imagery, of which the Stalin monument was the ultimate example, was driven by the Party's cultural intolerance fed by a fear of subjectivity, ambivalence and ambiguity, particularly in the symbolic realm where the complexity of interpretation made its scrupulously one-dimensional self-image vulnerable. In the eyes of the Party, Stalin's 'mistakes' compromised the very language with which the Party justified and framed its political aims and its 'objective historical necessity'. His true ideological crime, however, seems to have been to let his granite presence in Prague outlive its unambiguous symbolic purpose. In the nearly ten years between Stalin's death and the final demolition of the giant statue, a large number of public artworks were removed or remodelled throughout the country. This was not because the Stalinist heroic naturalism had run its course as the Party's style and become artistically obsolete, or because the statues and pictures lacked, in the main, any aesthetic merit, but because their ideological message were complicated by the turmoil of post-Stalinist power struggles.[9] As 'only art', the Stalin monument could have been dismissed as politically irrelevant. But irrelevance was precisely what the Party ideologues feared the most. The monument with its enormous scale and prominent position on the hill above the city became, above all, the personification of the ideology it was created by but which it no longer legitimately represented: inert, monolithic, remote, unloved, and ignored by the city made of sandstone, stucco and bronze. It became also what its own propaganda despised so much – 'the burden of the past [...] barbaric and savage', which must be disposed of 'definitely and for good'.

In its efforts to shed the image of Stalinism, the post-Stalinist Party showed a remarkable understanding of Stalinist thinking. Like in the show trials of the early 1950s, for which resignations and suicides were generally more desirable outcomes than expulsions, executions or 'fatal accidents' (so as to deny the system's own disruptions), the Stalinist 'ideological mistakes' had to undergo the humiliating public ritual of 'constructive self-criticism', to recognise its 'character faults' and to confirm the Party's 'objectivity' as the arbiter of history. Metaphorically, as well as posthumously, Stalin thus became the highest-ranking figure ever to be put on trial by Stalinist justice. Like many of his less lustrous former lieutenants, Stalin committed suicide: he blew himself up, piece by piece (in the still of the night) in Prague in the autumn of 1962.

'Modern demolition [...] is the opposite of a rocket launch,' declares Jean Baudrillard. 'What a marvellous modern art form this is, a match for the fireworks displays of our childhood.'[10]

My father never lived to see the destruction of the statue. He died some months before the demolition men moved in. I remember, vaguely, standing by the window of my grandmother's top-floor flat, watching in the dark the brief flashes of light on the horizon and listening to the thunder of detonations. The late-night adventure belonged for me to the new experience of a world in which mortality is the measure of things. My father was dead. Every evening at dinner time a place was still laid for him at the family table and for years to come nobody would sit in his chair.

1. Joseph Stalin, *The Tasks of the Youth*, International Publishers, New York, 1940.
2. Extract translated by Ewald Osers in Alexandra Büchler (ed), *This Side of Reality: Modern Czech Short Stories*, Serpent's Tail, London, 1996.
3. Eva Hoffman, *Lost in Translation: A Life in a New Language*, William Heinemann, London, 1989.
4. The expression 'when time stood still' has been liberally used by many Czech commentators to denote various periods of the post-Stalinist era. See for example Alena Potůčková (ed), *Art When Time Stood Still*, Czech Museum of Fine Art, Prague, 1996.
5. Angelo Maria Ripellino, *Magic Prague*, Macmillan, London, 1994.
6. Wiener's piece is 'site-specific' by coincidence if not by accident. The choice of the site preceded the invitation issued to Weiner, and the work chosen by him was an existing one.
7. I do not wish to contribute to the common, facile confusion of Nazi with Stalinist aesthetics and the different roles art and architecture played as propaganda tools within the respective ideological schemes. But talking to several people living in the vicinity of the Esterházypark in 1992, I was struck by their references to the tower as 'German', in the same way that the remains of socialist-realist monumental art in Prague are often popularly thought of as 'Russian'.
8. Doron Rabinovici, 'Poesie, Politik und Populismus oder: Literatur im Streit der Öffentlichkeit', paper presented at ELIA Symposium, Graz, 1996.

9. The iconoclasm of their removal would (ironically) confirm their status as 'only art'. Even though the definitions of 'art' (and 'public art') are permanently volatile, artworks are never destroyed because they are 'not art'.

10. Jean Baudrillard, *America*, Verso, London, 1988. I am indebted to my friends Rostislav Švácha in Prague and Julien Robson in Vienna for help with information on architectural history, and to Nikos Papastergiadis for an illuminating discussion.

David Harding and Pavel Büchler (eds), *Decadent – Public Art: Contentious Term and Contested Practice*, Foulis Press, Glasgow, 1997 pp.26–39.

WAR OF WORDS

What is 'writing'? What is 'making'? Both are processes of articulation. I could add that they are quite distinct – one is linear, the other not so, for example – but experience warns that I should resist the temptation. After all, as processes, they both traditionally involve the very same principle of tracing: an action of the human hand, usually equipped with or extended by a tool, leaving a trace on or in material. But particularly now, when tools have changed and linearity has all but vanished from writing as a result of cut-and-paste word-processing technology, the process of writing is moving ever closer to non-linear processes of making, such as modelling or drawing. And vice versa, with the invasion (or at least infiltration) of keyboard-operated digital technology into virtually every creative discipline, the process of making objects or images is increasingly like those mechanical operations involved in the making of texts.

To proffer insight from the specific characteristics of 'writing' versus 'making', it may be better to look at the two not as distinct processes but as conceptually different types of *thinking* and reflective engagement with the world – or, in academic jargon suitable, perhaps, for the gravity of this occasion, as *modes of enquiry*. True enough, even as modes, writing and making can be perceived as synonymous to some extent, at least in language, where the words properly belong. This very sentence, for instance, was *in the making* as I was *writing* it; and even in art, we often hear of 'reading' images and other material-artistic creations as though they had been written rather than made. (Indeed, the confusion is almost justifiable precisely because the written and the made are the outcomes of writing and making where the two are conceived as processes.)

To comprehend writing and making as modes, one must look not at the final product but at the potential contained in the original thought itself. There are undoubtedly perceptions and ideas that call for being articulated in writing, to become texts, and there are others which demand being shaped by making to become objects or images. But in the main, it is likely that thoughts, perceptions or ideas will contain a range of such potentials simultaneously (including, most obviously, the potential for nothing being done about them at all, the category to which, rather alarmingly, most of my ideas seem to belong); the hierarchy of the modes that may be deployed in realising a particular potential will be a matter of external priorities. In the social realm, these priorities reflect a range of values and symbols with which society supports its self-understanding as a culture. Again, in our modern society, these categories are linked to the segmentation of culture into various fundamental categories of specialist and mainly professional understanding (such as science or art), and the further subdivision of these into fields, disciplines, practices, genres and so on. (The academic parallel to these cultural categories and subsets is the organisation of the modern university, with its faculties, schools, departments, subjects and courses.)

As the separation of the various modes of enquiry, corresponding to the hierarchical organising principles of knowledge and understanding that have ordered society since at least the Enlightenment, remains one of the most enduring popular conceptions and academic orthodoxies of modernist culture, any question of the relationship between the modes of writing and making is a question of authority. This authority is always, of course, relative to any given field or discipline but it is not confined to them. It encompasses, as a political question, the whole of the cultural domain and manifests itself hierarchically through the authority of literacy, or the authority of experimental proof, or of physical evidence, or of the unique object, or the authority of physical attributes such as speed or weight, or of economical ones such as rarity or demand, and so forth.

Increasingly, the authority of the speed and data-manipulating capacity of digital technology is profoundly affecting the relative authority of the two modes within and across all cultural disciplines. This is particularly so where 'making' can be interpreted as 'image-making' (for convenience's sake, as I am going to do here, fully aware that I may be guilty of slightly twisting the argument) and where 'writing' can be confined to the language of words (as distinct from, say, the writing of a piece of computer software), but it is also true to some extent of all making and all writing, in any medium or language. For it is exactly the enormous extent to which *all* human existence and experience are in so many ways being transformed by the revolution of *image-language* technology, and the proliferation and all-pervasive presence of texts and images and their hybrid formats, no longer clearly identifiable as either one or the other, that is bringing about new authoritative relationships between the modes of writing and making. And the more any given discipline is engaged in the social world, which almost literally lives by the image-language machine, the more its internal hierarchies of authority between the two modes will be thrown into question by the effects of the technology on all cultural processes and all social relations – and the more the discipline itself will change.

Let me give you an example from an academic discipline that should be of more than a passing interest to artists.

Some months ago, I was taking part in a debate in anthropological theory on a topic quite close to that of the present conference. As the event was taking place in Manchester, the cradle and permanent domicile of visual anthropology and anthropological filmmaking, and as the debate concerned, broadly, the chances of the visual image in a contest with the written word as tools for methodically understanding society and culture, my presence there seemed appropriate enough. But even so, I soon realised that I was being cast in a role that was as privileged as it was distinctly uncomfortable: something of an invited trespasser. You can imagine that facing that gathering, I felt more like an anthropological specimen whose habits and behaviour were up for scholarly scrutiny than someone who could make a viable contribution to a discourse constrained by the narrowly specialist terms of an academic discipline. This was not because I am an artist rather than an academic, but because as an artist I am concerned with the *anthropos* and the *logos* in quite different ways than those whose job it is to examine, describe and classify the human with the word as their instrument of reason. After all, artists are commonly thought of as those who share with others their *vision*, their way of *seeing*, in the almost literal terms of ocular perception – those who meditate between the visual and the visible by making images – or such, at least, seems to be the task assigned to us by the conventions of language in which 'to *see*' means to understand and 'to *show*' means to prove.

The motion put it bluntly and with a disarming self-confidence that is very hard to argue with: 'In anthropology, the image can never have the last say.' But this short string of words had an interesting, if equally short history and as I was cast to play the devil's advocate on that occasion, and as the devil is always in the detail, I want to consider it here with a bit of a pedantic attention. When I was first asked by the organisers to take up the defence of the image, as it were, the proposed wording of the motion was: 'Images can never have the last word.' There was no mention of anthropology, and the poetic ambiguity of the phrasing (which I rather liked) made the motion in a strict sense quite irrefutable. Indeed, images cannot *possess* the word, the last one or any other, simply because they operate within a different regime of signification than that controlled by the rules of language. Images have conventions, visual idioms and certain established codes, but they do not have a vocabulary, a lexicon of agreed, defined and generally understood terms, each complete with etymology, context and usage. In short, images do not strictly have a language but they do have a *voice*. So I suggested to the organisers that the motion should be rephrased to read: 'Images can never have the last *say*.' It was less elegant but it seemed easier to dispute. There followed an exchange of correspondence exploring various alternative suggestions and by the time I received the definitive itinerary for the debate, the wording had changed again. The plural 'images' became the universal generic 'image', taking another bit of an already small rug from under my feet – for I could no longer so easily make use of the fact that images are members of a very diverse species, so diverse that maps and diagrams bear no resemblance to, for instance, photographs, which in turn are very different from moving images such as film. And finally, the word 'anthropology' had been added to clarify or, as I thought, to confuse the matter. Did it mean, perhaps, that the image could potentially have the last say somewhere or even everywhere else and that the attachment to language in the anthropological argument was different from other fields of academic enquiry? Or was this simply the organisers' ploy aimed at reassuring the specialist audience that no concessions would be granted to ignorant pundits like myself, that we all had to play by the rules?

The authority of language is conditional upon semantic precision. But this tinkering with and subtle shifts in the wording of the motion demonstrated that 'having the last say' implies not necessarily a final victory by the force of a reasoned argument but a conclusion or closure of an argument by the virtue of having the power to do so. This applies as much to the reality of academic discourse as it applies in principle. The questions that immediately arise, though, are ones of the legitimacy of the power to make final statements. Where does it come from? What is it underwritten by? How is it arbitrated? And so on. Whatever the answers, the next question must be: Is such a power held in perpetuity, is it continuous and permanent?

The motion put forward by the anthropologists seemed to claim as much. It said that the time would never come when any image could be authorised by the laws of the discipline to decide an argument. *Never*? How could they be so sure? Is it not rather the case that images can hardly have such decisive powers because the rules of the discipline stand the way they are, at the moment and for as long as they stay so?

The motion could also be taken as saying that if an image were ever allowed to conclude an argument, the concluding statement would never conform to the rules of anthropology. Those rules may not be written down but they are nevertheless hostage to language. As far as I can tell, they consist of a number of necessary language operations that one must perform in order to set up, conduct and conclude an anthropological argument: observed phenomena must be not only recorded and reported (something that images are quite good at doing), but also classified and interpreted and brought into language. Granted, this cannot be easily achieved by visual means alone.

But anthropologists should know better than anyone that rules, habits and conventions are always volatile and that they change over time. And so I argued that just as cultures develop or decline, so do the disciplines of human enquiry and the means and powers by which they are constituted and ruled. Anthropology is a dynamic discipline. Even though from the sidelines it often seems that it is bent on studying cultures that display a much slower cultural metabolism than the fast-changing culture which finally validates the anthropological argument, the subject of anthropology too must be undergoing a continuous change. There is some kind of reciprocity or cultural exchange at the very heart of the process. The discipline does not develop in isolation from the cultures it studies but brings about its own transformation in response to the experience of those cultures. And these are, in turn, affected by being studied. This means that anthropology cannot fully be the master of its own terms, its mode of enquiry or even its own destiny. The academic rules it is bound to and constrained by, dominated as they are by language, are only a part of what anthropology is or what it might become.

The other part – its dynamic side – is the way in which anthropology takes on and makes use of the modal exchange between the discipline and the subject of its study and opens itself to the import of the means of understanding, expression and ways of thinking, which do not necessarily derive their authority from any language-driven canon or practice. And as it is inevitable that anthropology will increasingly study cultures in which the most dramatic change is that induced or effected by the regime of the new image-language technology, disseminated partly by the cultures' contact with anthropologists, it is equally inevitable that the discipline itself will change.

So the question for anthropologists is *not* whether writing remains the dominant mode of anthropological enquiry, nor whether the 'language of images' (if that is not an oxymoron) can be fully substituted in any academic discipline for that of words, nor even whether anthropology is an exception, exempt from the massive change that is so radically affecting all human life. Rather, the question is whether and for how long it can afford to deny the image its growing cultural authority brought about by the technological revolution without losing its own dynamism.

You can perhaps put it differently. The recent and current changes in what we think of as 'language' are far more profoundly carried by the momentum of the conceptual and technological developments of the image than by the developments by which 'the word' *alone* affects the operations of society and culture and maintains its authority. Look at the respective technological histories. The revolution began with the separation of language from the image some 6,000 years ago, when the Sumerians developed the first system of writing using clay tablets. Since then, language technology has moved in giant leaps, quickly leaving the technology of the image behind. About 500 years after the Sumerians, the Egyptians came up with the papyrus. Then, about 900 BC, the Greeks invented the alphabet. With Gutenberg halfway through the fifteenth century, the revolution peaked and in a certain sense ended. Nothing much happened until speech caught up with the written word with Edison's phonograph and Bell's telephone in the 1870s and then the introduction of telegraphy and the wireless soon after. True, there was the first automated printing press in 1811, the invention of the Linotype in 1884 and the first phototypesetting machine in 1946, but these were merely refinements of an already established technological apparatus. Even the typewriter and its recent sibling the word processor have hardly changed the authoritative and authoritarian position that 'the word' has held for millennia. While extremely important in a great many respects, not least by facilitating literacy, all the modern language technologies have merely reconfirmed the dominant role of 'the word' among the means by which as a culture we negotiate our understanding of the world we live in.

Meanwhile, for 6,000 years, 'the image' had to take a back seat. True, there was the Renaissance invention of perspective, and the introduction of chiaroscuro in fifteenth-century Flemish painting, and through various manual graphic techniques, such as the woodcut or engraving, the image did share in some of the bonuses gained by language and writing from printing. But the great revolution had to wait until the 1830s and '40s when the invention of photography brought into being a completely new type of image and forever changed our perceptions and self-perceptions. Since then, the revolution has never stopped. Each new major development – the reduction of exposure times from minutes to fractions of seconds around the turn of the century, which enabled the development of film, followed by colour photography, television and video, and most importantly digital images – brought about something conceptually quite unlike anything that had been seen before. Each time, the relationship between word and image had to be renegotiated.

For a very long time, the authority of images (and of image-making) in Western culture had been, to an exceptional degree, dependent on texts (and writing). But with the shock of photography and the subsequent developments of the moving and then digital image, images have gained an enormous degree of emancipation. So much so that not only can they rejoin words on equal terms but it is no longer by any means certain that the language of words can still exist on its own. What is quite certain, however, is that the image's rise to power in our experience, as in the terms of the image-language technology of today, and the consequent shift in the relative psychological, political and social authority of writing and image-making are integral to the performance of the structures of specialist understanding and knowledge in our changing culture.

In this respect, the dynamic condition of anthropology and other social sciences is not very far removed from that which makes art (or the creative enquiry) an aspect of society's self-identification as a culture. Both social sciences and art must be involved with culture in ways that reflect their own performance within culture, by laying open to transformation their own discipline-specific premises, means and terms. The authority of anthropological writing, for example, must rely less on its adherence to the rules of academic discourse than on its ability to assimilate the momentum of the technological and cultural change; or, the credibility of art must depend less on the bind between specialist modes of making and the world of experience than on the interplay between the forms of participation that artistic practice can deploy and activate in the social world at large.

Joseph Kosuth – an artist with an exemplary record of bringing together writing and making within a unified practice – proposed over 20 years ago the model of art as *engaged* anthropology. In his text, 'The Artist as Anthropologist' (1975), he warns against modernist art's false claims to autonomy in the social world and demands that the practice of 'art must internalise and *use* its social awareness'. He sees the artist as both an agent and user of the symbolic apparatus within a culture, who should acquire 'the kinds of tools that the anthropologist has acquired' and 'obtain fluency in his *own* culture'. This should be achieved through 'a dialectical process which [...] consists of attempting to affect culture while [the artist] is simultaneously learning from (and seeking the acceptance of) that same culture which is affecting him'. (Sorry about the gendering of the artist – complaints should be addressed to Joseph Kosuth.)

For the topic of our discussion, this seems to imply that the modes of enquiry specific to art should no longer be those that fabricate 'other worlds' but those which are developed through practice *in the social world*. They are not taken from culture, nor are they given to it, but they are worked on as they already are and still remain in the very social destination of art. These modes of enquiry may subsume the traditional ways of making objects and images, or *thinking through* objects and images, insofar as the making of objects and images are a property of culture rather than autonomous preoccupations of creative disciplines within it. They may also subsume the modes that in an orthodox sense characterise other fields, such as writing, insofar as these are also aspects of culture. Indeed any mode of enquiry can be internalised and used within artistic practice as long as its internalisation and use is located as an agency within culture.

In a culture where the attachment of conceptually different modes of enquiry to values and priorities of understanding organised on the principle of discrete disciplines is quickly losing much of its former rigidity, the internalisation of writing into making and vice versa, aligns artistic practice with the growth of cultural parity and the shifting interdependency of images and words. And conversely, as the concepts by which various types of understanding are self-guarded, as discrete disciplines are fast becoming independent from the relative bias of the relationship between different modes of enquiry, the use of writing will not, *per se*, expand artistic practice beyond the confines of a discipline (be it 'painting', say, or 'artists' writing') or align it with the changing culture. What is at stake in the relationship between writing and making in the practices of art is the relationship they come to coordinate in the social world and the extent to which their separate or combined use in a given practice locates specific artistic understanding and knowledge in a culture and affects its social performance.

This is quite different, however, from seeking the support of writing to mediate among specialist discourses, as though they were a form of social interaction; or to form and occupy 'interdisciplinary' territories, as though these were already locations within culture. The use of writing was exemplified in 1970s and '80s art (and art education) by a wholesale import of rhetoric from a melange of specialist sources (the *uncritical* critical theory, as it could be called), and did often seem merely to use the loosening of the academic canon from its bounds to language as an excuse to transfer some of the surplus orthodox authority of 'the text' onto the making of images and objects. But it is not as if you could simply follow the logic of etymology and, from the humble *grafein* at the root of every graphic discipline, from drawing to writing, arrive through grammar at the glamour of an 'educated image'.

The artist, as Kosuth wrote, is 'a student of culture'. The job of the artist is 'to articulate a model of art' in the world. And in this world where the relationship between writing and making – as the fundamental processes of articulation and modes of reflective or critical engagement – is increasingly subject to negotiation, the artist could do worse than begin by asking: What *kind* of writing? What *kind* of making? And they are the questions I would like to leave with you today.

Point, no.7, Spring/Summer 1999, pp.7–9.

BUILT-IN OBSOLESCENCE

What brought us together today is an experiment that the organisers of this conference call the New Hull School of Art. My argument will follow the syntax of their title and will take the 'new' as my starting point.

The 'new' is the hallmark of the modern. The Big Idea of the twentieth century is innovation – the founding idea of modernism and the guiding spirit and light of what we do and how we do it. In all fields of social and economic life, in technology, commerce or administration, innovation is the driving force. But in modern art, and consequently in art education, it seems to have become a kind of self-perpetuating vortex. There is an inescapable contradiction. In the guise of the historical avant gardes, innovation was the very condition of modern artistic practice. But the practice of innovation was entirely conditioned by challenging the future rather than responding to the challenges inherited from the past. In other words, the 'new' in art is that which seeks validation on the basis of its inevitable future obsolescence (or, in the words of Monica Ross, in her paper at this conference, 'obsolescence is all that the system assures'). Unlike in most other fields, where innovation generally means an expansion of existing knowledge, technological standards or working methods and seeks to provide the foundation and tools for future developments, in art, in the avant-garde sense, innovation means speculation on the condition of the future, as it single-mindedly pursues the (contradictory) avant-garde tradition of anti-tradition while trying to reinvent itself ahead of its time.

It goes almost without saying that the practice of artistic innovation is incompatible with the culture of educational institutions. Yet in higher art education as we know it, the avant-garde pedigree of artistic innovation has nevertheless been claimed by the institutions and avant-garde discourse has been thoroughly absorbed. As a result, the built-in innovation only seems to work when it works – or is made to work – against itself.

British art education survives on a paradox: the academic system devised some 30 years ago is, in the main, obsolete, yet it is precisely its obsolescence that accounts for its occasional successes. It seems to act as a catalyst for some of the most motivated, independently minded students who feel compelled to find ways of working against the system – and so to make it work. They explore and exploit the gaps created by departmental tribalism, the bureaucratic segmentation of art into disciplines or 'media', the inflexible designation of space, the arbitrary diversions of modularisation, the oppressive hierarchy of 'year groups', the antiquated regime of 'professional' rules, codes and conventions and, indeed, the pitfalls of perpetual 'innovation'. Every school has a few such students who always discover the freedom of nonconformity even within the constant drifts of 'restructuring' and 'development' – a symptom and a feature of the system's obsolescence – with which institutions simultaneously acknowledge and try to ignore the need for a radical change.

The question is how to imagine a system imperfect enough that it continues to inspire those who seek new alternatives, but also one that provides viable opportunities for the meaningful engagement of all who work in it.

One way of addressing the question is to imagine a model art school that would be everything the established art school is not. It would be a non-hierarchical open space – constitutionally, spiritually and physically – where ways of thinking and working evolve from flows and collisions of ideas and interests among peers. There would be no departments or year groups, no competitive admission requirements, assessments and degrees, and no hierarchy of staff. Instead, the school would be formed organically as a focus of interaction within a community of students and artists, who would also share the responsibility for its running. The cooperative form would, in itself, provide the key educational content. It would do away with the despotic rule of professional managers, administrators and maintenance staff (although those wonderful people variously known as janitors, porters or 'house staff' may remain as indispensible as they are, in my experience, in the present system). Their jobs, from mopping the floors to controlling budgets, would be shared among students. Some might be undertaken by everyone in rotation, others by temporary elected committees or representatives, but there would be no concept of 'full-time' study or employment. Artists and experts from other fields would be invited by student groups to contribute their skills and knowledge, to participate in students' work or to carry out their own projects. They would be paid for their work at the same nominal rate as the students, and all appointments would be limited to, say, two years. The school would offer the use of its facilities and expertise to other educational organisations and groups in exchange for access to their courses and specialist services. It would be a public place, open 24 hours a day, with good workshops, a well-stocked library and an excellent bar.

This model, in all its imperfection, is a realistic one. Various aspects of it do already exist (or have at some time existed) and function (or have functioned) well in some art schools and academies around the world. It could work and should be tried. But even such a new open art school should only be seen as an interim step towards a radical reform of the whole educational environment in which art schools as separate, isolated entities would no longer be needed: where art is part of all learning so that it may become a part of all social life.

And here we are faced with a difficulty. What makes my somewhat anarchic, somewhat utopian model 'realistic' is the way in which ideas proposed by artists fall within the conventional expectations, and indeed requirements, of 'art' in modern(ist) society. The idea makes use of the identity of art as a paradigm of creative, expressive and even civic freedom, and of artists as providers of alternative, individual visions, who occupy a discrete domain reserved for them alone and operate under a special 'artistic licence'. This not only allows artists to envisage, present and, within the boundaries of the 'artistic domain', follow alternatives unconstrained by the priorities of economic realism or political expediency, but it also makes it their job to create visions and propositions which stand apart from the everyday concerns of politics, commerce or material production or the production of knowledge. The price that artists pay for the privileges of the 'licence' is, then, the lack of effectiveness of their ideas and visions as instruments of a structural change in the social destination of art.

These limitations become more obvious when we consider two interrelated (but not quite interdependent) conditions that parallel the concept of the 'artistic licence' and which affect the relationships between the broader 'social world' and the artists' own specific environments, the 'art world' and the 'academy'. The first is the concept of a 'professional mandate'; the second is one of 'academic qualification'.

Both of these, individually and jointly, have a bearing on the ways in which, and the extent to which, your use of the 'artistic licence' is socially, economically and politically effective. It is quite clear that from the perspective of the profession (any form of participation in the 'art world' – or anything you are likely to do as artists), you do not need academic qualifications to pursue your practices and goals. And conversely, from an academic point of view, the concept of the professional mandate, derived from the conventions of careerism rather than expertise, is (or should be) quite irrelevant. You do not become an artist by having graduated from an art school. Academic qualifications do not entitle you to a 'professional' career or success, nor does such a success necessarily enable you to make a meaningful use of your qualifications. But, in practice, the established model of art education nevertheless aspires to the condition of the professional mandate and such notions as 'professionalism' often underpin the achievement of academic qualifications in art.

While academic qualifications do not lead to the professional mandate, their very irrelevance (or vanity) reinforces the power of the 'professional' on the public perceptions of the role of the artist. Consequently, the current qualifications-based model of art education only further restricts the already limited contribution that artists, perceived as 'professionals', can effectively make to the transformation of society. This is true at least insofar as it can be said that society needs creative people more than it needs professional artists – and that for whatever creative contribution you might make to society, you don't need a degree. (In fact, you don't need much more that the ability to read, write and interpret information.)

If we look at it this way, the question of what kind of art education we need becomes largely redundant – or at least secondary to the question of educational needs in general, not just in terms of institutions but in the sense of the whole 'educational complex'.

The task of the artist/reformer then becomes that much greater: where do you start? The good news is that you can start almost anywhere. It is feasible to create small-scale alternative models, as long as they can function precisely as such and do not fall into the trap of thinking of themselves as specific solutions. It is feasible to work from within the existing institutional structures, as long as we can use them as flags of convenience and sail clear of the treacherous currents of arbitrary institutionalised 'innovation'. And it is possible to work from within the 'art world' or any other professional destination, as long as we remember that the destination of our efforts lies elsewhere.

But from wherever you start, you must remember that every 'new' has its own built-in moment of obsolescence and that the realisation of that obsolescence is the true goal of innovation. Working towards your own obsolescence is a noble mission – and something quite different from becoming obsolete through a lack of vision.

Conference paper, *Independent Art School Conference*, Hull, 2000.

BUREAUPHILIA: A LOST CASE

'Lost in the post' is one of the most banal excuses. But trains do run late, computers do crash, addresses do get mislaid, mobile phone batteries do go flat, watches do stop and letters sometimes vanish in the system. It does happen – and perhaps particularly when mail travels from one large institution to another.

About a month ago, I set out to write an article about a strange psychotic condition for which I coined the name *bureauphilia* and which I identified with certain characteristics of life at art schools. I finished the text in a couple of evenings, put it in an envelope and dispatched it to the editor of this journal. It never arrived.

The system has failed – or it may have been divine intervention. Thinking about it again, I feel uneasy. What if my observations of bureaucratic incompetence are no more than misperceptions caused by the myopic perspective of an insider? Or worse, what if my own interest in the subject is really a sign of falling under the spell of bureauphilia?

What is this fascination with the paraphernalia of administration? As with many other confusions of the soul, bureauphilia is a muddle of contradictions. Among its symptoms are as much an obsessive emotional attachment to non-productive work as a taste for 'outcomes', 'results' and 'answers'; as much an inclination towards formulaic 'solutions' as a weakness for intrigue of Byzantine complexity. In his public conduct, the sufferer is just as likely to draw attention to the guidance of policies and regulations as he is to proclaim loudly his dislike for what he terms 'bureaucracy'.

Bureaucracy has a bad name – and nowhere more than in the mouth of a bureauphile. The dislike for 'bureaucracy' so ostensibly displayed by the bureauphile is not entirely self-deluding nor does it simply mask the bureauphile's darker passions. We all love to hate bureaucracy but the bureauphile truly hates to love it (and always secretly hopes to be misdiagnosed as a bureauphobe). As he might put it, 'I can't cope with bureaucracy'. And, in a way, this is true. The bureauphile is generally not an efficient bureaucrat. Rather, he pursues the paths of bureaucracy to what can only be described as aesthetic ends: for the beauty of problem solving necessitated neither by problems nor by opportunities, for the love of order as a challenge in itself, for the thrill of classification practised as an abstract exercise. Like a child mesmerised by machinery but ignorant of mechanics, the bureauphile is drawn towards the outward performance of the systems and structures of administration but gets lost in the labyrinths of its logic and logistics.

In short, bureauphilia is a state of mind driven by frustrated creativity. Frustrated or trapped: creativity that creates nothing; innovation that makes nothing new; arbitrary imagination limited to the shifting of the goal posts.

Depending on the reader's disposition, the paragraphs above may seem unnecessarily cynical, irreverently flippant, or downright cheap – as feeble as easy excuses. They are all that and more. Bureaucracy is always a comfortable target. There is hardly a usage of the term which would have no negative connotations, from bungling inefficiency to red tape, obstructionism and the rule of undemocratic executive power. And there is hardly a social or a political position from which bureaucracy would not be under constant attack. It will always go down well with popular sentiment, borne by experience, to attack bureaucracy from whatever direction you care to choose (from the right, under the banner of the free market; from the left in the name of self-management; or from anywhere in between in the interests of openness, accountability or democracy).

If indeed what I call bureauphilia is especially at home in the environment of the contemporary art school, it may not be because artists, even lapsed ones, make bad administrators but because art schools instinctively resist bureaucracy. Even if bureaucracy is seen as simply a system of professional administration in the classical sense of Max Weber's definitions (hierarchy of responsibility, continuity, impersonality, expertise), it is difficult to imagine how it could ever make a comfortable bedfellow to creative independence. The spirit of 'originality' and 'self-expression', still at the core of the dominant model of art education, does not mix easily with the play-by-the-rules culture of bureaucracy. True, the relationship between opposites is often one of attraction. And just as surely as there is an aesthetic dimension to everything we do (as Roland Barthes insisted), the cold, systematic, precision of the bureaucratic process does have its charms. We all recognise something of bureaucracy's mannerisms in our practices and there is a trace of bureauphilia in all of us.

Although an art school is still a secure shelter, we are beginning to suspect that we may be fighting bureaucracy in its own field and the rhetorical weapons of our resistance may not be as sharp as we might like to think. Like bureaucrats, we too preach 'professionalism', pigeonhole what we do into 'disciplines', at least secretly believe in firm hierarchies of 'values', talk about 'diversity' but remain committed to systems of 'assessment' predicated on the notion that the criteria by which standards are judged are, if not universal, than at least essentially stable. And above all, we are often quicker to denounce the excesses of 'bureaucracy' than to defend the *limitations* of art: its never-ending doubts about its purpose, its vanity or its messiness.

So why do I hesitate to develop my argument and run for cover under the providential imperfection of the postal service? What am I afraid of? Perhaps, I don't really want to know the answer. Or the question makes me nervous. It is this: What if bureaucracy is just what we need to purge creeping bureaucratisation from our work? The very idea seems idiotic – but, in a sense, it may well be the case.

Sorry...

292: Essays in Visual Culture, no.1, February 2000, pp.37–48.

NEW ACADEMIC ART

Those of us who delighted on Wednesday night in the spectacle of one of the most improbable victories in the history of football may have forgotten our anxieties for a brief moment. That ball, guided by divine intervention into the net just seconds before the end of the match, may have reminded us of our hopes.[1] If Man United can do it, perhaps modern man can too. There may still be a chance before the whistle is blown on the twentieth century and we are thrown into that vast psychological space that we have always expected to open up in the year 2000. That space used to be known as 'the future'.

I know, my little witticism may be as precarious as Ole Solskjær's goal, but I can't resist. The idea that the future has the year 2000 written all over it is as deeply ingrained in my psyche as the notion that goals make history – and, of course, my thoroughly modernist artistic upbringing has a lot to do with it. It instilled in me the belief that the mission of modern art is essentially a progressive one and that the role of the modern academy is to strive for its inevitable future obsolescence – a most noble ambition even though, in reality, it may amount to little more than identifying where the goal posts are and moving them a bit further on.

Education is future personified. But from the vantage point of future's doorstep it is hard to pass such convictions on to students for whom our future has already become a history blessed by the academic curriculum. And since the sense of a 'progressive mission' seems neither sustainable nor justified by an educational practice in which the now incorporated ideals of the modernist experimental avant garde are about to reach their sell-by date, we seem to be discovering a last-minute substitute in the concept of 'research'.

So it comes as no surprise that I feel as if those in whose hands my immediate professional future lies – auditors, administrators and such like – wanted to release me from the grip of panic and, in the language of football, allow me some extra stoppage time, when they chose the year 2001 as the apex to which my thoughts as a researcher should be focused. The once-magic date 2000 would be business as usual, until 2001 when *Space Odyssey* would be forgotten in the name of the Research Assessment Exercise. A less cynical disposition than mine may have it that such coincidences are arbitrary, but I suspect that the timing of the exercise betrays a shrewd psychological calculation: forget 'the future', think on the scale of audit dates.

It is certainly my impression that just as education has become a short-term investment in a future measured by the declining working lifespan of a generation, so too what passes for research in academic institutions seems to have become, rather like football, a matter of scoring goals before the end of the season. (By which standard, no team these days would be anywhere near the research Premiership with players like Wittgenstein.) Yet this fixation on results and deadlines, and the almost cathartic effect that it may have on how we feel about what we do, may not just be a consequence of the inevitable bureaucratisation of the public sphere which modernisation entails. It may also be the reflection of our own conceptual frustrations and uncertainties, which cloud and confuse the vision of a research-oriented future of the modern art academy.

The first difficulty here is that the meaning of 'research' in the context of art and its practices is far less clear than many other concepts that the modern art academy has absorbed from the rest of the academic world. In the academic environment, dominated by sciences, research is usually defined as a systematic investigative activity which leads to new knowledge. The maximalist position expects research to provide an 'original contribution' to knowledge; the bottom line requires at least new 'informed insights'. All research is based on methodology. That is to say, research is not the product of sudden flashes of inspiration, or inspired discoveries, but a process which leads to knowledge in a methodical manner. The integrity of the method validates the resulting knowledge. The condition of methodology applies across the spectrum of research modes and fields from philosophical reasoning to laboratory or statistical analysis, and is a prerequisite whether or not the outcome of research is finally based on proof or supported by evidence, or whether the process leads to the formulation of a theory.

All research methodology comprises a number of steps, which lead from an initial observation, idea or hypothesis, through the collection of data and analytical or experimental stages and empirical or theoretical testing and verification, to the synthesis of partial outcomes and the formation and presentation of the final thesis. While research methods obviously vary according to the field and subject of investigation, they all share the same basic principle, which is that the methods of research are equally concerned with formulating questions as they are with providing answers. Indeed, one of the most attractive ways of describing research may be as a methodic link between questions and answers or answers and questions in whatever order.

Two common arguments are frequently put forward when it comes to the possibilities of applying the model of academic research to art and its ways of shaping our vision of the future. The first argument has it that innovative artistic practice is simply 'research' by another name. This view is supported not just by many practitioners (particularly of the modernist persuasion) but increasingly also by administrators on the basis of the growing structural proximity of the institutional environments across all subjects and academic fields. The second argument maintains that the established *aims* of academic research are quite different from those of art and that the appropriate parallels between the creative and academic fields and disciplines can therefore only be drawn within the concept of 'development' (or 'know-how' rather than 'knowledge'). This position is often taken by scientists who feel that art is founded in subjective empirical enquiry and that its practices are therefore unable to satisfy the necessary conceptual conditions that underwrite 'proper' academic investigation, and by those artists who are, quite conversely, concerned about compromising the direct communicative potential of the aesthetic experience (as much as about the potential loss of their 'artistic licence').

The recognition of 'research *through* practice' has perhaps settled these issues for the practical needs and purposes of the existing administrative and monitoring frameworks in our field. But it offers no answers to the questions of the ideological purpose of experimental, research-like artistic practices in the scheme of the art academy – nor does it help us, per se, to understand the aims, ambitions and the possibilities of one in the context of the other: research *within* practice and/or practice *within* research.

Research of one sort or another has always been a part of artistic practice, either as a preliminary stage in the making of a piece of work or, in a broader sense, as an ongoing activity aimed at the development of the conventional framework of an artistic discipline or genre. The outcome of the first type of research would be some formal or iconological aspect of the finished work; the outcome of the ongoing research would be a modification in the artist's overall approach or direction.

It used to be taken for granted that art was studied within the rules, codes and conventions of a practice and developed through a cumulative practical knowledge. There are no longer such certainties. The 'progressive mission' of the modern art academy has lead to the disintegration of that classic academic paradigm. By now, art is predominantly studied from the position of theory (or 'discussion', if not quite 'discourse') and developed through the constant reworking of its theoretical and ideological framework. This also includes the perpetually shifting definition of 'practice' itself.

Consequently, there has been a shift in the relationship between the experiential and experimental aspects of making, teaching and learning art. In the old academic model, the experience of practice within a set of rules and conventions provided the foundation for all experimentation and development. In the modernist model, practice became a dynamic point of reference for theory-driven experimentation, tied to the streamlined regime of ideologically framed 'disciplines' (based in an equal measure on administrative convenience as on quasi-academic assumptions of fundamental 'laws' governing perception and 'visual language'). The developments of art in the academic environment have thus become less founded in the experience of art making than in the constant questioning and self-questioning of that experiential foundation itself. While the old academic model could be described as one in which experimentation was embedded in experience, the modernist model is one in which experience is embedded in experimentation. In the old model, the outcome of artists' research used to be passed on through, and into, practice, whereas in the modernist model, the outcome of research tends to remain theoretical.

In the reality of the modern art academy, of course, the two models cannot be quite so separated. The remnants of the old academic model exist side by side with the half-corrupted modernist paradigm in a strange kind of symbiosis. Indeed, it is possible to say that what defines our – I hesitate to use the word – 'postmodern' institutions is precisely the tension generated by the simultaneous presence of the two paradigms. This is so, at least partly, because the experimental methods proper to art are still too narrowly tied to the notion of practice as it exists and develops independently *outside* the academic environment, subjected to the pressures of the art markets, fashion and independent critical appraisal. And even though that practice has become predominantly experimental, and has lost much of its experiential foundation, once transposed into the institutional environment of the academy it becomes canonised, in the old academic sense. Its diversity is reduced to a set of disparate 'professional approaches' and attitudes framed by academic theories, its purpose becomes literally 'academic' and its experimental efforts become a kind of a self-fulfilling prophecy. Finally – why not say it? – the 'art' prefix to the word 'practice' becomes largely redundant.

A key problem with the application of the concepts of research within *this* kind of practice is not so much the confusion between the separate professional identities of artists and career art academics/teachers (who, significantly, often describe themselves as 'practising' rather than 'professional' artists), or their very different social roles, but the lack of recognition for the value and purpose, and indeed prestige, of the experimental practice of art as a specific discipline in its own right within or outside the academic environment. There is an incompatibility of aspiration and purpose which is preventing the development of positive and relevant academic conventions – and which far too often manifests itself in the perverse view that 'research' is something like a preferred alternative to creative obscurity. (While in mathematics or philosophy, for instance, the general high status of research makes an academic career a pinnacle of professional success, I am yet to find one artist, in Britain at least, who would honestly prefer an academic career to an independent professional one for other than economic reasons.)

If, however, we succeeded in integrating or framing the notion of art as an experimental practice *within* that of research as a culture, we would get an altogether more promising set of possibilities. The requirement of a methodical approach could, for example, help us to reinvest the relationship between experience and experimentation with a new kind of tension beyond that created by the disintegration of the historical academic models. It could also help us to redevelop artistic disciplines as fields for experimentation without returning to their old rigidity. And, perhaps, it could even help us to at last turn the tired confusions and collisions between practice and theory into a positive confrontation. It could certainly give us a broader and a more open perspective on the purpose of 'academic' art.

My thoroughly modernist artistic upbringing has also left me with the conviction that art has a job to do in the making of society and its self-image, that it is a provider of a language which lends a legitimacy and a metaphysical support to society's perspective on its changing cultural conditions. And it is in this respect that I see a particular obstacle in the possibilities of the application of the concept and principles of academic research to the practices of art. Academic research and art do have different aims: the aim of academic research is the production of expert *knowledge*; the aim of art is the expression of *understanding* as an account of experience.

There are two basic (although not mutually exclusive) modes of enquiry in modern art. The first can be exemplified by Maurice Merleau-Ponty's argument that the 'artist is the one who sees that which others pass unnoticed and shows it to the most human among them', which identifies art with our search for the understanding of our existential conditions. The second can be illustrated by Jean-François Lyotard's maxim that the artist must pose the question of what art is – and that 'no other question is worth life's highest stakes'. This identifies art with our need to pursue speculative modes of questioning for their own sake, which is the need that activates our imagination.

Taken as such, one could be tempted to suggest possible parallels with numerous disciplines of academic research, from anthropology to theoretical physics, and the ways in which these make sense of the world as much as the ways in which they make sense in it. But this would divert attention from the question of the social purpose and the value of specific knowledge and understanding generated through artistic practices to the culture of production and object-centred 'knowledge hierarchies'.

Like academic research, art making is primarily concerned with the product – or 'creative production' – not necessarily in the sense of an 'artefact', but with a specific, singular outcome or an end result. Where this is so, means of research similar to those existing in other fields can be deployed in a developmental phase within the production of the artwork. But this kind of directly applied research generates new knowledge or new insights only internally. The outcome of the research – which is generally information – is integrated within the overall scheme of the artwork. The work may be able to tell me something about itself (which is what Lyotard demands), and it may be able to make me see the world differently (which is Merleau-Ponty's requirement), but it will be able to do so effectively only if it is 'good art' in a conventional sense: conceptually rigorous enough to deal with its own currency as art, yet not indifferent to the world outside itself. Clearly, the success of the work will not be tied to the academic criteria applicable to its research content. The knowledge gained through research will be subsumed in the final 'artistic' outcome or effect, whose self-conscious status as a product of the artist's creative labour will confirm any experimental aspects of the process as primarily instrumental.

This is further complicated by the fact that both art and academic research rely for their social prestige on the idea of 'originality'. And even though, in both research and art, the condition of originality is being relaxed and reframed by such softer terms as 'invention' or 'innovation' – a shift of attention from the source to the outcome – in the *practice* of art, the ideological requirement of originality remains the main index of the commercial and critical values of the artwork. The value of the 'research' involved in the production of the work is then inevitably relative to the work's success as something that all artists *do* but which no artist has *done* yet – which is not the same as posing 'the question of what (all) art *is*' and discovering 'that which others pass unnoticed'.

The potential for the application of the aims of academic research to art is rather different, however, in those instances where the emphasis is put on the *process*, or a working method, as an overriding determinant of a practice. There is, of course still a product – which may be in all material respects identical to a piece of work that comes out of the product-driven approach – but the relationship between the product and the process is qualitatively different. The greater the emphasis on the process, the closer the links between every aspect of the practice and the artwork – to the point where one may completely coincide with the other. I use the expression 'qualitatively' here to indicate that the difference is never absolute. Even in the most orthodox 'process art', there still is, of course, a material object, which under the established conditions of the distribution, dissemination and reception of art assumes a degree of autonomy. But in the academic environment, the product, as the material residue of the practice, can be of considerably less significance than the conceptual integrity of the process itself. As the art communicates on the conceptual level, it does not necessarily rely solely on the aesthetic criteria uniquely applicable to art (it does not have to be 'good art'). It can be put to the test by the respective (or combined) yardsticks of its relevance to our perceptions of the world and of its relevance to the questions of art, even without answering these questions in purely 'artistic' terms. But unlike the practice focused on the production of the 'artwork', it can also put to the test the very means of its understanding and self-understanding on which it depends as art, as purely experimental, provisional propositions without the burden of proof. Knowledge and understanding do not 'result' from the process but are formed and externalised through practice.

On the one hand, it would seem that such an emphasis on process as a practice should open up the possibility for the application of the *means and methods* of academic research to art beyond that covered by the notion of 'development', without sacrificing the critical capacity of art; on the other, it seems clear that a complete application of the *aims* of academic research (if it is at all possible) would inevitably compromise the cultural and aesthetic imperatives of the artwork and reduce it to an item of information. But this brings us back to the beginning.

So where do we go from here? Academic research has long been recognised as a domain in which scientific and scholarly interests can exercise a high degree of autonomy from the pressures of commerce and industry (including the industry of education). In this respect, research and experimental art share something of a common ethos and their academic practices can usefully learn from one another. The research bias of current art education can provide the framework, or at least a flag of convenience, not merely for new ways of doing things but also for new things to do. But the constant and often arbitrary demand for 'innovation', which treads so carefully between discredited 'originality' and the implausible ideals of 'progress', is holding art back from seeking academic alternatives just as surely as does the threat of 'methodological contamination' of artistic practice or the object-oriented culture of both research and creative production.[2] And alternatives are needed if we are to prevent the decline of our institutions into administrative machines for the manufacture of outcomes, or hiding places for practices uncertain of their social function. Alternatives are needed if we are to preserve and develop our institutions as spaces for critical debate and thought, where research *and* art share and shape a common language, and from where they can contribute a critical self-understanding to society and culture.

To get there, for a start, we would have to try and reconcile in some way such key polarities as experimental and experiential 'truth'; 'knowledge' and 'understanding'; 'objective inquiry' and 'poetic imagination'. We would need to expand the conventions, processes and methods of academic art and research, and focus on the common characteristics of their practices rather than the differences of their respective aims. Secondly, we would have to insist on the legitimacy of the 'purposeful uselessness' of academic practice, while remaining, as artists, actively committed to the social, non-academic, destination of art. Calling it 'research' will do nothing for a new academic art, unless such art rejects institutionalised avant-gardism and strives for socially active experimental models. Thirdly, in any attempt to reconstitute experimental practices into a new academic art we would need to negotiate not between but beyond both the criteria and standards of research and the conventional norms of production.

Ultimately, the culture of academic research will not be a good place for artists to inhabit unless we go there to do what we *do*. And the identity of our practices, which so often seems to make us strangers in the academic province, is also what will determine our contribution to that culture. The exclusive identification of research activity with 'outputs' (or 'works' – with what we *make*) has induced a myopic perspective on what there could be to do. And yet, it sometimes seems so simple. Perhaps, as we try to navigate these still unfamiliar waters, as we study the possible itineraries and ways ahead, we should remind ourselves every now and then that, after all, the most 'relevant output' of whatever we might do remains our students' futures.

As for my own immediate prospects and my consequent millennial anxiety, I will console myself with a vision of a future in which the term 'referee' is once again solely reserved for the discussion of football.

1. UEFA Champions League Final, Barcelona, 26 May 1999, Manchester United 2–1 Bayern Munich. 'God is English', commented the French sport newspaper *L'Equipe*.
2. While I have tried to retain the spirit of the oral presentation of this lecture, I would like to put on record my gratitude to David Connearn, artist and a doctoral candidate at Wimbledon School of Art, whose helpful critical comments have since inspired numerous revisions in parts of the text. 'Methodological contamination' is his term.

Antonia Payne (ed), *Research and the Artist: Considering the Role of the Art School*, Ruskin School of Drawing and Fine Art, University of Oxford, Oxford, 2001, pp.18–26.

Is it possible, all things being equal, to think of modern art as a socially meaningful mode of engagement with the world and with one another, independent of the conditions drafted by the institutional framework of culture? Can there be art, in contemporary Western society, without the institutionally sanctioned divorce between the roles of production and consumption, supply and use, making and reception? If art is a form of social interaction, a mode of enquiry directed towards understanding others, is it not futile to insist on any definitive formal requirements for the production of art? And if so, who needs artists?

In *The German Ideology*, written in 1845–46, Karl Marx and Friedrich Engels famously imagined how, one day, society would take over the organisation of the production of life's basic necessities, the division of labour would be abolished and every worker would be free to 'hunt in the morning, fish in the afternoon, rear cattle in the evening, criticise after dinner [...] without ever becoming hunter, fisherman, shepherd or critic'. If, from a vantage point at the doorstep of the twenty-first century such a bucolic idyll seems an unlikely prospect, it is not only because the social revolution, as Marx envisaged it, has evidently failed to deliver its promise; nor is it because the pastoral image is at odds with the techno-scientific bias that has largely fuelled the imagination of change in the material conditions of life since Marx's days; but because, in our culture, the forces of social and economic emancipation also bring about a crisis of identity and purpose.

Marx doesn't say that every sphere of work is commensurate with every other, only that all human activity and potential should be more than a means to an end. In his vision, it is the shackles of having to *be* what you *do* for a living, and having to remain so if you don't want to lose your livelihood, that hampers the development of 'what men ought to be'. Being trapped in 'one exclusive sphere of activity' makes every individual hostage to the interests and conflicts arising from the production and distribution of economic surplus. A better society, Marx argues, would refuse to perceive the individual as at once a component and a function of the machinery of work, whose every action is constrained by its direct economic utility. Having been freed from the perpetual submission to immediate economic imperatives, people would pursue their own temporary creative and emotional objectives without hindrance: 'one thing today and another tomorrow'. As for art, in such a society there would be 'no painters but only people who engage in painting among other activities'.

We now live in a world characterised no longer by communities but by interdependent industries and economic 'sectors'; not by a diversity of roles but by the diversification of means; not by 'useful work' but by the criteria of 'competitive advantage'; not by the distribution of surplus but by overproduction, excess and redundancy. Our immediate interests in one another are, to some degree, motivated and maintained by the considerations of the specific characteristics of the professional and economic identities of our neighbours (in the sense in which it is useful to know a good lawyer or to have a friendly joiner in the neighbourhood when, for instance, the community is gripped by an urge to improve the local playing facilities for its younger members). As a society, however, we rely on increasingly sophisticated systems of synchronised performance supported by a uniform infrastructure of communications, which have no direct bearing on individual goals, interests and aspirations (though, characteristically, we pay lip service to individual economic identity in such terms as 'stakeholder' or 'ownership'). Our dependency on coordinated, systematic expertise within the agencies of the state and the market has reduced the former certainties of our productive participation in the social world – our 'professions', 'careers' or 'trades' – to patterns of disparate approximations and 'hunting', 'fishing' or 'criticism' have become mere categories of detailed instrumental procedures, operating routines and specialist know-how. Under such conditions, it would seem that 'being an artist' can hardly mean anything very much – or can hardly mean anything much more definite than 'being an executive', 'consultant', 'contractor', 'sales representative', or any of the dozens of such provisional generic denominations. Why is it then, that the singular artistic identity ('the artist') should be so contentious and so contested?

What makes it difficult to negotiate the identity of 'the artist' is a widely held view (shared and promoted, as a principle, by many in the artistic 'community' and latently supported by the dominant models of art education) that modern art is functionally autonomous – that it *necessarily* exists at a distance from all other practices. And further, that the practice of art can only make sense of and in the world, as much as of and in itself, from the irreducible distance between art and all practices of living. And furthermore, that only when art can keep faith with the human and resist being dragged into the social – when it resists the commodified practices and forms of mass culture and corporate enterprise that drive the human and the social further and further apart – can it perform, indirectly, any critical function. The view that art can only function as an autonomous practice always casts the identity of the artist in the terms of self-determining difference, whether this view is underwritten by those philosophical ideals that seek in art an antidote to instrumental rationalism, or, conversely, whether it is founded in the notions of 'objective' aesthetic enquiry that have largely governed the quasi-scientific modernist paradigm of formal plastic and pictorial experimentation; whether it comes from the idea of a seamless continuity of art as per the idea of its 'transhistorical' nature among the constant flux of everything else; whether it reflects something of the paradoxical logic of the avant-garde tradition by which bridging the gap between art and everything else demanded a negation of all given norms; or whether, finally, it acknowledges the avant garde's historic failure.

Self-determining and self-justifying but not self-evident. 'The artist' is always a generalist (for art is an abstraction and each artist's practice is a model of art). Sure, there are 'painters', 'sculptors', 'photographers' and others who describe themselves by a reference to their use of particular materials, media or techniques, or by the nature of the objects that they produce. And it is true that these descriptions are commonly taken to mean specialist activities in the field of art. But this is precisely the point: 'being a painter', for example, clearly implies the pursuit of certain activities within certain norms and traditions, which distinguish the work from, say, the pursuits of photography or fishing, but the application of paint on canvas has no necessary connection with art. It is neither the 'aesthetic quality' of the work, nor the natural gifts of the painter, nor skill, nor, in itself, the tradition of pictorial art, which distinguishes 'the artist' from 'the painter' (the distinction is, of course, non-hierarchical – and the question as to whether a painter is *also* an artist is not the issue here). 'The artist' is not, strictly, another name for a maker of paintings even if 'paintings' are thought of as a universal self-defined category of aesthetic endeavour – and much less if they are seen against the background of the actual history of painting. The paint, the domain of the painter, is the simple truth of painting. The domain of the artist is the surplus, the rest, what remains to be seen after the simple truth has been told: the *difference* that art makes. If it is to be found *in* the painting – or exclusively in the painting, as some would claim – then it is in all probability the property of the painter (of the artist as a painter); if it resides elsewhere, as others would have it, in the act or context of reception, for instance, in the destination of the work, then why should we attribute it to the painter? Why not say that it is the viewer who is then the producer of art (the artist to the painter)?

If it were only so simple! As the strategies of modern art so often call into question the functional status of artistic practice itself, the overt distinctions between the production and reception of art, its source and its destination, become unreliable, as do those between the work and the institution of art or between the latter and the 'public domain'. The course of action through which the artistic intent is channelled, realised and recognised becomes unpredictable. There are no longer any safe guidelines for the forms of engagement with an audience, as indeed there are no definitive formal requirements by which the 'simple truth' of the work could be established with any degree of certainty (the 'simple truth' whose absence perennially provokes among some onlookers the perplexed question, 'but is it art?'). Hence if there is anything left in the work from which, always with difficulty, the identity of the artist could be derived, then it is the uncertainty of the difference in the work of art, in art as *work*, in how art makes a difference, which remains the only distinct feature of 'the artist'.

When the German artist Joseph Beuys insisted a quarter of a century ago that 'everyone is an artist', he did so to make us reflect on our collective conditions and individual human potential: how we live and act as individuals and as social beings, and how we could or should live and act otherwise. He was not proposing that everyone should make works of art. And when the Austrian poet, Beuys's contemporary, Hans Artmann announced as a 'well-known fact' that 'to be a poet one no longer needs to write poetry, or even be able to read and write', but that 'a more or less conscious intention to make a poetic gesture is enough', he tried to challenge the definitions of poetry and its ties with the productive/receptive institutions of literature and literacy. But he did not dispute that the *realisation* of the 'poetic gesture' would still amount (more or less) to making poems. Removing the object or gesture of art from the interplay of difference, or reducing them to things that can't be materially demonstrated, would silence art as well as liberate it. The idea of artistic freedom, which already provides for such a possibility, would then be fully subsumed in the ideal of human and civic freedom. But what if Beuys and Artmann's statements are the works of artists (they made them) who are self-conscious about their own 'impossible' condition? What if they are acts of resistance to being what the artist has to be?

While the production of works of art remains the main characteristic of 'being an artist' in the accepted sense, as well as the main pretext for the popular acceptance of such a category (somebody's got to do it), it does not provide us with more than instrumental definitions ('artists make art' or 'art is made by artists', for example). It does not justify the existence of the artist, nor does it suggest a particular critical function in the social world. It makes the artist's labour 'useful' in sustaining the industry of art, which, in turn, is of 'use' to other industries; it reconciles the production of art with the product of art and aligns it with the value systems of a market (or 'the market' – there seems to be only one). The only difference then is the precise and demonstrable difference between one work and another, one practice and other practices, the diversity of production indifferent to the difference of art. This difference, the variable quality of all art, its transformative power, is what the artist must try to realise (both to understand and to make) by continually testing the conditions of the production of art as a means of acting upon the world. Even if, in the materiality of the work of art and the reality of production, such an ambition must always end in a compromise – a compromise between making something and making something happen. The social significance of 'being an artist' lies in the artist's determination to resist the identity of a producer, even if that is the only identity that the artist can have. 'Being an artist', then, does not mean doing different things than others do, but instead doing things differently.

Modern society undoubtedly needs creativity, critical imagination and resistance more than it needs works of art. It needs artists with their ways of doing things more than it needs the things that they make. It needs them for what they *are*, rather than for what they *do* – and if it needs them for what they do, then it is in the sense that artists are producers of culture rather than of discrete artefacts that characterise that culture. Society largely relies on artists to be agents of culture who provide an index of human experience as well as a critical support for social practices and ideologies from which the concepts of culture are developed. And here again, it is the work of art, the actions and consequences of art, rather than works of art, that is the active ingredient of culture. I use the word 'culture' here in that time-honoured sense of the term, which associates it with the symbolic and expressive side of collective human life and relations, as a matrix of conventions through which people share and develop their mutual understanding and attitudes towards one another. I also use it in that generalised sense in which it is possible to speak of culture as such without claiming that there is one unified overarching culture, but simply because there is, in this world, a continuity among the many individual symbolic and expressive systems, cultures and subcultures that coexist and confront one another in society, just as there is a continuity among languages or systems of communication.

This notion of culture, 'our culture', endows the artist with a double identity. Artists exist in our society to experiment with the conventions of culture, licensed by tradition and consensus to define their practices, their particular criteria, specific methods and aims, independently from the dynamics that drive change in the conventions that prevail more generally in that same culture. At the same time, the existence of the artist is also something of a social experiment in itself, subject to the authority of conventional assumptions, beliefs and expectations, as much as to the apparatus of enterprise and economic selection from which the practices of art are expected to stand apart. Thus on the one hand, each individual artistic practice, each model of art, is by definition unique and non-representative of the culture at large. While on the other, all artists and their practices share in the eyes of the public certain common, externally identified characteristics and traits (creativity, critical imagination, resistance, for example) and these collectively represent the place of art in the make-up of that society's self-image. The image that society has of itself as a culture is, then, less the product of artists' individual efforts or experiments (their works, propositions, observations, statements) than it is the outcome of that society's attitudes towards the value of the 'non-representativeness' of 'the artist', manifest as the diversity of practices, for the social experiment of art.

This applies equally whether we conceive of art as representation, i.e. a picture of the world, or as expression, i.e. a subjective statement of the artist in the world. Whether 'the world' is the outer reality in which the artist partakes with others through observation and intervention, or whether it is the subjective inner world of private experience, it is always *this* world (there cannot be any other) that art acts upon and in which the transformation of art takes place. Either way, the artist is generally expected to provide a private response, which is at once non-representative and representative of the culture's concepts of art. To achieve this, the artist must assume a particular position (perspective, point of view) within the 'others' world' or let the others enter the intimacy of his or her unique 'private world', while also maintaining at all times the necessary distance (speculative disengagement) that is needed to understand the artist's practice as a model of art. Art is a game whose rules are entirely made of exceptions. The artist is expected to act as an independent agent of direct experience, as if that experience were a denominator of general principles, *and* to exemplify general principles, as if they were subjective and socially authentic departures from the norm. The friction between the two requirements grows with the rising levels of mediation, which are characteristic of modern social formations. The more this world becomes the 'world of information', or the more culture becomes identified with integrated networks of distribution and communication, the more remote, indirect and abstract the models of art become; the better synchronised the links between the individual and general interests and the greater the dependency of social contact on social institutions, the more society tends to learn about itself not from the observations of artists but from observing the artist.

The development of 'socially active' models of art is then taken over by intermediaries who 'deliver' art to the public, or who facilitate public 'access' to art – curators, critics, producers, administrators – and whose role it is to negotiate the practical and ideological terms and conditions of the 'services' provided by artists in society (as much as it is to serve the institution of art). This 'resolves' the troubling questions of the place, function and identity of the artist by proxy – the preferred form of all social engagement.

It has been said that art is a job that no one has asked you to do. Yet in the reality of this world, the artist has to gain a special mandate to do it with any sense of purpose. This mandate, the 'artistic licence', stipulates what artists can do. To earn it, however, the artist must make a difference: do differently what all artists are permitted and able to do – indeed, what anyone could have done but nobody has done and what is thus left to this one artist to do. To find out what needs to be done, the artist uses the 'artistic licence' as a kind of a passport into the social world. The artist is always an itinerant, a messenger, an explorer, who operates in or among others' territories. The artist comes and goes, takes away and brings back. As an itinerant, the artist always remains a stranger whose temporary presence disturbs and contaminates the familiarity of the place. But that presence of a stranger may be just what it takes for the rest to feel at home.

Dolan Cummings (ed), *Art: What Is It Good For?*, Institute of Ideas and Hodder & Stoughton, London, 2002, pp.23–32.

YOUR DISCIPLINE IS DEAD

'Is she dead?' asks Samuel Jackson as a shady gun-pusher in Quentin Tarantino's film *Jackie Brown*. 'Pretty much,' replies his somewhat retarded accomplice played by Robert de Niro.

A similar exchange takes places between a juvenile kidnapper and a hardened mercenary in the first series of the HBO drama, *24*. 'Is she dead?' the mercenary demands to know. 'Sort of,' replies the young man. 'There is no such a thing as sort of dead,' reasons the mercenary, 'either she is dead or not. Here, let me demonstrate…' and shoots the young man in the chest.

This precarious state of 'pretty much dead', or 'sort of dead', must have been what the French painter Paul Delaroche had in mind when more than a century and a half ago, upon seeing his first Daguerreotype, he notoriously declared the death of his discipline: 'As from now, painting is dead!' And this too must have been what the proposers of the topic for our debate today meant by their provocative hyperbole. A more charitable way of putting it would be to say: 'Your discipline is in a critical condition and you shouldn't harbour much hope for its recovery.'

To address the presumed crisis of disciplines – and of disciplinarity – in the visual and plastic arts we first need to know what a discipline is. Following the logic of our proposition, 'Your discipline is dead', a discipline can be provisionally defined as something that can die. But this will not get us very far. In the field of human creative endeavours, which is where our attention is focused today, any particular manner of doing things can become irrevocably obsolete. Painting in any or all of its manifestations and guises can conceivably die – but so can, for instance, any form of a cross-disciplinary practice. Painting is a discipline; a cross-disciplinary practice is arguably not.

It seems that it is not mortality but vitality – in the sense of necessity – that characterises a discipline. According to the dictionary, a discipline is a set of particular conventions, system of methods of practice, an area of learning or a school of thought. It is kept alive by the evolution of the necessary expertise, knowledge and know-how specific to the discipline's role in culture. Discipline is that part of a practice that must be learnt and mastered so that it may be taught, passed on from an expert to the discipline to be perfected further.

If it seemed once that painting was 'sort of dead', it was undoubtedly because certain aspects of its specific expert know-how had become unnecessary, outmoded by the automatic operations of the photographic camera, the speed of the chemical reaction and the superior accuracy of photographic optics. What was the point of disciplining the eye and the hand to learn how to do things that machines could do better? Up until then, painting was the sovereign arbiter of the rules by which the visible world was reproduced in pictures and the expertise of the painter played a vital role in the articulation between the visible and the visual. It had a purpose, authority and responsibility. Now, photography had demonstrated that the visible could be reproduced without the expert intervention of the painter's hand and that a box of mechanical tricks could take over the responsibility for the norms of producing the visual with an equal confidence.

The crisis of painting brought about by the new technology of mechanical picture production finally made another French painter, Maurice Denis, point out something rather obvious. In 1890 he wrote: 'It is well to remember that a picture – before being a battle horse, naked woman or some anecdote – is essentially a plane surface covered with colours assembled in a certain order.' And it was the pursuit of this 'certain order' that gave painting a new lease of life. Painting did not die. Rather, with the advent of photography it became not just unnecessary but literally 'useless'. As Rosalind Krauss puts it with reference to Walter Benjamin, 'obsolescence frees the outmoded object from the grip of utility'. This liberation from the 'grip of utility', in turn, made painting free to pursue the unnecessary and purposefully useless goals of art, to emancipate the search for an inner aesthetic order from the utilitarian logic and systematic rationalisation of both material production and cultural consumption, which is one enduring legacy of the modern age.

Less than a century later, we heard much the same being said about photography's most important progeny, the cinema. Since the 1970s the phrase 'cinema is dead' has signalled the growing irrelevance of the specifically cinematic aesthetic and sensibility to our experience of a world saturated by all manner of moving images and the omnipresence of the television monitor and the computer screen in our daily lives. When painting died, when it became 'useless' as a technique of reproduction, it lived on as a form of art; when cinema died, it died as an artform, as a 'separate and complete structural form', not merely a visual medium but 'the great art of painting in motion', in the words of one of its most distinguished critics, Rudolf Arnheim.

Painting has, since the Renaissance ('painting from life', 'imitation of nature'), been essentially a modern discipline. Its values, until recently, were derived from a progressive improvement in the process of expert work. The application of expertise to production is the source of all values in the modern world. Photography, as a discipline, is not modern in the same sense. (Although this is not to deny that, in its performance, photography remains the modern medium par excellence.) As Vilém Flusser persuasively argues in his writings on the subject, photography is not a separate form but a function of a technological industrial apparatus whose operations and possibilities are preprogrammed. The photographer is a functionary of the apparatus who operates the camera. In terms of expertise, the photographer is an expert user: 'the camera', says Flusser, 'does the will of the photographer, but the photographer has to will what the camera can do'.

The development of the photographer's expertise and know-how consists of learning 'what the camera can do' in a never-ending struggle against the development of its preprogrammed possibilities, that is to say, against the development in other disciplines, those of the fields of science and technology, such as chemistry, optics or mechanical engineering. But the discoveries made by the photographer in the process of mastering the camera are constantly fed back, by the photographic industry, into the design improvements of the apparatus – and so, even as it is being developed, the photographer's expertise is being made redundant by those who control the programming of the possibilities of the camera. It acts as an agent-informer for the industry to the detriment of the internal necessity of the discipline. This entropic feedback loop is called 'knowledge economy' and is the source of values in, and a defining characteristic of, the postmodern stage of capitalism.

In its early days, the norms of photographic practice were imported from the conventions of other disciplines, particularly painting. The same was the case, later on, with film. If Arnheim was justified in describing film as 'the great art of painting in motion', it was precisely because it initially took from painting the 'useless' pursuit of a 'certain order' of the visual properties of the image, which, by the time cinematography entered the stage, had become painting's sole preoccupation. To the extent that photography and cinematography remained artisanal practices, they soon began to develop disciplinary conventions of their own – even if the development of these conventions, from photographic pictorialism to the structuralist cinema, more or less paralleled the logic of painting's own self-identification as a specific art form. (In fact, the structuralist filmmaker, Peter Wild, claims that it was the development of technical images that influenced the grounding of painting on a quasi-scientific method and depersonalisation.)

In the majority of their uses, however, photography and cinematography cannot be thought of as separate – or authentic – disciplines. (It goes without saying that in their domestic, private uses they are simply modes of consumption and do not belong to this debate.) This is because the 'systems of methods of practice', the particular rules and conventions and the evolution of the necessary expertise that characterise a discipline are developed externally as specialist functions of coordinated industrial expertise. And it is not only the technological nature of photography and film that erodes their respective specificities as disciplines, it is also their cultural forms and social functions. The association of photography with the printed page, for instance, has forced the visual language into dependence on text and imposed the rules of journalism, graphic design and a host of other disciplines onto the production of photographic images. In cinema too, and even more clearly, the collective methods of production with their division of labour and organised hierarchy of individual tasks, inevitably contaminate any notion of a separate discipline, and indeed invoke another meaning of the term 'discipline': subordination.

At the same time, these technological visual forms also compromise the disciplinary integrity of other types of images, and their status as the means of mechanical reproduction radically alters the condition of the other arts. Walter Benjamin explained that reproduction and reproducibility force the individual work of art, and therefore the separate arts, into the condition of general equivalency. Whatever is particular to a given art, including that which is necessary to its production, becomes subordinate to the principle of exchange and the law of commodification, that is to say to the forces and interests of the culture industry which 'now impresses the same stamp of everything'. (This damnation of the culture industry by Theodor Adorno echoes what Karl Marx had been saying all along: 'All that is solid melts into air'…)

Against this background, disciplinarity in the visual arts, as in the rest of the creative cultural activity, suffered something of a decisive blow in the late 1960s and early 1970s and has remained in a critical condition since.

From within the art world itself, it was the emergence of Conceptual art and the rise out of the debris of Greenbergian modernism of various forms of process and intermedia art, especially the introduction of video; and from the field of theory it was post-structuralism and deconstruction that began to dismantle the 'metaphysical fiction' of self-identification and internal unity on which any notion of separate disciplines largely depends. Both the developments in art and the writings of post-structuralist thinkers such as Jacques Derrida, Michael Foucault and Jean Baudrillard demonstrated that it was no longer possible to sustain any belief in the specificity – or authenticity – of cultural processes and products. They showed that there are no 'separate and complete structural forms', as the arts were for Arnheim, because everything, every interiority, is always contaminated by an outside, just as the meaning of every activity is constituted by its context, and therefore there is no possibility of an autonomous aesthetics form, nor a definite boundary of a given discipline. In the words of John Latham, the archetypal 'interdisciplinary' artist, 'context' is always already 'half the work' – and artistic disciplines are 'pretty much dead'.

It would be hard to argue against our proposition if we only analysed it from the perspective that I have sketched here with perhaps too much expediency. But not least because of what I have just said, I must acknowledge the context in which the proposition is so confidently uttered and look at what it means when in a university we say, 'your discipline is dead'.

One way to take the context into account might be to revisit my gangster fiction references and translate the short sentence in the spirit of James Gandolfini's Tony Soprano: 'Here (your discipline) don't mean shit.'

It captures the sentiment with a forthright honesty but while the institutions of the criminal underworld settle arguments 'with a kind word and a gun', academic institutions are the intellectual battlefields of the undead where arguments can never be laid to rest and everyone lives to fight another day. And when among the 'plurality of discourses', which still, somewhat contrary to appearances, distinguishes academia from the mafia, a kind word rises above the argument, the voice is quite likely to be that of the PR department. So a more fitting translation of the phrase might be: 'Here we recognise the diversity of individual needs and interests of our academic customers by providing a flexible menu of educational opportunities in a structured multi-specialist environment where you are encouraged to develop a personalised portfolio of skills that will enable you to seek employment as an adaptable creative practitioner in today's dynamic job market.'

No, I wouldn't really put it like this either. It is too easy to mock the detestable language of spin that frames our institutional agendas and priorities and the jokes quickly wear thin. Rather, I will say that from the mouth of an academic the proclamation of the death of another's discipline often amounts to the dismissal of the discipline in principle, an exclusion of its values from the system of expertise on the grounds that they cannot be measured or otherwise aligned with the prevailing principles, conventions and values. It therefore amounts to the demand to disassemble the given discipline's specific expertise into the generic components that make up the academic knowledge system. To my ears it says: 'Conform or die.'

It is the combination of bad faith, resignation and cynicism which lurks behind such dismissals that forces me not so much to oppose the present proposition as to object to it – while being fully aware that, in the circumstances, I may be truly flogging a dead discipline and my objection may be received as quite 'academic'.

It is this: the veneration of interdisciplinarity, of hybrid forms of practice implied in the proposition and the false equalisation of the general and the particular that it entails, is but an abdication of responsibility to a system whose own closure and structural rigidity dominates over individual interests by lessening every qualitative difference. At the same time, it is a demonstration of an uncertainty of a clear cultural purpose within the academy, including the uncertainty of what or how to teach, and a sign of resignation to the industrial model of culture. For the university's academic principles, conventions and values, which have been imposed on the arts and creative education and assimilated by it in turn, are already heavily contaminated by the dominant concerns and priorities of the market economy and the self-interest of the culture industry.

Structurally, the academic system has not changed much for centuries (just think of the arcane and somewhat embarrassing nomenclature: professors, lecturers, fellows, masters, bachelors…). The system is and always has been solidly disciplinarian. Indeed, and for a reason, the academy is the guardian and patron saint of disciplinarity, rather than a frontier post of some new brave post-disciplinary world, even if it no longer believes in individual academic disciplines as self-evident and self-perfecting epistemological domains. Even if we see everywhere the break-up of traditional disciplines into a proliferation of incomprehensibly designated courses, programmes, modules or units that bear little resemblance to anything in the living world, the system still thinks along disciplinary lines. And it is not only in its structures but also in its operations that the institutional academic system shows its commitment to disciplinarity.

These proceedings, for one easy example, are taking place within a cross-cohort postgraduate programme evocatively titled 'Testing Time'. What could be more disciplinarian than the concept of testing? Testing demands criteria – and 'criterion', like 'criticism', comes from the Greek *krinien*, which means to divide, to separate, to break up. Testing requires rules, yardsticks, systems of measurement and standards, and these have to be appropriate to what is being measured. There is about as much point in testing the products of one discipline by the standards of another as there is in measuring time in inches, distance in gallons or volume in minutes – unless, of course, the qualities of the object in question are irrelevant and what is being tested are the norms of the exercise alone, or, unless we believe that all criteria are essentially interchangeable, all equally 'academic'.

The concept of the discipline is the means by which a philosophical distinction can be made between the particular and the general. In our field, this concept can be used to distinguish the arts, which are particular disciplines, from art, which is general. And by the same means, we can draw distinctions within other categories of visual and plastic production, such as design or craft. Typographic design, for instance, is a discipline, at least in an academic sense, while design as such is a general category.

(This brings us a little closer to where some corpses may be buried or where skeletons may be hidden in the departmental filing cabinets, for in practice, a great confusion reigns on this point. To take this institution as a measure of conceptual and semiological chaos: 'Fine Art', which is not a discipline, is treated as one; 'Media Arts', which is a technological category, is treated as a raft of disciplines; and 'Art as Environment', which sounds like something akin to a discipline, is treated as a branch of cross-disciplinary science.)

The very denomination that you will soon be using to describe your qualification, Master of Arts, implies the particular and the general. The established pedagogical truth has it that in mastering your discipline you proceed from the general to the particular. In the old art academies, where the arts were separated into painting, sculpture and architecture, the learning of the particular was always present in the general since the general itself was specific to the discipline, proper to it, as in 'vision is proper to painting', and axiomatic. So the general axioms for painting (flatness/colour) were different from those for sculpture (material/volume/space), and those again were not the same as the general axioms for architecture (structure/interior/exterior).

The same progressive logic persists in the new university-based provision, except that the particular is now itself confusingly general. You started your creative education with a foundation course where you learned basic picture- and object-making skills. You progressed through an undergraduate discipline-specific stage, perhaps a course in painting or photography, where you were guided to hone those skills in such a way as to establish the rudiments of an individual practice. When you entered the master's level, that individual practice, no longer necessarily recognisable as belonging to any given discipline, was your new starting point. You are now expected to perfect that practice and put it to the test through an independent critical reassessment of its means and premises, as a mastery demands, but the tools for such a reassessment appear to be rather general: the common critical, theoretical or methodical points of reference that can be established in a contact among disparate practices, whose lowest common denominator may be nothing more solid than the much abused concept of 'research' or the equally battered notion of 'experiment'. As a result, the particular often tends to be borrowed from other academic and social practices – 'the artist as ethnographer', 'the artist as archivist' – while being hardly recognisable by them.

Academic institutions tend to group and fit practices together without any gaps, so that disciplinary boundaries become arbitrary and the disciplinary character of a practice is defined by its proximity to randomly placed nominal reference points (closer to painting, say, than photography) and has almost nothing to do with the place of that practice in culture. Yet the structure itself has a lot to do with the world we live in. It is not difficult to recognise in this structure of tightly fitting components the patterns of the capitalist market logic and the systemic needs of management. For the market, any gap is a niche of economic opportunity and will be filled as soon as it is spotted; for management, it is like a break in an electric circuit.

The cultivation of individual practice within this framework then mirrors the economic concept of 'cultural individualisation' or 'mobility' and the political construct of 'creative industries'. The former simply means self-exploitation in your readiness to forego the security of employment in exchange for a vain promise of creative independence, and the latter are merely subsidiaries of the culture industry, collectively branded and co-opted by corporate and civic agencies. And just as on a university campus where variously grouped (and oddly shaped) academic disciplines are allotted their physical space, so too in the external world these 'creative industries' are marshalled together into 'cultural quarters' by town planners and local governments for the benefit of private developers. Meanwhile, in the academy, academic managers are busy filling gaps in the market by devising courses for those 'cultural producers' or 'entrepreneurs' who, having failed to find an outlet for their creative energies in a culture manufactured to plan, come back for another academic degree manufactured to the same plan. Chances are good that the curriculum will include a critical studies seminar to make the students reflect on Adorno's observation that 'what parades as progress in the culture industry remains a disguise for an eternal sameness'.

I am beginning to sound as cynical as those whom I have accused of bad faith. Indeed, I have to admit that, in some respects, I find myself in agreement with them. I too believe that in the production of culture, the concept of the arts, that is of separate disciplines, has little real relevance left. As an artist, I cannot advocate the resuscitation of self-sustaining artistic disciplines. But as a teacher, I am not ready for a disciplinary euthanasia.

I know that this exposes my argument to all sorts of criticism. If my job as a teacher is to help you define the knowledge and skills that each one of you will individually need to function in the contemporary world on your own terms, then how can I justify the system of disciplines that my own form of artistic practice is helping to undermine? If the vitality of artistic disciplines cannot be constantly refreshed by the works we make, how can there be any active feedback between the disciplines and a living culture? And how can the notion of a discipline be anything but an empty abstraction? Or for one last time from the repertoire of Hollywood mobster wisdom, to paraphrase Jack Nicholson as Charley in John Huston's *Prizzi's Honor*: 'If (your discipline) is so fucking smart, how come (it) is so fucking dead?'

Fair enough. Yet it is not the discipline itself but its symbolic function in creative education that I plea for. Learning how to negotiate the dialectic between the particular and the general against the norms of a discipline, however outmoded they may be, means more than merely learning practical specialist skills. It also means learning to take responsibility for determining the value of what you do with those skills. Giving up on this responsibility means giving in to the external values underwritten only by the false conviction that the wholesale emptying out of the particular into the general, in the academy as in contemporary culture at large, is something like a 'natural' tendency arising spontaneously from social practice and human creativity in the conditions of postmodernity. It is a feature of a project of a neutralisation of culture by the culture industry in the service of economic expansion and political stability – a project internalised and reproduced in the academy by precisely those whose values you have to borrow to 'test' your individual practices when your discipline has been proclaimed dead.

Your disciplines, in and of themselves, may no longer have the normative powers that they once had to put your skills and work to the test. Not even in the relative safety of the academy are they all you need, let alone out there in the world. They may be no more than signposts. But as long as they do not all point in the same direction, as long as your testing does not become an exercise in smoothing out disciplinary differences, they will give you a better chance to find your own way than the indiscriminate label that makes you all, in the institutional newspeak, 'creatives'. Your discipline may be dead but it should not be buried before we find something more meaningful to put in its place.

Conference paper, *Your Discipline Is Dead: Testing Time Symposium*, Manchester Metropolitan University, 2003.

OFF THE PEG

Like those school photographs of a year group, long out of fashion, degree-show catalogues are mementoes of a time spent together. They are souvenirs, small investments in future memories (she went out with him, he never bought his own cigarettes, and this one… whatever happened to him?). They are also, like the photographs, displays of brave faces. Every year, dozens of degree shows all over the country mark the first tentative steps into the public domain for the work of thousands of aspiring artists, who all strive for recognition and all want to make their mark. For many, this is one of their first opportunities to publicly exhibit what they have to offer; for some, or perhaps for most (let's be honest, for once), it will also be their last; and for all it is a moment of heightened anxiety.

The professional culture of art has assigned degree exhibitions a straightforward role: to provide indexes of 'emerging artists' – a shorthand for those whose work is yet to undergo the test of critical endorsement – and to indicate new tendencies and directions, strategic positions and tactical approaches. Such expectations are, at least in part, the result of deep-rooted assumptions that surround the reception and appreciation of works of art in our time. Both inside and outside the art community, we have come to see art in terms of artistic argument and conflict, driven by the 'logic' of aesthetic and conceptual discourses and the canon of confrontation and challenge. Caught in the crossfire of 'post-' and 'neo-' and negotiating the minefield of paradigms and contexts, we have learnt to debate precedents before a single work is discussed. As our critical curiosity seems to need schematic classification more than it needs individual works of art, there is no escape from the regime of '-ities' and '-isms' – so much so that even the self-proclaimed 'pluralism' of recent debates is beginning to look like another dogma.

One of the most enduring orthodoxies in our approaches to new art is the notion of the 'school', which unites the comfortable bearings of 'tradition' with the homely dimension of 'provenance'. And whilst the metaphorical usage of the term is perhaps no longer current, in its literal sense the word still resonates with the same connotations in a culture saturated by corporate identities and brand names.

It is particularly difficult to escape the obsessive branding when it comes to degree exhibitions and their paraphernalia. True enough, there is an identity of mutual formative influence to any group of artists who have worked alongside each other for a few years, formed alliances and allegiances, and developed an understanding of each other's work (even if only by endlessly talking about themselves). There is an identity to the time and place of their generation, their culture with its mannerisms and fashions, which does affect what they do and how they do it, even when it is not immediately visible in their work. There is, too, a definitive identity to the successive generations of graduates of this or that college, school or university, the inheritance of their cumulative failures or successes to respond to tradition without falling hostage to its mythology... But any label weighs down the work of an 'emerging artist'; the designation of a 'school' does so perhaps the most heavily. Too vague to reflect the autonomy of individual perception and integrity of experience, too constrained to acknowledge the spiritual independence which is the condition of any creative achievement, and far too loaded with the unpleasant connotations of academic self-importance.

If the regime of the degree show inevitably imposes the brand of a 'school' on the graduating students' work, then the degree-show catalogue can be a token of identification while also being an attempt to moderate, bypass or even subvert its institutional terms. In these days of fiscal austerity and streamlined institutional priorities, degree-show catalogues are more often than not produced by the collective initiative and efforts of the 'emerging artists' themselves. They take over, organise themselves, form committees, argue, fundraise, beg and borrow, go to any length to see their own group identity in print: to see themselves, that's to say, as they want to appear to 'the world'. On occasions (and this is the best scenario) they manage the opposite and show how the world appears to those who perhaps realise that to 'emerge' is to leave one's self-image behind. Or in other words, the best degree-show catalogues manage to declare a position and abandon it at the same time. In the main, though, like in the photograph, they just strike a pose.

To select an exhibition from degree-show catalogues is, above all, to call the 'emerging' artist's bluff.

Off the Peg (exhibition leaflet), Mid Pennine Gallery, Burnley, 2003, np.

AFTERWORD: BUT IS IT LIFE?

Art is a job that no one has asked you to do. This simple observation, so obvious that it is hardly ever mentioned, provides a key to understanding the 'radical art' processes whose motives, interests, commitments and aspirations are at the heart of *Cultural Hijack: Rethinking Intervention* (2012). This book sheds some light on the purpose of experimenting with personal and creative freedom through 'another kind of art', one which defines itself here as cultural hijacking. It also sets the tone: the first-person mode of the individual testimonies, self-evaluative accounts of projects and strategies, extended 'artist's statements', personal anecdotes, stories and one-to-one conversations. It puts into perspective the desire for recognition and affirmation of the artist's identity in a world in which this identity has perhaps become the main field of contestation for practices which strive to keep so close to 'everyday life' as to be indistinguishable from it and yet to make a positive difference in it in ways that only art can – or in the words of the Fluxus artist Robert Filliou, 'art is what makes life more interesting than art'.

The struggles of the avant garde for acceptance of art as a kind of work that puts in doubt what is acceptable as art have ended in victory for artists. Yet their victory has made the integration of art and life that artists of Filliou's generation advocated and pioneered all the more difficult. When anything can pass for art and anything that can be done can be done as art, the construction 'art-as-life' loses its radical tension. The closer art 'lives out' life, the less effective it becomes as an arbiter of meaning for lived experience and the more it tends to reflect on its own condition.

With the demise of any reliable criteria by which a work of art can be recognised as such, it may have become easier to act as an artist but it is harder to know what to do. As a consequence, much artistic production today has turned towards the analysis of the operational frameworks and operating systems of art. It consists not of making but of revealing the internal functions and relations of art in society and history and the attendant discourses of theory and philosophy, in art's institutions and markets, in mass and popular culture, in the culture industry. In its more radical manifestations, it examines the social functions of art and the possibilities and conditions for society's engagement with, and of, art as a transformative agency. There seems to be a growing interest among artists and those who orchestrate our encounters with art in transposing social reality into the domain of art and vice versa, simulating social structures, promoting connectedness, participation and dialogue, and giving real-life concerns a publicly discussable form and a public forum. Projects that experiment with working models of collective organisation, strategies of self-reliance and resistance, social and economic research, or with education as a platform for creative and critical exchange, for instance, break down the conventional relationships between art and life in favour of an inclusive aesthetic paradigm concerned with neither objects nor critical judgment but with communication. Invitation, hospitality or communal solidarity are often the guiding concepts in projects which develop this paradigm by engaging the audience as the producers of the work. In yet other examples, the expertise and labour of professionals from all walks of life, or the dedication of amateurs, may be enlisted in the production of an artwork so as to make 'work' the active communicative ingredient in the experience of art and so on.

Such and similar initiatives, in and outside the institutional setting and patronage, stem from the tradition of framing the progression of modern art by a critical narrative of 'problems' and 'solutions'. One part of this narrative, and a part of the history of the avant garde, is a progressive search for a 'social' solution to the problem of the identity of art itself, to the point where the concept of art can host and endorse almost any form of social interaction.

For politically committed and socially engaged art, which takes it as a given that art is only meaningful as a social activity, this solution is, in a sense, once again a cultural problem. It poses a particular challenge to the extra- or anti-institutional artistic practices and anonymous and spontaneous creative interventions, 'neither framed [by] nor recognisable as art', which can no longer be sufficiently validated by their status as art but only in relation to the processes of legitimation, which lend purpose and meaning to the aesthetic action, always provisionally, in a concrete social situation, at a given moment and in the specific circumstances of the encounter. In other words, such practices need to demonstrate the value of their unsanctioned and sometimes unwelcome interference with everyday life by what they contribute to the perceptions of how and where we live, how we go about the 'project of daily life', what we can be and need to do, and how we recognise and grasp the possibilities that we may be passing by. They need to not only inspire and incite imagination but to empower. Above all, they need not merely to hijack the literally exclusive freedom licenced in this society to what is recognised as art but also to extend and transfer it as an instrument for individual liberation and a meaningful expression of creative freedom onto our collective social existence.

The practices of *Cultural Hijack* discussed here position themselves both within and outside the broader field of activist art. Their projects and interventions are tactical, even opportunistic, rather a strategic, distinguished by self-motivated action initiated and carried out by the artists, rather than acting on behalf of a third party, supporting a cause or devising something for the benefit of specific – typically disadvantaged – target constituencies. While activist art tends to utilise the political power of art to bring about, or lobby effectively for, a real tangible change for the better where the actual political will and powers fail or do not work, the self-styled 'tactical practitioners' prefer to work in the interstices and gaps left unclaimed by both politics and art.

In taking action where nobody else will or can, the artist acts under the prerogative of art to propose a specifically cultural understanding and solutions. To the extent that the action provokes a reaction, the self-identification of the artists' action as art, or its disassociation from other forms of activism – or, for that matter, from social research or cultural politics – is as instrumental as it is paradigmatic. It provides not merely the means and 'licence' but also the primary critical context, even if this may lie beyond the horizon and interests of formal art discourse. While the impetus of the artistic action may be ethical or political, rather than aesthetic, and while the action may follow an agenda for social or political change that may be independent from, or indifferent to, the aesthetic nature of the artist's activity, activist and interventionist art is still, and perhaps above all, a form of critical aesthetics.

The ultimate goal of all revolutionary praxis is its own redundancy. The ideal of activist art practice is to establish model situations or relationships that can function in such ways as to transcend their identity as (only) art, often by adapting extra-artistic processes and structures only to reintegrate these adaptations more or less seamlessly into their original social contexts. It strives to provide the tools and resources not for doing whatever can be done as art but simply for doing what needs to be done.

This is where the practices and projects compiled here depart, in the main, from the orthodox notions of artistic activism. They prioritise 'invisibility' and 'impermanence' and value anonymity but their goal is the recovery of art as a vital presence in everyday life; they emphasise proximity but aspire to a role for art both integrated into the everyday and at a critical distance from its pragmatic concerns. This critical distance is what defines an alternative. It is what makes it possible to think in ways that span the familiar and the unfamiliar, the visible and the ignored, the expected and the unexpected, art and 'non-art', the regulated and the contingent.

In general, they also aspire to a critical distance from the 'art world' as the space reserved for art in the liberal-democratic political order and the global capitalist economy, which over the last 40 years or so brought about an almost total corporatisation of the cultural field and the loss of the autonomy achieved by modern art. The specific artistic values that characterised the relative success of modern art as a site of resistance to the market have been displaced by the quantitative criteria, logic and power of corporate interests. With the complicity of the public and private institutional structures which, heterogenic in themselves, largely monopolise and normalise the production and mediation of contemporary art, art is increasingly both produced and managed by a new type of professional who appears to resemble ever more closely every other member of the professional class. The professional corporate 'art world' suffers from many ills, not least from vanity, self-indulgence and greed, a loss of faith in the revolutionary potential of art exemplified by the acceptance of, and the demand for, subversion as an essence of art-making, ethical complacency and the symptoms of self-denial. The aim of *Cultural Hijack* is neither to provide a cure nor strictly 'another kind of art' for another kind of world, but a perspective.

Insofar as it is meaningful to identify common trajectories among practices and projects that stand as far apart from one another as a Paris squat from an office at Harvard, some of which feel just as comfortable in bed with major institutions as others do in the margins of official culture, *Cultural Hijack* points towards the potential of art to reclaim a space for independent imagination. It calls for a rethinking and reinvention. It offers some guidance on how to interpret our encounters with art in everyday situations but it wants us to think and act for ourselves. It is 'a book of ideas', not of recipes. To prescribe the paradigms and models for others to follow would counter the open spirit of the contributions and the practices they represent.

Ben Parry (ed), *Cultural Hijack: Rethinking Intervention*, Liverpool University Press, Liverpool, 2012, pp.307–313.

SECTION THREE

I HAVE NEVER HAD AN IDEA IN MY LIFE

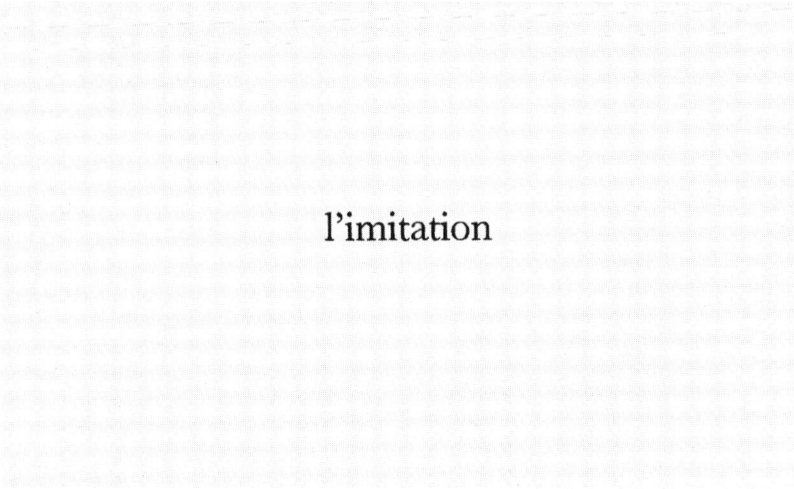

l’imitation

Limitation (No. 2), 2008, ink on paper, 13 x 22 cm

In five separate drawings the same ten letters have been meticulously hand-drawn with a 'French' pen, the nib of which maps the finest of lines. Each version isolates those letters on a uniform sheet of paper, centre of frame. Only the dimensions of the letters change through the sequence of sheets, scaling down from 9 millimetres tall in caps height to the size of 12-point type. The only thing that complicates the simplicity of the repeated content in these drawings is an apostrophe. Is that apostrophe bonding a definite article to a stem word in the form of a French-language contraction, or has that apostrophe slipped in (slit open) a previously complete word? Is this continual script one-and-a-half words or two? In the confusion of potentially being both, this set of drawings poeticises the limitation of imitation as it plays out between word and image, English and French, history and repetition.

A process note published by Büchler describes *Limitation* as an exact drawing of a misquotation of the English word 'limitation' spotted in an essay about Marcel Broodthaers, redrawn five times until the last drawing matches the scale of the printed extract. The Belgian artist struggled during his first career, as an aspiring poet, with the literary side of a national anxiety now known as *belgitude*, the root of which was spelt out by one of Broodthaers's inspirations, Charles Baudelaire in the mid-1860s: 'There is no Belgian people, properly speaking'. According to this socio-psycho anxiety about being defined by something you are not, Francophone Belgian writers could only ever be second-tier French *littérateurs*, limited imitations. Throughout Broodthaers's second career, the gaps between the thing-itself, the image of that thing, and the concept of that thing, gave space and charge to his art work: representations are both less and more than the things they represent. As such, images of words or words as objects short-circuit the proper linguistic function of communicative language: 'I use the object as a zero word', Broodthaers said in a 1974 interview.

Over-attending to a misquotation, slip or glitch is typical of Büchler's work and the genealogy to which it often foregrounds references. In *Limitation*, this reflexivity is linguistic as well as contextual and materialist. *La limitation* would describe the limit of an action, and *une imitation* would describe a reproduction. The translation *l'imitation* fails grammatically at being either, yet the words 'imitation' and 'limitation' are both exact cognates – they are spelled the same and mean the same in English and French because of their shared etymology in Latin. In fact, their use in English is an act of lexical borrowing from French.

Therefore the content of Büchler's drawing is a borrowing of a borrowing of a borrowing of a borrowing even before he cannibalises it through redrafting, yet all five drafts are also a one-off drawing. As one of Broodthaers's other great inspirations, René Magritte never quite said, *ceci n'est pas une imitation*.

THE END OF WORDS

JIŘÍ KOLÁŘ

The age of the finite world is now beginning.[1]

As we are entering the last decade of a millennium, it is becoming increasingly plausible to think that this century may, despite – or perhaps even because of – the all-pervasive penetration of images into the body of culture, be distinguished in the history of Western art as the Century of Language.[2] It has been a century in which the coherent environment of the picture has been fractured and fragmented, intruded into by both image and language. And language, which, together with the picture, had cohered those certainties of humanist thinking that had underpinned Western society's self-conception since the Renaissance, was itself fractured no less radically than perspective or the picture plane. Language was reduced from the security of word or sentence to the insecurities of a sign in the multi-planarities of cubist composition, exploded into non-sense by Filippo Tommaso Marinetti and Kurt Schwitters, propelled into vertiginous new formations in Carlo Carrà's collages. (Indeed, the very possibility of collage issued from this determined assault on the unifying structures of the humanist consensus.) Such actions prefigured those developments in twentieth-century language technology, which, from the wireless to the word processor, have progressively disintegrated language into a multidimensional environment of information. The solid, sure state of language has been made first elastic, ultimately liquid.

Each new state, each new method for the storage, transmission and dissemination of information has been followed, once established, by a quantitative leap in the way we interact with language. The momentum of these developments has been such as to challenge the primary function of language as a means of formulating, discussing and analysing the knowledge, perception and experience of the world and through such a process, to construct a world view of some coherence and foundation. Instead the modern world identifies with the ability of language to generate data, units of information in themselves devoid of significance. The ability, and capacity, to process information at an ever-increasing speed and in an unprecedented volume has developed to the extent that this society no longer finds common focal points or a unifying perspective. It can move in language, so to speak, in all directions at once, expand language through a limitless manipulation of data. The linearity of words has been supplanted by a 'network', without a centre and without an edge, multidimensional – and silent.

As the primary function of language in society ceased to be the meeting point of reality and thought from which concepts are born and through which they are examined, to instead become a point of access to the 'liquid' field of information, society has generally lost the use for art as a provider of a vocabulary of symbols through which a sense of communal understanding and identity could be secured. Through the technology of reproduction, a process analogous to that of generating data in language, the art of the past became a resource for the new needs of this world, its history a pool of information. But the history of art is a finite resource. True, art does not diminish with consumption, but that does not mean that the continuity of consumption can be sustained without a continuously renewed supply. Such demand is being fed by the supply of reproductions. As Walter Benjamin demonstrated, with traditional modes of art such as painting, which is not specifically intended for reproduction, the functioning of the reproduction is dependent to a great extent on its relation to the original, its 'origin'. The more prolific the supply of the reproduction, the greater the distance between it and the original, to the point that the two completely separate. It appears that a point can be reached at which the relationship of the reproduction to the original becomes reversed: the source, the original, becomes the only version that is *not* a reproduction. The original derives its significance from the reproduction and not vice versa. Its context becomes its availability as a mass-produced image. This in effect means that the function of the original as a source becomes exhausted. It gains a new multiple existence in a simultaneity of images (and of course texts). Propagated like a rosebush through cuttings, it now belongs to a different, expandable world of information, a different history. As a consequence, the history of the previous world has contracted and compressed.

> My relationship to the history of art is like that of a son to his dead mother – it never dies.[3]

Through the transformations of language and its functions, our century distanced its connection to that tradition in European culture, particularly of painting, which was dependent to an exceptional degree on literature. The continuity-in-change was disrupted; the tradition, itself perpetuated by a constant remaking of its own inheritance, came to an end. The new culture, needing information more than literature, finds an art whose content is released through the process of linear, 'literary' reading to be of little necessity. As the speed of the 'language machine' dictates a very different mode of perception and thought, it meets its reflection in art as an open space into which anything can enter and which can be accessed at any point; art liberated, in other words, from the sequentiality of text.

The beginning of the century saw the birth of the avant garde, a concept that, for better or worse, has subsequently dominated the history of art. As Rosalind Krauss has pointed out, the constant claim of the avant garde, which over the years has 'worn many guises' and 'preached a variety of creeds', is the claim to originality 'conceived as a literal origin, a beginning from ground zero, a birth', which 'is the way an absolute distinction can be made between the present experienced *de novo* and a tradition-laden past'.[4] The 'originality' is then the self-originality of the source. On this general assumption, the early twentieth-century avant gardes set out to find the means by which to claim the 'essence' of art. The key question became the very question of definition.

The language in which the metaphors for the abstract concept of art began to be formulated became one that no longer derived its existence from the language of words but from precedents outside its tradition: a language of material, of process or of attitude, not of *iconography*... of something much older than the history of art...

The works of tradition were to be expelled from the new era. They were to be banned (together with pasta, in the case of the Futurists), museums were declared 'cemeteries' and were to be destroyed. The old was to be disposed of to allow the new truly to begin. Yet, paradoxically, it was precisely the 'new' that enabled the works of the past to claim the new space of art: they did not creep in from the quiet of the museum or the cathedral, they roamed in through reproduction. Stripped of their 'aura', their 'here and now', as well as emptied of their significance previously formulated in words – they were no longer the vehicle of tradition and instead became *precedents of images*.

I write because I do not want the words I find.[5]

But why would one introduce a body of work produced in Czechoslovakia of the 1950s and '60s with a discussion of the situation of language and of the international avant gardes? Particularly as the work seems at first glance quite at odds with most of the vanguardist art of the same period from Western Europe and the USA. Is not the Eastern European experience far too specific to be implanted into such a context, to be addressed in such (almost global) dimensions? Surely, the most obvious feature of the conditions under which this work came into being is precisely isolation, the divisive impenetrability of the 'iron curtain' and the consequent loss of access to both technological and artistic developments in the rest of the world. And, finally, is it not true that the separation of contemporary art from its own tradition (and from its audience) came in postwar Eastern Europe by means of the ideologue's official decree rather than as a free, as well as liberating, gesture of the artist?

The intention here, however, is neither to portray Jiří Kolář as an 'international artist' nor to suggest that 'art knows no boundaries'. The distinctness of expression of Kolář's work and that of many Czechoslovak artists of his generation cannot be seen simply in contrast to developments elsewhere – just as it cannot be understood as a simple parallel. A direct comparison would not escape the schematism of the 'grand designs', which have seen the East/West division of Europe as a matter of two homogeneous 'blocs' (a myth at last being brought into question). Looking for parallels would result in an equally schematic search of artistic movements and isms. The context of an isolated *milieu* is revealing only to the extent that it reflects the more general situation and conditions of the world. Whilst the work of any artist belongs to his 'locale', at least so far as this is a deliberate and manifest consideration in the work, presumptions of contextualising 'provenance' in terms of a national culture – or even a culture of a geopolitical, supranational 'bloc' – do not help in attending to work which is, above all, remarkable for its single-minded commitment to the twofold nature of human experience: the individual *and* the collective, the lived *and* the relived, the conceived *and* the received.[6]

The importance of the questions of language and of the avant garde becomes apparent if one considers that even the very recent adjustments to the 'political map of Europe' can, at least partly, be explained as a product of the crisis of language that has characterised this century. It has been widely accepted, for example, that the media and other products of language technology – typewriters, telephones, fax machines and computers – had played an exceptional role in maintaining and finally raising popular consciousness in Eastern European countries. (And it has to be stressed that original works of literature circulating as photocopies had contributed at least as significantly as the broadcasts of the BBC World Service!) But also, and perhaps more importantly, the roots of the current upheavals can be found in a reaction against the 'rationalisation' of culture. Stalinist regimes of the 1950s and their progeny promoted what they called a 'scientific view of the world' – anything in the world can be rationally explained *in toto*, as 'natural'. This, of course, disabled art from pursuing its critical function of challenging the hegemony of generally held assumptions and in reality it meant that 'understanding' was a matter of compliance with a doctrine, an unconditional suspension of disbelief, an absolute prohibition of doubt. Hence, every cultural product, and especially art, had to obey the commandment of *comprehensibility*. It had to guarantee a singularity of reading. Consequently, the reader lost his right to differ, the right not to understand. As a definitive 'meaning' was being built into the construction of the work, the reader was as a result denied participation (just as he was denied any meaningful participation in political life). Yet, 'meaning sticks to man'; it cannot be imposed on him, it can only be offered as an open option. There is a paradox at work. The man who stands in front of a painting and thinks that *he* does not understand it is asking, 'What is the meaning of *this*?' The one who faces a painting whose meaning is exhausted by an outside prescription – be it the dictate of ideology or the reductive authority of interpretation – may well be asking, 'What is the meaning of *art*?' This question is the same one that avant gardes have consistently been asking themselves.

In such circumstances art in society was reduced to a historical convention. Its sole purpose (in theory) was to help the political organisers to shape the new socialist man. But, the contradictory requirements of social and cultural experimentation and that of an unquestioning adherence to a dogma made any artistic contribution virtually impossible. The Czech art critic Jindřich Chalupecký observed that because the doctrine of Socialist Realism arrived in Czechoslovakia after 1948, when it had already degenerated into academism, and because it disrupted artistic developments linked closely with contemporary tendencies found elsewhere in Europe and re-emerging after the Second World War, a more liberal tendency soon evolved among the new establishment, permitting the freer approaches inherited from the aesthetic of expressionism. Such a moderated doctrine, however, was no less outmoded: the academic art of the 1880s, on which the work of Soviet painters and sculptors was based, gave way to the academic standards of the 1920s as a model for their Czechoslovak counterparts. Chalupecký comments on the inevitable feeling of loss of contact and continuity with 'living art' among younger artists, and quotes one of Kolar's generation: 'Perhaps [the recognition of this] gradually led to the awareness that you have to begin with what is. In other words, you have to start with practically nothing.'[7]

The new history of art in Czechoslovakia started with 'nothing', or 'practically nothing'; the new art was born almost as if from within itself – or better, from trying to *define itself anew*. In practice, of course, the continuity had never been lost completely. The artists of the 1950s were not unaware of the previous developments or uninformed about the accomplishments of their contemporaries elsewhere, but there was a delay and a disruption caused by the 'silence of the Muses' during the war, followed almost immediately by the strict controls imposed on all aspects of social life by the postwar regime. By the time the artists could again see their work in the framework of the culture of art, as opposed to a culture of 'social commission', their work had already begun to develop independently. Concurrently with the official culture promoting art as *artisanal* production of articles of use, there began to evolve an 'avant garde by accident', whose search for 'originality' was defined negatively, by exclusion.[8]

For Kolář's generation, to 'begin with what is' meant to begin with a *distance*. The avant gardes of the first half of the century were still able to provide an important reference point, but it was too far removed to be really trusted. The distance itself had to be taken into consideration. Kolář, who by the 1930s was closely acquainted with the work of Marinetti, Schwitters and TS Eliot, and who was for a time influenced by the work of Max Ernst and the Surrealists, already began to realise this unbridgeable distance during the early 1940s – the distance that he perceived between the historical paradigms of his art and the reality of his world. It was the same distance that separates the language of art from lived experience, or indeed language from poetry. (And it is this distance that is so powerfully expressed in Theodor Adorno's dictum, which Kolár often acknowledged, that after Auschwitz, lyrical poetry should not be attempted.) To Kolář, poetry cannot be found in language, it is not a property of language. Language resides in man, poetry comes from outside. 'The artist is the one who arrests the spectacle in which most men take part without really seeing it and who makes it visible to the most human among them.'[9] Yet, without a language, poetry cannot be expressed.

In his desire to 'express poetry' rather than necessarily to 'make art', to make 'perhaps something, perhaps nothing, almost like art', as Mallarmé said, but in any case to search, to collect, to witness, rather than to 'create', Kolář was by no means alone. There were a number of other artists who in their own way recognised the 'impossibility of creation'. The most notable example among Czech artists of the 1950s and '60s was probably Vladimír Boudník who, like Kolar, turned to the 'poetry of the city', to its fabric, not simply to find inspiration, nor even material, but for the questions that it posed to art. (And, just as many of his fellow poets initially labelled Kolar a 'primitive', Boudník was seen as a 'gentle barbarian'.)[10] Nor was Kolář isolated in his quest to find a vocabulary with which to express poetry in the visual languages of images rather than that of verbal poetry. A tradition of poetry that works close to the visual stretches back to the 1930s and there were, and are, Czechoslovak artists like Ladislav Novák and Rudolf Fila who scrutinise found imagery just as relentlessly.[11]

Kolář's transition from written language was gradual, the result of a process of almost manic experimentation lasting a decade. By the early 1950s, he was aware that a new *vocabulary* could not be found within the coherence of written language. His initial and fascinating experiments with 'rapportages' and 'confrontages', in which he juxtaposed images culled from magazines and art history books, were superseded by a more urgent search for possibilities. Incomprehensible fragments of texts in foreign languages and scripts, individual letters of the alphabet, musical notes, Braille characters, hieroglyphic doodles, knots, pebbles, razorblades, became the potential elements of this vocabulary of an 'unknown culture'. At first these were to substitute the elements of writing, but soon they enabled Kolář to break away from the conventions of text altogether.

'Breaking away from language', however, does not necessarily entail leaving language behind. In Kolář's case it meant breaking away from language's descriptive and interpretative faculties. Many of the formal attributes of language have remained constantly present in his work, some have even become a hallmark, not least the sequential nature of language, which is simultaneously acknowledged and challenged in his 'evident poems' and his 'rollages' and 'prollages'. (And it is worth noting that in those works where complete sections of literal text are used, as in *Diary* from 1968, for example, these are always conventionally positioned the right way up.) Kolář's attempt was to find a position *within* from which to question language and its functions.

Kolář's questioning (oscillating, in classical interrogatory mode, from the benign to the brutal) could not stop with the literary text. It extended to the whole itinerary of historical/philosophical concepts embedded in the history of art, and indeed the broad history of visual expression. From the early 1960s, images from art history, already deployed in the earliest collages, especially from 1952, became recurrent. As with the verbal language of poetry, this material has been subjected to the inquisitive treatment of de-structuring, its place in the real and everyday world has been confirmed. To avoid confusion, a comparison is perhaps necessary. For Kolář, his material is what he 'comes across'. It is found, salvaged perhaps, but not appropriated. This found material is not *used* in the sense that found imagery is used in the services of a postmodernist critique. Unlike those strategies, Kolář's interventions are not concerned with concepts of authorship, ownership or cultural and political status. His is not the culture of quotations in which everything can be unsaid and undone. He does not attempt to align his inquiry to the current state of 'culture', which, through most of its production, seems to be aiming at its own demise. There is no piracy and no purposeful violation of copyright in Kolář's work. And, above all, there is a respect for human achievement. His attitude to images is of a different order. He takes his source material neither with resistance nor with passivity. He is a witness as well as interrogator, consumer as well as producer, and he is 'not indifferent to anything'. Kolář's response to the modern world is in this sense affirmative rather than confrontational.

The material is a point of access open to anyone. He chooses these readymade elements for their potential for immediacy, which derives from their availability. They are images of an unspecific context, cultural orphans, 'mere' reproductions; they do not command, they silently expect. There is a built-in instantaneity at play in Kolár's work: the better known the image, the more familiar, the less it is weighed with particular connotations and the quicker the response. Such instantaneity is both particular to and a product of the functioning of the modern world. This seems important to Kolář as he does not seek a dialogue with the viewer but rather their participation. His questioning is a way of pointing out new possibilities. He did not want to liberate himself from the tyranny of language for the sake of being free. He turned to images not as an alternative but as the only adequate option. He wants to be free to unearth the unexpected and he wants to be free to find it anywhere.

But did not Kolář himself say that 'great works of art withstand even mutilation?' And does that not mean that even dismantled and reordered they still formulate *particular* propositions? Does he not do just that through the 'grammar' and the 'vocabulary' of his methods? Are his attempts not rather like that of Tristram Shandy's father trying to understand Erasmus: 'he had got out his penknife, and was trying experiments upon the sentence, to see if he could not scratch some better sense into it'?

Kolář does not see the language of art, both that which he speaks and that which he constantly refers to, as something composed of elements of content. He believes that the meaning of art is with us, as is the place we reserve for poetry in our lives. It lies in our ability to see, to recognise and to remember; our will to question the validity of separations and to negotiate distances; our right to resist the fragmentation of culture and of experience. Kolář has revolted against tradition, against its rule, against the ends to which it is being used, but he has not forgotten history. In rejecting tradition, Kolář rejects the passivity of consumption. The language of art has long become a fluid state. It is a space that he is trying to open up even further through his cutting, scratching, tearing, crumpling… and, at the same time and by the same means, to invest it with a human dimension, a human destiny.

1. Paul Valéry, *Reflections on the World Today*, Pantheon Books, New York, 1948, p.22.
2. The framework of history aligned to the conventions of the decimal system – divided into decades, centuries, millennia – is not used here to add to the current and already excessive 'fin-de-siècleism' but rather to submit to a general art-historical fashion. It seems quite pertinent both in relation to Kolář's attitudes to the history of art and to his 'diaristic' working methods.
3. Jiří Kolář in a letter to Charlotta Kotík, 25 January 1978, in *Jiří Kolář: Transformations*, Albright-Knox Art Gallery, Buffalo, 1978, p.11.
4. Rosalind Krauss, 'The Originality of the Avant-Garde', *October*, no.18, 1981, pp.47–66.
5. Roland Barthes, *The Pleasure of the Text*, Hill and Wang, New York, 1975, p.40.
6. Kolář himself sees the transition ten years ago from one political system to another, from Prague to Paris, in terms of a change in personal rather than 'cultural' circumstances. He feels free from the restraints of a citizen under a dictatorial rule, not from the commitments of an artist.
7. Jindřich Chalupecký, 'The Lessons of Prague', *Cross Currents*, no.4, 1985, pp.323–34.
8. This is perhaps why some of Czechoslovak art of the 1950s and '60s displays such a strange mixture of influences often incorporated into a single work – from essentially romantic variations of Surrealism to the experimental commitment of Lettrism – and it is also why it often seems to anticipate 'strategies' employed by artists in the West only many years later.
9. Maurice Merleau-Ponty, 'Cezanne's Doubt', *Sense and Nonsense*, Northwestern University Press, Evanston, 1966, p.18.
10. Jindřich Chalupecký, 'The Path of Jiří Kolář', in *Na hranicích umění* (On the borders of art), Karel Jadrný Verlag, Munich, 1987. The term 'gentle barbarian' comes from a novel by Bohumil Hrabal inspired by Boudník's life.
11. The sounds and stuff of the city, the vernacular images and expressions seen and heard in the street had, of course, posed the same fundamental questions and provided a similar range of primary material for several of those artists who had transformed Kolář's perception of possibilities in the 1930s – Filippo Tommaso Marinetti, Kurt Schwitters and TS Eliot. This fascination with the street had subsequently developed, most intensively under the gaze of the Surrealists, into an almost canonical preoccupation. A wealth of resources, particularly amongst the signs of decay and destruction, were exhaustively mined, most notably in photography. It was unsurprising that this vein, exemplified by Brassaï, Cartier-Bresson and the photographic reproductions in André Breton's *Nadja* (1928), should have reached Czechoslovakia given Breton's prolonged sojourn in Prague, and there is a direct link with Kolář through the photographs made by Miroslav Hák in Prague in the 1940s, about which Kolář was to write in 1959.

Pavel Büchler and James Lingwood in *Jirí Kolár: The End of Words, Selected Works 1947–1970* (exhibition catalogue), Institute of Contemporary Arts, London, 1991, pp.7–15.

PASSING BY AND BEING THERE

ELISABETH BALLET

It was the twilight end of a winter day. A couple of nights before, a TV news crew had made it into a remote Highland village to film the arrival of a snow plough followed by an ambulance, the A66 over the Pennines was closed, and the 0800 train from Euston arrived at Glasgow at midnight. Even – and quite against the rationale of its subterranean scheme – the underground had been shut down for two days, as if 'snow cover' was just an euphemism for an imperceptible penetration of frost deep under the earth's surface, like corrosive salts. But on that evening, the memory of snow was kept alive only by the conspicuous dry rectangles on the edge of the road where cars had been parked during the day.

In the gallery (a converted tramshed which still shelters the city's last stretch of tramway rails), eight tonnes of food-grade salt had been carefully dispersed in an inch-deep layer on the floor, leaving only a strip of bare concrete by the walls. The fine white crystals formed a vastly enlarged reversed image of the evidence of recent weather changes on the road outside, frozen in a shimmering stillness and undetermined history by the bright artificial light, inert and pristine – as if this 'snow' had fallen before the building was erected and as if nothing else had happened yet.

I arrived early. Like the Land Surveyor in the opening chapter of *The Castle*, 'I did not want to miss the chance of a walk through the snow'. Like him – 'a stranger here', facing this image of a 'brilliant winter morning' – I was reminded of my (and K.'s) native town, Prague, which I 'had not seen for such a long time' and where church towers soar above snow-covered roofs 'with a loftier goal and a clearer meaning than the muddle of everyday life'. But also like in Kafka's novel, there seemed to be no certainty in familiar appearances, other than the familiarity of strangeness, and no indication of any exterior dimension, except that which is assumed from the logic of incomprehension and always only waits to be recognised.

How relevant are such first impressions for an understanding of Elisabeth Ballet's work? Why should my private nostalgic reverie – incited less by the work itself than by the fragile meteorological coincidence – open up any viable possibilities for a reflection on (let alone interpretation of) the ostensibly public intentions of the artist? How can I justify, writing seven months later (at the end of another summer), the fact that it still dominates my recollections of the exhibition? After all, the salt-covered floor was a tactical device for the presentation of a number of autonomous pieces of sculpture rather than a self-contained 'work'. Its main purpose was the conversion of space into a field of activity.

The potential of space is every sculptor's concern. But for Ballet it is the abstract capacity of space, rather than its measurable dimensionality, that defines and is defined by her sculpture. The simple geometry of her constructions regulates not just the perception of space but also its denomination. Volumes of sculptural space are marked out as enclosures within a volume of spectacular activity, which, in turn, is generated by the presence of the visual and physical demarcation. Despite its formal precision, the demarcation of space is proposed as a matter of provisional qualitative distinction. The sculptural space is confined and structured by the surfaces and edges, sides and faces, of the individual pieces of sculpture, but it remains open in the sense of being negotiable as an aspect of the social space where things happen. The human scale of the works provides the basic ratio of imaginary interchange. Moving around or between and among the sculptures becomes an act of integration and reclamation. With every step we claim the space that the sculptures 'occupy' as the one that we 'inhabit', and from every vantage point we 'take over' the space that they 'take up'.

In a few hours, the gallery floor became a maze of footprints. Over the next weeks and months, it turned into a cryptic register of transient activity like the pages of a visitors' book. The cumulative traces of passing by and being there contrasted with the still undisturbed areas of salt within the sculptural enclosures. In this configuration of design and accident (on this building site of meaning), space was being remodelled in and by time, invested with the temporalities of 'then' and 'now' within a history of looking.

As it operates in a perceptual time zone of simultaneity – of a past and present that permits no outside position – Ballet's art resents symbolic interpretation. There are no models and no chance of disclosure. Nothing is concealed in what her sculptures look like – large honey-coloured perspex 'vitrine', modular 'doorway' hanging above at a right angle to the floor, metal 'railing' painted industrial grey, elevated circular 'walkway' made of a steel frame and floorboards, circumscribing a small rink of cold light – and nothing is suggested beyond formal facts. But in any act of 'reading' the dialectic of resemblance seeks to reassert distance and retrospection (and, at any rate, the invitation to the contemplating mind to participate in the material presence of the work also includes the license to conjure up images of the world outside). Even where all is confined within the space of the work and the time of looking, and where observation is part of bringing the work into being, nothing can stop memory from playing the role of a passing stranger. Salt becomes snow not by visual analogy but by an imaginary spatial and temporal shift of perspective. This also makes it possible for us to recover, in our experience of the work's here and now, a sense of that which we 'had not seen for such a long time' and which, in those rare moments when the wandering metaphor stumbles upon the determination of precise form, can be suddenly glanced, as if for the first time, right under our feet.

(Since then, I saw Elisabeth Ballet's gunpowder magazine in Berwick – an island of mid-eighteenth-century English military architectural design surrounded by a raised plywood floor painted the chroma-key blue of the Mediterranean sky contained by the perimeter walls; an image resonating with fantasies of flying castles and dreams of southbound voyages, and quite Shandean in its eccentric ingenuity and 'bowling green' setting.)

Sugar Hiccup: Elisabeth Ballet, Sam Samore, Richard Wright (exhibition catalogue), Tramway, Glasgow, 1997, np.

HERE'S HOW IT WORKS ...

CHARLES SANDISON

Language is a labyrinth of paths.
– Wittgenstein, *Philosophical Investigations*, 1953

Here's how it works. 'Staring at a blank sheet of paper is the hard part.' According to a paper manufacturer's advertisement in a recent issue of an art magazine, 'once you start, it is easy and rewarding'. My rewards, according to the terms suggested by the French publisher of this catalogue, will amount to €75 for every thousand characters which, at a guess, will translate into something like £500 by the time the 10,000 allotted characters have been variously grouped together to form, give or take, 1,700 words. If my quick calculation is anywhere near the mark, this looks like easy money – except that, by a contractual implication, the publisher will only honour his side of the bargain if the words thus formed can be identified, perhaps with some exceptions, as those belonging to the vocabulary of the English language and arrive at the publisher's desk in an order that conforms to the conventions of (English) syntax and grammar, so that the semantic relationships between them can be explored by the reader to some sort of intellectual benefit. Furthermore, the arrangement of said characters into said words and the sequencing of the latter into said intelligible text should adhere to the logic of discourse and so be definitive and final. Fair enough, you might think, for, after all, this text will be translated from one language into another – and translation, a modal shift without a loss of meaning, is really the art of understanding and maintaining the conditions of the definitive text. (Although strictly speaking, it consists of reorganising the same set of characters within a different set of rules – and *voilá...*)

At any rate, the quantitative basis for the proposed economic exchange – letters for euros, words for pounds, so many syllables and no more – is here to give me just enough incentive and impose a limit on what I may do. The contract is, in fact, nothing but an expiry note attached to the temporary licence to use the word processor keyboard, a reminder that I will have to stop somewhere. There is a good reason for this: life is too short. In the extreme, way beyond the human capacity to provide an experimental proof, all the possible permutations of the permitted number of characters (keystrokes), albeit finite and constrained by the rules of language, would eventually produce every word and every sentence ever written plus all those yet to be written and those that will never or can no longer be written (for there also are such) as well as an unimaginable amount of random nonsense besides. Every secret ever kept would be revealed. All that is, and will remain, beyond discovery would be put in writing, every name of every person living, dead and unborn would be listed – and all this in every language and writing system that uses the given set of letters (the Latin alphabet for instance), including languages and systems of writing long forgotten and not yet developed.

Or in other words, the alphabet is a field of endless possibility. Disarranged on the keyboard in front of me and accompanied by the space bar, it already contains the code of the entire word-generating apparatus of language. All that needs to be done to produce a word (to bring a word, which already lies dormant at my fingertips, into the open) is to calculate a combination of symbols. Words themselves accumulate and fill page after page through the same process (hence word processing – the procedure for developing words much like the processing of the latent image on the photographic film). Machines can do it – and indeed frequently do – for next to no cost. It goes without saying that the publisher would not really want to purchase just any old words that I might care to process out of the characters at my disposal, but only 'good' ones (what I am being paid for is not a word count but selection), those that best express what I intend to say or what you might like to read. This is not a matter of precise typology or classification (as in what the dictionary calls 'derog.', for example). If a sentence is 'well written', if it 'reads well', it is not because the words are accurate, let alone 'correct', but because they perform well, they are good at their job. They have to be chosen for their ability to do the 'right thing' in the right place at the right time. They have to be 'good' in an almost ethical sense: they have to know what to do. How do I find them? Words have to be put to test by writing. Writing is a way of giving words things to do.

Imagine a complete language with a readymade vocabulary of less than ten words (mother, father, female, male, child, old, dead, food, virus) governed by a combinatory scheme of merely seven syntactic formulae – the kind of language that a machine might use.

Here's how it works.

> male + female = child; male becomes father, female becomes mother;
> male + male = 50% chance of either becoming dead;
> female + mother = move out of each other's path;
> female + father = move out of each other's path;

mother + child = move closer together;
father + mother = move in relation to each other but not always closely;
virus + male, female, father, mother, child, old = dead.

The words come from the English dictionary but, for the moment at least, they have left most of their lexical baggage behind. In this pared-down language, there are no synonyms, no nuances and no connotations or multiple meanings. It is a closed list with no further use for the alphabet. Female, male, old and dead are nouns. No adjectives, no verbs. Food and virus do their best to compensate for the absent categories but they can only do so much. Even a master of haiku would have a hard time here and all intentional thought would soon give up in frustration. Compared to this, the compressed language of teenage text messaging with its monosyllabic shorthand of abbreviations seems like a gold mine of expressive potential.

The verbal poverty and the roughness of the rudimentary rules are not the only difficulties. The very functional identity of the system is uncertain. The language has no spoken form. There is no voice, no diction, no intonation, only a silent passage from one word to another. The term 'writing' does not capture the concept very well either. Writing forms texts; what can be 'written' in this language is not a text but texture alone. The difference is, above all, one of directionality. In a text, expression and understanding follow the semantic 'thread' in two directions: horizontally along the logical progression of the sentence and vertically across levels of meaning (we can only speak of writing when we can also speak of reading between the lines). The horizontal tendency of the text and its vertical axis are trajectories of motion: the text flows, runs, stumbles, it has a rhythm and a pace. Texture is the quality of the movement of the text. Here, patterns of movement are legislated for as predictive operations ('move out of each other's path'; 'move closer together'; 'move in relation to each other' – like commands for a linguistic exercise yard). Direction is arbitrary where disposition is the only principle. The movements here, always tangential, produce textures without the support of texts. This, then, is not writing but dispersion: display.

Words stand for things (or so it is said), but these words seem to stand (stand up) for themselves. The vocabulary is like a dramatis personae, a cast of 'characters' – the words 'act' rather than signify, destiny is their mode. Female breeds, male competes for female, mother guides child, father defends a social unit, child eats and grows. Dead is a case in point. It does not even seem to belong to the 'vocabulary'. Rather, an odd thing for a word to do, it takes on the walk-on role of the smallest character of the writing system: the full stop, period. Children become males or females, grow old and die. Females find male partners, produce children, become mothers, grow old and die. Males fight among themselves for females, those who lose die, those who win become fathers, grow old and die. Being unto death is the single grammatical rule.

Food and virus is the nearest this language gets to verbs. Food is a passive recipient of action (it is eaten); virus is an active agent of mutation (it makes words go mad). That's about all.

And yet, there is so much more.

White luminous words progress along the four walls, floor and ceiling of a darkened room. Some are restless, moving faster than others, some proceed in a jittery kind of way or run maniacally in all directions, falling and rising, agile and tired, some converge in dynamic formations, some travel alone. A cluster of words climbs up along the edge of the doorway like a swarm of insects. Words flicker and vanish as other words descend upon them to feed like sparrows on crumbs of bread. Every collision between the moving words produces a response, adjustment, transformation. In every contact there is something that demands to be described as mutual awareness, even communication: rumours spread, memories of the dead remain among the living until they are whipped out by the passage of generations. This is language on the brink of coming alive; an organism, a culture, a world of words as conscious beings, trying to overcome their condition.

How can the words of a language, one that barely deserves to be recognised as such, aided by nothing but the on/off, yes/no of binary calculation, do something that, until now, only the languages of poetry or metaphysics could hope to do? It may seem simple: everything in the world is a manifestation of infinite possibility (some call it 'chaos', others speak of 'chance events'). The world itself is open to calculation but not to discourse. This is why the binary code and not dialectics can create worlds out of symbols ('words') which parallel the order of things in the living world of our perceptions. But this explanation is inadequate. And it is inadequate precisely because it is an explanation. It is just something for words to do.

Larys Frogier (ed), *Charles Sandison: Between Heaven and Earth*, La Criée centre d'art contemporain, Rennes, 2002, n.p.

In a text entitled 'Possible', published in 1991 in Thierry de Duve's edited collection *The Definitively Unfinished Marcel Duchamp*, Jean Suquet introduces *The Large Glass* as a 'blueprint for a machine'. To find out what this machine does, he suggests, 'the best we can do is to make it run'. But a sceptical objection immediately follows: 'How are we supposed to make it work since it appears inexorably stopped?'

The answer, for Suquet, lies in a green cardboard box, scattered among the 94 scraps of paper bearing the engineer's plans, drawings and notes, 'as if offered to the blowing winds', which accompany this thing like an instruction manual: 'the machine runs only on words'.

At the end of the text, having skilfully disassembled Duchamp's linguistic machine and put it back together, word by word, comma by comma, ready to go, Suquet quotes two propositions from one of the notes: 'le tableau est impuissant ... le langage peut' (the picture is impotent ... language can).

Not having any better tool at hand, I want to use this ignition key to the mysteries of one work like a crowbar to prise open the secrets of another project – that of the other enigmatic Marcel – Cinéma Broodthaers. Forcing the device into the gap between the subtitle of Broodthaers's film *La Pluie (Projet pour un texte)* (1969) and the word 'silence' stencilled on the walls in the *Section Cinéma* (1971–72) of his own museum of modern art, I want to offer to the blowing winds the following misquotation of the well-known phrase with which, in 1964, the 40-year-old poet announced to the world his intention to 'succeed in life' as a purveyor of images.

L'idée enfin d'inventer quelque chose d'impossible me traversa l'esprit et je me mis aussitôt au travail.

Tanya Leighton (ed), *Impossible Cinema*, Centro Cultural Montehermoso, Vitoria-Gasteiz, 2007, pp.22–23.

PAINTING 'SOMETHING'

What makes abstract painting difficult is that the painter is not painting an image of something and yet the painter is painting 'something' – a painting. The question of what this 'something' is puts to the test the painter's *a priori* assumption of what painting is. But the answer that the painter seeks from the painting is to show what painting can do.

What makes it possible to see what painting can do is the painter's skill in rephrasing the question of identity as one of performance – an effect of a painting that can be observed rather than an abstract concept that can be thought: a picture of painting at work.

What makes some paintings good and others indifferent is the painter's ability to release the 'something' from the constraints of the conceptual intentions of painting, so that the results are not predicted by the initial question. To achieve this, the painter proceeds as if there was nothing to paint. There is no picture, no representation, nothing to start with and nothing to go by apart from the material ingredients and conventional limitations of the painting yet to be made. It is no more than incidental to the efforts of the painter that in the process of painting these are transformed into textures, colours and shapes. They are not the painter's aim. They are, rather, challenges and obstacles presented to painting by the persistence of the picture and our demands for it.

What makes painting full of interest and possibility is the improbable picture it may produce in the face of such obstacles.

Unpublished, 2012.

A HALF-FINISHED PAINTING

'The right-hand side is finished,' says the painter pointing at a cluster of brush marks on what appears to be an otherwise empty canvas. 'I realised it when this happened.'

'Do you have any thoughts yet about the other half?' asks the gallerist.

'Some kind of object, maybe a curtain, but we will see what it does. It may change this half again.'

The 'other' half awaiting the 'object' is, at the time of the conversation, almost entirely white. Save for a small accent of red in the top left-hand corner, it has been covered with an uneven coat of white oil paint rather than left in its basic white-primed state, as if the ground had to be tested in anticipation or else invested with effort before it could be covered again, perhaps, by a painted curtain. Or it may be that the painterly incident which brought one half of the painting to a halt demanded the erasure of all (but that little bit of red) that had preceded it. In any case, more painting activity seems to have taken place here than on the completed portion of the canvas but so far without a conclusion.

The expectant half and the finished one are separated by a black vertical line through the centre of the canvas. Or perhaps, the line connects them: it could belong to either. It was clearly there when the white oil paint was applied and is possibly the residue of something made redundant by the unexpected success of the marks on the right. In fact, it seems that the whole of the left half (excepting, again, the dissonant red corner) may have been painted black before it recovered its former whiteness, making the line a negative image of this recovery. Is it finished? Is it not?

These are facile questions: nothing is finished in a painting finished by half. All the possibilities remain open. 'We will see what it does.' But when?

When is a painting finished?

In a contract with his dealer Ambroise Vollard, Picasso insisted on having the last word on the matter. His paintings were finished when he said so. But Picasso was the kind of impatiently prolific artist who wants to get rid of the painting so that he can continue to paint. Others prefer to think of paintings as if they were sentient beings equipped with feelings, intentions and desires. They follow the painting where *it* wants to go and they stop when *it* wants to stop. Yet others talk about an indefinable 'something', a 'this' or an 'it', and conceive of the act of painting as a process which prepares the conditions for 'this' or 'it' to occur. Their paintings are less finished than they are ready to surrender.

Picasso's mastery was in his power to stop painting, to interrupt himself when he saw fit. But his resolutely authorial stance may betray signs of anxiety beneath the show of confidence. He claimed to have been haunted by the ghost of Frenhofer, the 'greatest painter of his day' from Balzac's story 'The Unknown Masterpiece' (1831), who after ten years of work reveals to his perplexed admirers a painting which appears to be nothing but a 'dead wall of paint'. Only one detail in the corner of the canvas suggests an unfulfilled promise. Among the mess of lines and chaos of colour there is a single delicately rendered bare foot of a young model, the last remnant of a picture concealed by coats of paint. Frenhofer's masterpiece is a work of faith ruined by the quest for perfection. It is not a painting which failed to stop and went too far nor is it one whose formlessness is the failure of the creative process. Rather, it is *the* perfectly finished painting, so complete, definitive and resolved that the very idea of painting itself, 'the means by which the effect is produced, fades away'. Overcome by the painter's efforts, it has nothing left to show. And while the incomprehensible results of Frenhofer's art undoubtedly incite imagination, it is the artist alone who, unable to separate from the work, perceives the ecstasy of his highlights and shadows in the vague fog of paint.

Where Picasso assumed the sole responsibility, Sigmar Polke wanted none. His 1969 painting *Higher Powers Command: Paint the Upper Right Hand Corner Black!* is merely a dutiful execution of the directive. Besides poking fun, all at once, at the authenticity of Expressionism, the austerity of hard-edge abstraction and the anti-aesthetics of Conceptual art, the fact that this disarming disclaimer of authorship is the least painterly of all Polke's paintings (even the text of the instruction is painted as if it was mechanically retyped) makes a fair point: the painter's job is simply the application of paint. The painter makes paint marks, not paintings. The variations, shapes, colours and textures, highlights and shadows, introduced by the painter in the progression of the work, challenge the paint to declare its own authority. They are the painter's way of gradually distancing himself from the painting, stepping aside and finally breaking the bond between his work and the painting, so that we can see what painting does by itself.

Having been asked at the age of 63 how many paintings he had made in his life, Polke replied, 'One good one and the one I am just working on.' Though the anecdote may be apocryphal, the eloquent message is borne by every painter's experience: the painter never knows if the work is done. The most he can say is that a painting is what happens in the process of painting and what does not stop happening. It is a continuous event, not a definitive thing, a work in progress, not a solution. It is not what is left behind by the painter but the living potential of the neither finished nor unfinished work that counts – not what he has made but what is. (As for the single 'good one' in Polke's reckoning, he may well have meant the unambiguous black corner of 1969, the one that dismissed its author from the start while also being indisputably his own.)

Rafal Topolewski (exhibition leaflet), The International 3, Manchester, 2013.

And what? The conjunction left loose at the the end of the incomplete phrase could be an invitation to conjecture, I guess. And if so, then not just because of the hidden pun but also because the original meaning of 'conjecture' is the interpretation of signs and symbols. In any case, the promise that there is something unspoken to discover is leading me into a maze of symbolic associations and meanings where the elusive 'time' poses a constant challenge: the harder I try to grasp it, the more it refuses to stand still.

One of Evangelia Spiliopoulou's *Office Drawings* (2009–11) shows an outline vertical column or tall cylinder with a four-word annotation: 'EVERY NOW AND THEN'. The words run conventionally from left to right but are spaced wide apart

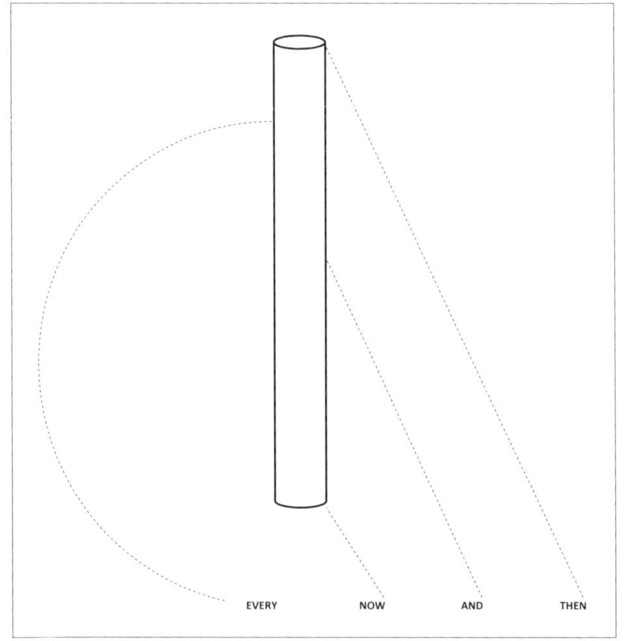

as if to loosen their semantic bond. Each word is connected by a dotted line to a part of the column. 'THEN', 'AND' and 'NOW' point to the top, middle and base while EVERY is linked by a curve to the body of the object. It connects to the column in its upper half, permitting me to read from top to bottom: 'THEN EVERY AND NOW'. The picture could be a graph for spent time: the amount of time available 'THEN' of which nothing is left 'NOW'. Borrowing terms coined by Marcel Proust in his novel *In Search of Lost Time*, I could read the 'EVERY' as the 'essence of the past' and the 'AND' could stand for a moment of 'involuntary memory'.

Proust's project was to represent recollection as a creative process in which the writing itself dissolves and recomposes time. It never lets me forget that time is 'lost' in the distorted mirror of language, a linguistic play with those remembered minutes that seem like an eternity or days and years that flash in the mind in a fraction of a second. This is the kind of imaginary dimensionless time that seems to flow according to its own subjective laws through Spiliopoulou's drawings – at least every now and then.

Then again, it could be that the phrase 'EVERY NOW AND THEN' simply denotes a mundane repetitive occurrence when every 'NOW' and every 'THEN' are the manifestations of time as I know it; not the time of poetic imagination, scientific concepts or metaphysical beliefs but the humble hours and minutes on the clock that separate one activity from another in the relentless but never the same flux of routine and minor variation – in short, the time of the unexceptional and the everyday. It could be, for instance, something as simple and direct as a reference to the time I find to make a drawing or write a few words, every now and then, among all those other things that occupy my days.

This is where my search for clues about Spiliopoulou's drawings turns from Marcel Proust to another master of the word play, Marcel Duchamp. His 1915 readymade, a snow shovel, carries an enigmatic reference to a future time inscribed along its lower rim, which doubles as its title: *In Advance of the Broken Arm*. For Duchamp, this annotation 'added verbal color' to the purity of the industrial form. The words suggest a potential accident or perhaps violence concealed in the design of the tool and in its use. In Spiliopoulou's *Office Drawings*, it seems that the logic of this addition is reversed. She begins with words as if they were readymade immaterial objects from the production line of language. Then she adds basic geometric shapes, patterns and tints to activate the random suggestiveness of the phrase. These graphic elements come from the limited 'vocabulary' of the Microsoft Word Office software, a tool originally designed for 'processing words' but used by the artist intuitively and somewhat subversively, almost against its intended practical function, like a snow shovel which could be used as a weapon.

Just as the snow shovel evokes manual labour aligned with the changes of seasons and the vagaries of weather so Spiliopoulou's drawings call to mind the Monday-to-Friday, nine-to-five pattern of office work. Their graphic economy and the instrumental efficiency of their execution gives a picture of organised time, measured by the hierarchy of recurrent tasks and punctuated every now and then by a coffee break. Yet their resemblance to technical drawings and diagrams is a tactical ploy in which the promise of information turns my sense of time into a play of perpetual delays and diversions.

The drawing that prompted my questions looks, give or take, like a schematic sketch for a thermohydrograph, an instrument that measures and records temperature and humidity over a period of time and charts the data on a revolving cylinder. There is one of these in every museum. But in Spiliopoulou's *Thermohydrograph* two of these identical devices stand side by side – not the real thing and a decoy, but rather both. There is no original and no duplicate. At once a time piece and a drawing machine, the thermohydrograph is a metaphor for our efforts to articulate and make sense of the observation of our surroundings. Doubled-up, as it is here, it perfectly unites the metaphorical and the functional in an endless exchange of cross-reference. It demands interpretation but resists explanation. It leaves me with a question.

Evangelia Spiliopoulou: Of Time And (exhibition leaflet), Bury Art Museum, Bury, 2013.

THE SHOW

'Art used to be beautiful, now it is merely interesting', says a hastily scribbled note in an old notebook. The quotation is attributed to Lefebvre but in a reckless reliance on memory I didn't care to record its provenance or even note M. Lefebvre's given name. More than a decade has since passed and with my memory being what it is I am at a loss. The sentiment holds true whoever made the remark but the news of the centenary of the death of Jules Joseph Lefebvre, the French painter of alluring female forms, accidentally encountered in an airline magazine, has thrown my certainty into confusion and makes me think again about what seemed so obvious.

It would have been in keeping with Jules Lefebvre's preoccupations and subject matter to mourn the displacement of an ideal by a 'mere' idea or to regard sensual pleasures rather more highly than intellectual ones. At the time, perhaps, of late Courbet and early Monet, it would have made sense for a salon painter to voice a longing for what art 'used to be'. Chances are high that with his commitment to the self-contained illusion of the picture, rendered 'from life' but only to compete with it, he would have been weary of 'interesting' art – an art which is 'merely' bound to betray the illusion.

Still, it is more likely that whatever it was that I was reading all those years ago had something to do with the Marxist philosopher and one-time associate of Situationist International, Henri Lefebvre, than with a painter mostly ignored by the critical wing of art history. After all, what is of interest to a Marxist, let alone what a Situationist finds beautiful, is surely not the same as what intrigues the voyeur. If this Lefebvre was indeed my source – and it is a big *if*, I know, but why not? – then what would be at stake would not be just the identity of art or the kind of attention it calls for but the liberating potential of aesthetics and its capacity as a mode of resistance to any resignation to the ways things are. A 'merely interesting' art would have been of no more use to the philosopher in his own contribution to this struggle than the old bourgeois ideal of beauty corrupted by the values of cultural and economic elites and denounced by the Situationsts as an ultimately nihilistic obstacle to cultural and social liberation. From the perspective on the philosophical left, the aesthetic deficit of 'merely interesting' art is the product of alienation, which prevents true aesthetic experience and which, under the existing social order, 'merely' cultivates indifference instead of unbiased contemplation. It is an art that incites curiosity and stimulates the pleasure of affirmation but only to entertain us by playing games with what we know and recognise; it attracts attention 'merely' by reproducing the distractions of the culture industry. If art is to do more than this, if it is to make us reconsider our assumptions about the world, then cognitive interest is not enough. It has to take us beyond the reach of rational analysis and engage us in a poetic exchange, which takes place not on the canvas but reconciles, dialectically, the dimensions of sensibility and thought in individual lives and social situations where works of art inform the expression, interpretation and transcendence of lived experience and the imagination of other possible ways of living.

Beauty has a history and a sociology. The banishment of beauty to the realm of nostalgia, its displacement by interest, parallels the shift in modern art from the autonomous object to context to the point where the context has become the key or sole factor to differentiate works of art functionally and conceptually from other objects. It is no longer the aesthetic appeal of the object but the conditions of our encounter with it that arouse our interest in the work of art and from which, in turn, the work of art derives its meaning and its aesthetic effect. The context is not universal but it is largely generic. We come across works of art not simply in the world but in particular kinds of places, some solely reserved for the purpose, some closer to the fabric of social life, but all in some ways adapted for the presentation of art. The presentation of art and its presence, its placing and its symbolic place in our world have now become synonymous.

Throughout history, artists have created works with particular social environments and physical locations in mind, to transform those sites by the presence of art, to invest them with artistic beauty and significance, sometimes in the hope of having their work seen but rarely with the explicit aim of exposition as an end in itself. The salons of Jules Lefebvre's days notwithstanding, the idea of a temporary art exhibition as the primary, not to say proper, destination of the work of art is a relatively recent innovation. The enormous rise in the production of works specifically for just such events in recent decades is an aspect and a manifestation of the ever-growing dominance of the provisional context of presentation as both the mediator between the subject and object and the medium of aesthetic exploration. No longer the preserve of the avant garde or post-studio institutional critique, the self-consciously exhibition-oriented practice has now become virtually the norm for all contemporary art. As temporary presentation becomes the focus of artistic practice, so the exhibition of the work, 'the show', becomes not only a location and agency but also the model of art and the essence of the aesthetic experience.

The show is the site of exchange where interest is produced, cultivated, socialised and organised. The organisation of the show is a comment on art and on the wider context of culture, economy, history and politics in which the show is taking place. It is a means of managing perception, disrupting or reinforcing perceptual habits. It presents us with a specific but conditional situation in which the world and art as its image are at once clearly separated and structurally interdependent. The physical setting of the show provides the spatial coordinates for the viewing of the works of art as well as the 'necessary' distance from the concerns of everyday life; its temporality and its place as a social event activates the collective aspects of our subjectivity as an art audience – and, by contrast, as spectators and participants in social reality – dividing those of us who have seen the show from those who haven't, and uniting us again in a communion of communication.

Ultimately, however, the show is a paradox. By placing the work it tests the work's capacity to resist its placing, the provisional context of its presentation – to resist, in other words, its reduction to the 'merely interesting'. In some sense, the work in the show is always displaced. It is then in the experience of its power to manifest this displacement that the beauty of the work of art can perhaps be recovered. It is also where the genuinely interesting is revealed.

Mallarmé, who believed in beauty as independent from the world in which his poems existed and who advised poetry to be made not 'with ideas, but words', quipped that 'everything can be summed up in aesthetics and political economy'. (Again, a chapter and verse citation is missing from my notes.) His 'everything' is the world: all that is, all that 'has a place'. It includes the little we add to nature as the 'inventions of our making' and the little we isolate from it as art. Art too can be 'summed up', talked about and understood in such terms. But the work of art is an act of negation. It is the 'object escaping' everything that 'has a place' – or at least it used to be for Mallarmé.

'The Show', Le Grand Balcon, Sylvie Fortin and Philippe Pirotte (eds), La Biennale de Montréal, Montreal, 2016.

WORDS MEAN NOTHING

INTERVIEW WITH PAVEL BÜCHLER

NICK THURSTON: *One of the things that artists of your generation inherited was a need to tackle the privileged status of both art objects and the mysticised work of making art. How and why artistic products and production were or are privileged was very different in 1970s Prague from 1980s Cambridge, let alone twenty-first-century Manchester. Could you start from the centre out, as it were, by talking about the kind of work you do, the kind of work you are interested in, and the kind of work that you think art to be interestingly capable of?*

PAVEL BÜCHLER: I usually describe what I do as making nothing happen. What I mean by that is that I try to make you notice those small and neglected things in the world that you would have otherwise passed by without noticing. These things, circumstances and situations are what tend to be dismissed as 'nothing' and our job as artists is to make that 'nothing' count. Metaphorically, you can imagine that job as the closing of the gap between the 'no' and the 'thing' – where there seemed to be no thing, there is now a perceptible nothing. This is not to say that art is made out of nothing; rather, that it is made out of what is in that gap between nonexistence and existence.

I am interested in what art can make of the world, what it makes possible to realise in both senses – 'to think' and 'to do' or to 'act upon'. Good art makes the world as you know it seem different; and at the same time, it makes you wonder how the work is what it is and how it does what it does. It does not rise above the world or step aside from it. Instead, it seems to be at once in and of the world and in a world of its own. It makes you realise that the world is not a given, but something that we make and that makes us. In some sense, art is the world upside down. The world the right way up is just reality.

Or to put it differently: the critical job of a work of art is to stand up to 'the ways things are' by putting its own identity to the test. The tension that the work creates between what it proposes about the world and what it suggests about itself encourages you to reconsider your habitual views. The work works when it takes something that you already know and understand, shows it to you in a manner that you perhaps recognise, yet still it manages to surprise you and provoke your curiosity. Ultimately, it tells you something about yourself while it also somehow slips from your grasp. It frustrates your questions and resists conclusions. Every time you look at it, you see something a little different and think something a little different.

You can find this enabling quality in old masters – I am a big fan of Vincenzo Bellini, Lucas Cranach the Elder, or the Flemish Primitives, for instance – as much as in modern and contemporary art. Regardless of its age, I am particularly attracted to art that achieves these effects by the most modest means. It is fascinating to see how little it takes to shift perceptions and turn something familiar, ordinary or banal into something wonderful or strange – to see how easily something obvious can become something unexpected. This is the kind of experience that I like and that I would like my work to give. But in order to discover what it takes to make the work work, I have to work. I have to work to give you something to work on in turn. Art is not for lazy people.

That said, I am not really interested in a 'kind of art' or a 'kind of work'. I am only interested in the individual artist and the individual work and the specific effort that has gone into a specific piece of work. I prefer the particular to the general; I am interested in singular facts more than in categories. One of the points that a good work of art proves is that there are no such things as a 'kind of art' or a 'kind of work'. When we are talking about the 'kind of work' I do or the 'kind of work' art is capable of, we are not talking about works of art. We are only talking about the conditions and circumstances of production and reception. Which is to say, we are talking about ourselves.

NT: *One of the influences or echoes that registers most strongly in* how *you work and* what *you work on is an Adornean Marxism. Central to that line of thought is something like a version of art-working that is* purposefully useless, *which would produce kinds of artworks without prefigured interpretations or applications. You addressed this explicitly in 2004 in conjunction with an exhibition that you co-curated at Rooseum, Malmö,* Whatever Happened to Social Democracy? *How do you think about your own making in those terms now?*

PB: In *The Heart of Darkness* (1899) Joseph Conrad says something like, 'I don't like working, nobody does, but I like the chance to find yourself that work gives you.' I suppose that when I was sixteen or seventeen I decided to try and become an artist because I could see no sense in any manner of useful work. I was very influenced by reading Johan Huizinga's ideas about play and by an obscure Czech Nietzchean philosopher, Ladislav Klíma, who claimed that all work was forced labour and inconsistent with voluntary and free activity. I read Robert Louis Stevenson's 'An Apology for Idlers' (1877) – 'It is surely beyond a doubt that people should be a good deal idle in youth' – and I was into the Situationists' *ne travaille jamais*. I became interested in the passive musings of Zen, filtered by the 'turn on, tune in, drop out' counterculture of the late 1960s, and I came across the playful provocations of Fluxus, which somehow rhymed for me with the home-brewed early twentieth-century tradition (or rather, mythology) of the artist as a work-shy bohemian and social outsider. It was a thoroughly incongruous mix of influences, but it made a lot more sense than the drudgery of labour celebrated under communist rule as heroism – 'The Mother of Progress', as the Party slogan went – a constrictive model of labour that was avoidable only at your greatest peril: 'Let him who does not work not eat'.

My doctor asked me recently how I became an artist. 'How did you become a urologist?', I asked in return. 'I have no imagination,' the doctor said, 'and that's what my neighbours were and that was what they did.' 'Similar with me,' I told him, 'I also have no imagination and I also saw my neighbours, but I knew that I didn't want to do what they did nor be what they were.' What I did not tell him was that the next-door neighbour and another one further down the street were both sculptors whose front yards were full of variously shaped pieces of stone, metal and terracotta. These objects were obviously not useful in any ordinary sense but the labour and skill that went into the shaping of those materials seemed to have a useful function in the process of coordinated production and the hierarchy of values that came with it. You knew that the work of these people had a function *not* because the things they made were self-evidently valuable but because their work was granted a level of public visibility – you sometimes heard their names on the radio and saw them on posters – which in those days could only be achieved if you had the right qualifications and the approval of the Artists' Union. This gave them a licence to work for themselves and to produce things that were a little different from other products. Nevertheless, the value of those things was predetermined by the *a priori* official endorsement of their maker's competency as an artist. These men were makers but it didn't seem to matter what they actually made – one worked in the academic tradition, the other was a committed modernist – or how their craft and ability was demonstrated in their output. What mattered was that they were officially sanctioned professionals and their labour had a recognised place, even if only as an exception, in the machinery of production. Professional artists produced useless objects that were ultimately ideologically and socially useful. So, becoming a professional artist like my neighbours would have defeated the object, as it were.

At that time, I did not yet understand that the promise of self-realisation through working is predicated upon understanding the social character of your work – what it makes you among other people, what it does in the world – not merely its purpose in the formation of your world view or in the construction of some inner world. I saw art as something private, my own, an excuse for not taking part in what 'society' then meant for me. As an activity, art made sense in itself or on its own terms, and I saw doing those things that are worth doing for their own sake almost as a type of anti-social behaviour. It only dawned on me very gradually that by insisting that our private activity be recognised as work, people like me were not only making a subversive demand for the freedom to act individually, but also recognising that making the private into a matter of public work was a necessary condition for maintaining some sense of integrity in a society like ours.

For me, the question was then, as it still is now, what kind of work is art? This is probably the defining question of art today. The making of artworks is certainly work, but is art something we make or is it something we do? And is it really possible to say what artists do? To my mind, if it is work, then it is work that needs doing only so that it may be recognised as work. It is a kind of work that fills a gap, a gap which the working itself constantly creates. In a culture where all identity is derived from work and where labour is rated as almost the highest value, the ambiguity that surrounds the notion of art as work is the source of its privileges and its limitations, of its freedom and its vanity.

NT: *I am interested in an idea you raise in 'New Academic Art' (2001) that making art (the work of making art) cannot be a method; that it is, instead, better understood as something like a* mode *of working. Mistaking its mode for a method creates a problem or misconception, one which we in art education and the art industries describe using the term 'practice', which is an uncomfortable holding concept, one that maybe misdescribes what an artist does. The modes of your professional working life are various. Could you talk a little about what they are, how you distinguish between them, and if or how they overlap?*

PB: Art is an activity. It has become fashionable to refer to the activity by this rather unhelpful term 'practice', perhaps to somehow limit the processes of that activity, to give it constraints and a sense of coherence or commitment at the time when almost any human activity can be presented as art. Claiming the creative work you do to be a practice is now what qualifies your activity as an artist's endeavour. We often hear about 'practising artists'. This rather desperate denomination sometimes gets used in descriptions of people who make artworks that have not yet achieved public exposure and critical endorsement. Even though the outcomes may be unmistakeably recognisable as, say, paintings, it seems clear that it is not the activity of painting that makes the 'practising artist' an artist or their painting a work of art. It seems that it is neither the activity itself nor the artist's self-identification of their work as a practice that matters, but rather the participation of their work in the discourse of art.

Professionally, in the colloquial sense of what I do for a living, I participate in that discourse as a producer of artworks, as a teacher and as an occasional writer or critic. These forms of participation differ in obvious ways and do not even necessarily overlap. But they are nevertheless connected and so add up to one identity or one practice, if you like. If, for convenience's sake, I call myself an artist, it is not because art-making is the dominant activity or the job I am the most committed to, but because it is the least contaminated by the 'professional' characteristics of my other two roles, and therefore it best tallies with how I think about what I do. Art is the subject that I teach and it is generally what I write about. The teaching and the writing are inevitably influenced by the thinking that goes into what I do in my studio. In some way the experience of teaching and writing also has a reciprocal bearing on the studio work, or at least it can sometimes get in the way. But in both the teaching and the writing there are principles for action, akin to a rudimentary method, which are founded upon interest. I teach out of interest, and it seems obvious to me that some deep-seated interest has to be at the heart of any viable pedagogy. In writing, my interest sustains my arguments, it helps me to give the piece a structure and a flow, it helps me not to get lost.

The artworks come about in a quite different way. There is no method, no strategy, no theory, no technique, and there are no firm disciplinary divisions between the bits of knowledge or know-how I put to work in the studio. There is not even a starting point; or if there is one, it almost always turns out to be false and getting lost is usually the best thing that can happen. I may set out to find something but it is only when I accidentally trip over something else that I realise what I should have been looking for all along. I really work like an incompetent electrician who connects tangled wires at random until a spark jumps somewhere… If it causes a short circuit, so much the better. The interest that sustains the work is something that I discover in the process of working, and it shifts and changes as any one piece takes shape. The only constant in all of this is my curiosity. Alongside boredom, curiosity put to work as a way of paying attention to what so often appears obvious seems to drive artists towards those chance discoveries that then really get the work going. Inspiration comes later. Inspiration is what makes you see what needs to be done. It is not the start but something you try to get to by putting one thing next to another. The rest is just whatever it takes to get rid of the things you make as a consequence.

If art is the product of the mind, then it is the product of a mind thinking differently to the mindset used by a teacher or critic. Art is the product of a mind thinking without syntax, aimlessly wandering.

OUR MODES OF MAKING

NT: *Your artworks have recurring traits: the conceptualist distillation of form and an economy of material means, or gestures of absenting and appropriation, for example. Could you say something about how your oeuvre coheres?*

PB: I am not sure that what I do or have done amounts to anything as grand as an oeuvre and I am not concerned with coherence. The recurring traits that you identify in my work may be nothing more than a reflection of my inability to focus on anything for very long. I get bored, my attention drifts and that makes me change my mind and notice new opportunities or suddenly see something which may have been staring me if the face for years. With me, one thing almost never leads directly to the next in a straight path. They are all diversions.

The only characteristics that my artworks seem to share is that they demonstrate that something always remains as-yet-unknown in those situations (objects, places, mental and emotional contexts, etc.) where everyone has looked or been before. This is perhaps where and how what you call 'distillation' and 'appropriation' and my preference for a technical economy all come together and amount to the same thing. I like to keep things light and simple, without any surplus or extra weight, not because less is more but because just enough is plenty. Elaboration is not the precondition of complexity just as boredom is not the same as ambivalence.

NT: *In a 2010 interview with Patrick Van Rossem you claim that artworks are semantic. Using semantic models to interpret art is a contested method, so could you sketch out what you mean by that claim, given our focus here on your writings?*

PB: Art is semantic in the sense that it is concerned with meaning and meaning is subject to interpretation. But that is not to say that all art in any form, shape or material should be apprehended as though it were a 'text' or that meaning is only ever what can be 'expressed'. The meaning of any work of art largely depends on, or largely is, what your experience of that work of art leaves you imagining or thinking – in the associations that it provokes you to make – rather than in what that work of art (or its maker) has to say or how the 'message' of that artwork is encoded and transmitted. When we talk about 'reading' works of art we are using a metaphor that implies a kind of studious, analytical engagement with the artwork, with which we mentally disassemble and recompose the work to understand perhaps not what it means but how it can be made to mean something. We want to uncover the code encoded in its material makeup. But another metaphor from the same stock would reflect the semantic condition of art just as appropriately: 'listening to'. It evokes a different kind of immersion in the work, a different kind of attention and a different kind of experience. It lets the work of art play a more active part and creates a different situation for engagement. In the different situations they prompt, 'reading' treats the artwork like a text and relates it to a context, whereas 'listening' isolates the artwork within an ambiance. The questions that listener-ly encounters pose to the interpreter are not 'what does the work mean relative to its context?' or 'how is it affected by the act of interpretation?' or 'how does it reflect upon itself?' and so on, but rather 'what does it mean to be with this work?'

Artists are not without blame when it comes to the methods of reception and interpretation of their works. The tendency to treat works of art as 'texts' is directly encouraged and legitimised by the paranoiac contemporary convention of artists' statements. The ostensible purpose of the statement is to make intelligible the artist's process and intent, but it often seems as if the statement makes the work speak like a ventriloquist's dummy, as if the work is determined by the words of the accompanying text. Pre-empting our fear of uncommunicativeness, which we equate with stupidity, such paratexts give the work the resources of speech by proxy. One particularly telling example of this is the frequently heard allusion to the 'intelligence' of the work, typified by claims that some or other work is 'investigating' a topic or 'interrogating' an issue. While it is certainly possible for an artist to work systematically on an idea in some sort of an inquisitive manner, art is not an instrument of cognition. It cannot be the aim of the 'artistic inquiry' to reach answers. Artistic intelligence should not seek solutions. It should cause problems. I have always wondered why anyone would think that a terminology best suited to the practices of the police or the holy inquisition would give the work of an artist any intellectual dignity. To say that the intelligence of art, its questioning nature, is founded on an intuition bordering on blind ignorance is probably a more honest way of putting it.

NT: *One of the characteristics of your artworks is a switching back and forth between analogue and digital media. Concerns with media and mediation seem to run through all of your writing and art-making. How has writing about those concerns allowed them to surface? And how have your opinions about media and mediation changed since the late 1980s?*

PB: I am very interested in the message of the medium, as it were. For me, this interest has developed as much from writing and reading – Marshall McLuhan, Vilém Flusser or Jean Baudrillard certainly have a lot to answer for in this respect – as it has arisen from everyday observations. This interest was probably latently present already in my earliest work, in my collages for instance, where the technique makes you aware that the image is in fact a physical thing. But it was not really until the late 1980s, via the close involvement I had with photography at the time, that the mediacy of particular technologies became a conscious concern of mine. The identity of photographs, as material traces of moments – the time embedded in the physical object and the simultaneity of the past and the present that it proposes – is something that has fascinated me ever since. I was, and still am, interested in what photographs are and in their ghost-like presence in the world. I am not interested in taking pictures. In the late 1980s I was making a lot of work through re-photographing tiny details of found newspaper images, enlarging them to a macroscopic scale, playing with ideas of retention and obliteration, identification and the loss of individuality, continuity and fragmentation, and I was also exploring the same topics in writing. My studio work soon moved on to other things (I told you that I have a short attention span) and the writing and art-making parted ways, but it was certainly an important phase. What has remained from then in the work I do now is a tendency to reuse industrially produced and machine-made materials and objects that have some sort of a token history inscribed in them by their prior use or function.

During recent years I have been preoccupied by a historical link between cryptography, the Morse code, letterpress printing and the frequency of letters in a language. The idea of letter frequency is sometimes attributed to two artists: Edgar Allan Poe, who used it in his 1843 short story 'The Gold

Bug' as an aid to decipher a cryptogram; and the English painter Samuel Morse, the inventor of Morse code, who around the same time needed to know the letter frequency in English-language messages to make the transmission of codes efficient. To understand how to assign, economically, the combinations of one to four dots and dashes to the letters of the alphabet, Morse sent an assistant to his local printer to count the stock of type they kept. He realised that the experience of the printer would give him a more reliable indication than if he had counted the letters in a text, as any given piece of writing will have a letter frequency that is subject to its writer's vocabulary and style.

The binary Morse code was one of the most important inventions in history. It was the first step on the way to our contemporary digital language technologies, and even today the calculation of the relative frequency of letters and symbols is of interest to computer science. Morse's invention holds its place right alongside Gutenberg's invention of movable type. Yet of all the language technologies, from the Sumerian cuneiform and clay tablets to computers, the moveable type upon which letterpress reproduction depends is the most limited one. Theoretically, it does not enable you to say everything that you might potentially like to say because the total stock of available letters is always finite. There are only so many 'A's and so many 'B's in the world at any one time, let alone in a particular printer's particular fount case. A million monkeys with a million typewriters might perhaps succeed eventually in producing all the works of Shakespeare, but they would not get very far with printing type.

In my own writing (which sometimes resembles the monkeys' strains), these ideas and any insights they might lead to are still waiting to enter. For the moment, they provide a fodder for the studio work and for my ways of thinking; for me for now, artwork is the way of working these things out. By which I mean, art is a place to think without consequence.

NT: *We have shared a transgenerational yet epochal change from pre-digital to born-digital technologies. Now, new technologies don't stay new for very long. Sometimes their obsolescence is planned, sometimes not. You have written on camera and print technologies at length in essays and short reviews, plus many of your artworks involve mechanically reproduced type or put the hardware of relay devices on show. How has living and working through this epochal change affected the production of your art and art generally, do you think?*

PB: What makes the change so dramatic is not just the almost immediate obsolescence of every new technology but above all the social, cultural and political disorientation and disruption that technological 'progress' creates and promotes. Already in the late 1950s, Hannah Arendt warned about the consequences of the technological contraction of space and duration for our understanding of humanity, and so also for our humanity. These consequences have since become a reality. The Frankfurt School thinkers before her envisaged the dissolution of the individual into the hegemonic regime of institutions, consumerism, mass communication and mass production. Their pessimistic vision has come true, too, to a degree even beyond their expectations. Information processing, communication technologies and knowledge industries have displaced material production as the core principles of social organisation. 'Social media' have now irrevocably transformed all social relations. The demise of the old analogue world and the advent of the new digital one has brought about a loss of any sense of coherence in what used to be called 'objective reality' on the one hand, and a vertiginous acceleration and proliferation of uncertainty and impermanence on the other. The old world was still to some extent solid and measurable, it had not completely 'melt[ed] into air', it had some outline, structure and scale; the new soft or liquid world seems to have no definite proportions.

It is difficult to generalise about how the production of art – once the domain of durability and imperishable values – has been affected by these still new, post-everything conditions. Recently, I have come across the term 'post-contemporary'. Idiotic as it is, it does explain something. Contemporary art in its original meaning signified a commitment to the actual political and social reality of its time. Later the term came to be used to distinguish current practices from historical modernism, to give those new practices some semblance of temporary relevance via their de facto- or quasi-periodisation as 'contemporary'. In our times, it seems, the relevance of art to its time and place is not an issue. But this is not the same as being timeless. Whatever the term 'post-contemporary' might mean, I suspect that it implies that there are no real challenges for art. Nothing is really at stake for 'post-contemporary' art. It is just something that is going on in the world among other goings on.

Everything can stand under the umbrella of art now: from resistance to resignation to complicity; from work that reflects the times we live in by its overblown scale or inflated production values and exorbitant prices, for example, to art that does exactly the same by its deliberate flimsiness and lack of substance; to art made by artists who have given up production altogether in favour of pure presentation. There is a genuinely critical vein of art, there is a cynical vein of art and there is a lot of patronising art. The one thing you can say, though, is that in much recent art opposition and complicity, divergence and indifference, are hard to tell apart.

My own technological backwardness, the use of outmoded processes, technical devices and materials, is partly expedient and partly critical. I like the control that comes with the limitations of analogue technology. It is simple, I understand how it works and I can modify or fix the machines if I need to. It can also be cheap. Besides, every artist's work is somehow biographical, always a self-portrait of sorts, and these things belong to the background of my life. The critical part is that those things have little, if any, practical use left in them. Therefore, they prompt you to consider the qualities and characteristics of practical life and our technological conditioning that you had ignored when you used these machines merely as functional objects. The slowness of the old technology, for instance, offers a measure and perspective for seeing differently the scale of our experiences in our high-tech society; their relatively unreliable mechanical operations mirror the human imperfections that are increasingly being eliminated from life by virtualisation; and so on. One of the keywords of relentless technological change, and the rapid obsolescence it drives, is 'power'. A more powerful processor, more powerful memory chip and more powerful software put more power at your disposal – if only, perhaps, the power to hold on to all your holiday snaps indiscriminately and still have plenty of gigabytes to spare on a storage device the size of your fingernail. Yet these excessively powerful tools leave less and less for you to do. The old technology is now powerless. There is something potentially powerful in that image.

TECHNICS

NT: *Technical and biographical matters get entwined here because you started your artistic life as a student of print and typography in communist Prague, right?*

PB: Right. Though the beginning of my 'artistic life', as you put it, was a reaction to rather than the consequence of my training and studies. Typography is a humble art and you always serve multiple masters: the client, the text itself, the needs of the printing process, the requirements of legibility, sometimes fashion and so on. At its most basic, typography is simply a reorganisation of existing material in such a way that it conforms to the constraints of the printing technology. All this suited me well, not least because I believe that what designers call 'problems' are always opportunities and I believe that the acceptance of all those constraints can be as, or more, productive than a creative *carte blanche*. But it gave me little freedom to improvise.

I have always envied musicians for whom improvisation is a matter of course. This may be why many of my early artistic exploits had the form of improvised and mainly collaborative 'actions', where the process may have been loosely predetermined in advance but the results depended on chance and random human interaction. There was nothing in my training that equipped me for that kind of experimentation, but that was liberating in itself. So, the true beginning of my artistic life started with an effort to forget my profession and be an amateur – one who loves the work he does, from the Latin, *amator*, a lover – and I hope that something of that amateur sentiment is still in my work today.

NT: *But to rewind for a moment: you have described to me before the very rigid atelier model of your artistic education. Could you do so again, for the record?*

PB: In 1970s Central Europe, the common denominators in all art education were observational drawing and art history. Courses in the theory of colours, principles of composition and anatomy were also common to all the visual and plastic arts disciplines. The pedagogic model had not changed much since the nineteenth century except for supplementing art history with the history of the working-class movement and something called 'scientific communism', which you can imagine as a version of catechism adapted for the purpose of saving our immortal souls as much as our vulnerable arses (lest we say something stupid). While the culture of individual ateliers differed, the pedagogy was fairly uniform. The studio teaching was strong on practical know-how and specialist skills. It was based on step-by-step assignments and the progress of the students' work was measured against standards determined by the interests of the professor. For example, my professor benchmarked Hans Holbein and Bridget Riley with not much in between. What we now call a 'crit' was then called 'corrections' and the period of preparation of the year's final work was called 'clausura' ['confinement'], which I think speaks for itself.

Students were students, not artists. Their work was an exercise conducted under expert supervision; it was not art. There were various competitions organised for us and the annual exhibitions of the year's final work were opened to the public. But as a rule, we were actively discouraged from trying to do anything on our own. It was as if the society that gave us the privilege to study should not be inconvenienced by any art that came out of the hands and minds of people not yet fully trained.

Yes, the model was rigid but it was also rigorous and no worse than the technocratic system of uniform values and generic academic conventions imposed on all students in today's university-based art education. In the end, my training gave me a lot to unlearn and that is always a good thing.

NT: *Your experience in the atelier and afterwards as a 'professional of the state' must have set up a strange contrast to what you found in Cambridge, England, in 1981? There must have been countless shocks of contrast between there and here, but could you reflect on those that pertain to the different status and cultural presence of art? What were the principle differences between Czechoslovakia and England in the discourses that surrounded how new art was being made, presented and represented?*

PB: The shocks were indeed not worth counting but my first impressions of art in the West can be summed up in a single phrase: too much. My first stop *en route* to England was Paris where, in the Centre Pompidou, Panamarenko's airship, *Aeromodeller* (1969–71), was dwarfed by the scale of the architecture. Soon after, I saw *A New Spirit in Painting* (1981) at the Royal Academy in London. These two experiences, which stunned me in close succession, left me numb. I knew, or thought that I had known, many of the works that I saw in Paris and London but I could not recognise them. Everything was much bigger, brighter, more colourful and visually more aggressive than what I had seen in magazines and catalogues. And there were acres of it. I just could not digest it.

Back in Czechoslovakia, all the interesting work was being produced discretely if not clandestinely by a small number of artists in the background of official production. The artists were often no longer young, they had lived through Stalinism, the hopes of 1968 and the disappointments of its aftermath. There was a genuine conviction in their need to keep art going so as to resist the degradation of all cultural values under the official regime of 'normalisation'. The art had a modest scale, modest aspirations and minimal visibility. Much of it openly acknowledged its debt to developments in the West and by the early 1980s some of the artists had first-hand experience of Western European and North American art. I had not and I had kept an open mind about what to expect, but I was unprepared for what seemed to me the sheer vanity of it all. This was the free West, I thought, but free for what?

The second thing that took some getting used to and gradually displaced 'the shock of the new' was the encounter with art criticism and critical argument. In Czechoslovakia, criticism was a 'historical' phenomenon, familiar from the interwar battles amongst the various factions of the avant garde, but almost entirely absent from the discussion of current art. All writing on current art was reduced to description and to an art-historical or journalistic account of the work's precedents in the orthodox genesis of modern art, regimented into trends, schools and -isms; or of its semblance or otherwise to the work of the artist's peers. It was never polemical and it never expressed a judgement. This was, unsurprisingly, the case with writing published on officially approved art in the official media. The critic would simply dispense with all critical responsibility by using a superlative or two in the description of the artist's brushwork or by drawing the reader's attention to the 'humanity' of the artist's subject, but would safely assume that the very fact that the work was appearing in public testified to its qualities and merits. Evaluation was the job for the authorities; the critic's job was to renounce criticism.

Less obviously, you would find pretty much the same avoidance of argument in the writing that used to appear below the horizon of official literature – the material distributed via samizdat networks or in small semi-official publications. This was because to criticise means to take a position and the available positions were hopelessly polarised, making it impossible to escape a conflict of interest. It would have been difficult for a critic to express any reservations about a work in the unofficial context for that could be misused in the official context as a self-admission of the work's inferiority and a justification for its exclusion from public view. But an unreserved approbation of a work, no matter how accomplished, would have inevitably been seen as partisan and equally open to misuse.

My 'discovery' of art criticism as the means by which, however questionably, the experience of 'good' art can be separated from the indifference of the rest, may have helped me to overcome the initial shock of over-production and recover my own taste for making artworks. It also turned me towards writing. It may be that there is indeed far too much art jostling for critical attention, and there is certainly no shortage of opinion, but the dynamics of critical debate need a constant supply of both. Without it, the discourse of art will become a canon – as it did in old communist Czechoslovakia.

MATERIAL HISTORIES

NT: *One of the ideas that seems to surface because of your bewilderment, and which becomes a stance common in all of your critical writing from the early 1990s is a commitment to a particular idea of modernism. It is the idea, strongly influenced by Theodor Adorno, of working against useful production. We have touched upon the reusing of extant material but I wonder if you could say something about how and why you seem determined to squeeze more meaning out of already 'used' things in your art and writing?*

PB: Because they are never used up if you can imagine their relation to the world differently. The Western 'exchange society', in Adorno's vocabulary, is organised around the satisfaction of human wants in the process of production for the sake of exchange. The engine driving this process is an ever-growing economy fuelled by technological innovation and by ever-growing scales of consumption. Innovation is the production of desires, consumption is the production of waste. The useful life of everything is measured by the rate at which innovation renews desire and utility itself equates with usability, that is, the fitness of the thing for consumption. The machine works perfectly as long as we either leave out those things that cannot be turned into waste through use or find ways of absorbing them into the exchange economy. Art, being one of them, is then assigned its discrete corner in the aesthetic sphere where it can experiment with how things could be without actually changing anything, while the entire aesthetic sphere is simultaneously integrated into the economy as an industry for the preservation of the ways things are.

This scenario is not entirely pessimistic. As long as art can assert its autonomy, even within the industrialised aesthetic sphere – as long as it remains genuinely distinct, not just structurally separate from useful production – it can be a good home for 'used' things. It can provide the space where their cultural significance as things rather than exchange commodities can be partially restored. Once their exchange value has been exhausted then they can become a material for artistic transformation, one enriched by the very process of use and exchange.

NT: *I have mentioned Adorno or the Adornean but there are many influences that echo unapologetically in your work, from Marcel Duchamp to Marcel Broodthaers, from Franz Kafka to Kurt Schwitters, from Samuel Beckett to Flusser, from pragmatist politics to concretist poetics. You nominate quotidian materials and ideas and put them* *in the foreground. In many ways you produce echo chambers. Could you talk about the importance of some or all of those echoes and about how you try to do something productive with them rather than pretend to work* sui generis, *as it were?*

PB: Adorno was an admirer of Beckett, as am I. He believed that the play of contradictions in Beckett embodies the absurd truth of the modern world. For me, Beckett means perseverance in the face of inevitable and even deliberate failure. He is a bit like Kafka's protagonists, who insist on their right to take part in hopeless situations. Something similar goes on in Broodthaers – think of his film *La pluie* (1969). They all insist on trying again and again because, rather than despite, there being nowhere to go and nowhere to get to. There is some kind of a positive scepticism in this eternal struggle against the impotence of hope. It is an aspect of European culture that I feel very close to.

These figures and authors, among many others, are my contemporaries. I am conscious of their presence in my life and in my world. They are like people I have met; what I call my world is a fabrication that has come out of those encounters. Lawrence Sterne, for instance: his *Tristram Shandy*, published some 250 years ago, around the time when art became art as we now know it, is for me the ultimate postmodern novel. Or Galileo Galilei. These old men have just as much to tell me about my world as they have to tell us about their own. Or Vladimir Nabokov, an arrogant reactionary genius. You can dismiss him but he will not go away. Even if you do not want to listen, you cannot help overhearing the murmur of his brilliance. They may be voices from the past but life brings them together in one place where their various confrontations and discordant exchanges can never be concluded and therefore remain current, like everything that is open to questioning or still not entirely understood. And the more familiar and the better 'known' it is, the more there is to discover and the closer the attention it warrants. There is an endless amount of it, of course. How we select from this infinity depends on circumstances; and the same circumstances – the choices and accidents that bring us into contact with certain things and not others – are also the source of what we do.

Drawing on such sources in my work is perhaps my way of finding myself and stepping outside of myself at the same time. It makes it possible for me to be uncompromisingly authentic without making any claims for authenticity. It is my world but it is still an external world, the existence of which can be corroborated by many. Art is always an echo of the outside and artists should work with what is around them, from observation, not from introspection. Echo rather than Narcissus should be the artist's proper deity.

I do not believe that there can be original art in the absolute sense of art without a reference and influence. Even Ad Reinhardt's purest 'art-as-art' is a reference to the specific possibilities opened up by the history of painting. It is an observation on the state of culture. It does the same as Robert Rauschenberg's *Erased de Kooning Drawing* (1953).

What is productive about this way of working with echoes is that it potentially brings together conflicting and incompatible perspectives. It creates unreasonable connections, hazardous conditions, slipperiness and slippages, like black ice that makes you skid and swerve just when the road and journey start to feel familiar. (Though this does not quite explain why the alert drivers, the critics and the theorists, so often end up in the worst accidents.)

NT: *Your artistic production has been marked, for better and worse, by significant upheavals in where and how you could or could not choose to make art. You have touched on some of the matters about emigrating, but could you expand upon what it meant for you to focus on making something that we call 'art' as opposed to any other kind of cultural product? Art is a specific field of cultural activity with specific histories, epistemologies and practices, especially if you teach it as the discipline fine art in Europe. And you were a jobbing graphic designer before being an artist seemed a viable career choice, right?*

PB: Graphic design was a good way of making a living. It was never a way of thinking about the world or commenting on it. This was not a creative compromise either, just a different thing. You always get pleasure from doing something that you are good at doing and I was good at it. But eventually, maybe because I was good at it, I got bored and started doing things that I was not good at, like writing. So in that sense, yes, being a designer was a viable career choice at the time.

It was also viable from another perspective. The confidence I had in my skill and craft helped me to find my bearings in my new situation in Cambridge. I could hardly speak English when I arrived here but I had another 'language', typography, and furthermore this 'language' was culturally quite specific. Working as a graphic designer here required being sensitive to sometimes very subtle differences between the design and typographic traditions I had traversed. Coming to understand what those differences were gave me a better insight into where I had arrived than almost anything else.

HISTORIES OF ART

NT: *Conceptual art is a category delineated by art history but often misused as a descriptor for any conceptualist approach to making art. In both of those senses, it is often used to contextualise or even define your work. The history of that movement as well as its legacies, as well as the more basic principle of a conceptualist approach to making art, clearly resonate in what you do and how you do it. You narrate your connection to that tradition through a funny phrase in a 1997 lecture, 'Studio Irrational': you say that your approach to making art was formed, in Prague, by the mistranslation of Conceptual art. Could you expand on the hows and whys of that narrative?*

PB: In a talk that he once gave in Manchester, Joseph Kosuth uttered the words 'Conceptual art', paused and then continued, 'Well, when we did it, they had to invent a new term for it, but now we can just call it art.' This impromptu remark, made in passing in front of an audience of undergraduate art students, was something of a landmark for me. It ended years of confusion by wiping the 'Conceptual' off the slate at a stroke. Kosuth, whose early writings made him the arbiter of what was and what was not Conceptual art, was the right person to break the news that the term had become superfluous. I did not know if I should feel sorry for the young students: they were given a history lesson, clear and authoritative; at their age, I was living through something that was defining my own time and for which the lessons of history were seemingly of no use.

Or should I have felt sorry for my young self in that I did not realise at the time what it was that felt so urgent, what it was that was in my world yet beyond my grasp? It needs to be said, however, that the bewilderment and confusion was not entirely due to the unprecedented forms of art that reached my generation of students in communist Prague in the early 1970s in the shape of various Western publications. The unpredictable whims of censorship complemented by the ostensive disinterest of the authorities also played their parts. We had good reasons to treat with suspicion anything that we could access in art school libraries, but we had no way of knowing if magazines such as *Studio International* or more sporadically *Flash Art*, for instance, had either somehow escaped the censor's vigilance or were actually on the shelves because they were deemed harmless or simply too esoteric to worry about. It is confusing if you cannot at least trust the integrity of censorship. We had information but not much orientation. This, combined with the difficulties posed by the language barrier, geographical distance and restrictions on travel, made us miss the critical and emancipatory point of the changes that were then taking place in Western art. We did not understand the specific cultural conditions that produced those artists and their work, nor the new possibilities for art that those artists and artworks in turn produced in those conditions. What inspired us was not the radical contemporaneity of this new art but, on the contrary, the fact that from our vantage point it did not seem to have any real temporal dimension at all. This seemed to make idea-led art adaptable for our own unchanging times, for the moribund void we lived in, where art had lost its sense of time, as it were, and was not much more than the tradition of applying paint to canvas confined in its own art-historical framework.

Censorship cannot suppress thought. It tries to control thought to suppress action. Even in a culture of general apathy, where most people believed that 'nothing could be done', it was still the thinking that prevented the doing. The new pared-down form of this art, which seemed like something anyone could do in any place at any time, when stripped of its context, seemed to provide the tools to *do* something just for the sake of feeling alive. It was a different art, so we felt that we could do something different with it without having to justify it as a cultural activity, while also having the excuse to claim that our actions were 'only' art. What else could they be? The abstract character of 'art as idea' gave us something like 'ideas for art' – not so much a concept as a conception, fertilisation, initiation – which, paradoxically, could be turned into actions because those ideas were wholly abstract. It was not the proposition but the realisation that mattered. After all, if the magazines were to be believed, those artists in the West were actually *doing* these very ordinary things.

Initially in my mind, 'Conceptual art' was indistinguishable from a whole array of practices that stretch way beyond those enumerated by Lucy Lippard in *Six Years of Dematerialised Art* (1973) or those gathered together by Harald Szeemann in *When Attitudes Become Form* (1969). The range of this art extended to such things as concrete poetry or certain types of performance theatre and experimental music. This was partly because of the printed format in which we encountered all such work – the black-and-white reproductions with obligatory austere, minimalist typography made everything look similar and gave everything an equal status and authority – and partly because you could reduce the work to information. The works were stories and stories could be passed on just by talking around the table in a café. It was not until 1974 when I spent a small fortune on an overpriced bilingual anthology of artists' texts *On Art/Über Kunst*, published by DuMont, a few copies of which unexpectedly appeared in a specialist foreign language bookshop, that I began to understand the singular position of Conceptual art. I struggled to comprehend texts by Sol LeWitt, Art & Language, Douglas Huebler, Kosuth, Lawrence Weiner and a few others, but with the help of a dictionary I eventually deciphered that 'all ideas are art if they are concerned with art and fall within the conventions of art' (LeWitt) and that 'art is the definition of art' (Kosuth). It made me see that art as a pure concept was also a pure ideal. It was not a recipe for action in the absence of an active artistic culture, as we had originally embraced it. Talking about ideas in a cultural vacuum was not enough. I still remember that, from then on, I felt embarrassed whenever the expression 'Conceptual art' cropped up in our café conversations.

NT: *This all bleeds into the long-standing tension of the art–life question. One of the reasons why I am so interested in your work is that we probably both agree with Robert Filliou when he says, 'Art is what makes life more interesting than art.' Right?*

PB: Right. He is as right as Ad Reinhardt was when he said, 'The only thing that needs to be said about art and life is that art is art and life is life…'.

ART EDUCATION

NT: *When you lived in Cambridge you began teaching on Stuart Brisley's strange MA Media programme at the Slade in London. From then on your artistic career was significantly framed by your relationship with British art education. Could you tell us some of your afterthoughts about your time at the Slade?*

PB: The word 'media' in the title of Stuart's course needs quotation marks. The disciplinary identity was only nominal. In reality, it was everything that was not already something else. The work that the students produced was formally and materially just the same as what you would have found in any of the other programmes, anything from performance to texts to films to drawings or objects, except that in all the other programmes a performance would be understood as, say, a form of sculpture, or a film would be seen as a form of painting. In 'media', there were no privileged ways of thinking and there were as many models of practice – and therefore also of teaching – as there were students. Having no positive identity, the course was the Slade's Cinderella and it was treated as such. It certainly felt that we were not an entirely legitimate part of the Slade establishment; rather, that we were tolerated out of respect for a tradition of free-minded benevolence. There was no proper studio and not much in the way of any other dedicated work spaces, save for an airless broom cupboard with a couple of battered Betamax video decks. The only space large enough to accommodate all of us together without too much of a squeeze was the Jeremy Bentham, a pub around the corner.

A few students found various ways of making virtue out of necessity and made those conditions an ingredient in their work, but most went off to do their own thing. Being active outside the institution made them think about their individual interests in different ways than an academic studio practice would have done. The institution itself was a location of social contact, a place to meet and talk before going to the pub to talk some more.

Although it was not really quite like this, at the time it did feel like there were as many visiting students as there were visiting teachers, and what those students brought back with them others could learn from. There is a lot to be said for learning how to work on the move. Since 'doing' art consists of producing things that are not attached to a place or time but have the capacity to exist in the world by themselves, it seems fitting that their makers also acquire that capacity.

NT: *Then your time at Glasgow School of Art put you in a very different context and in a very different role, as Head of Fine Art from 1992 to 1996. Could you reflect for us on that period of your life and, theoretically, what changes it prompted in your thinking about how we do and might teach art?*

PB: My contract at the Slade was less than marginal, a day every alternate week. It made teaching a welcome distraction from the routines of my daily life in the cultural isolation of Cambridge. The job in Glasgow was a full-and-a-half-time commitment. The School had a prominent presence in the life of the city and what was happening in the city had a presence in the life of the School. The students and young artists of early-1990's Glasgow cared about their place, associated with its history and its culture and wanted to contribute to it. They figured out how to assert their belonging to the place without making a fetish of it in their work or letting their work be constrained by it. They also cared about the School and claimed it as theirs. The question of what defined the School was one of constant contention. Contestations and conflicts were part of the daily reality of the School and spilled out into the local art scene and beyond. The School was a forum for a confrontation of ideas as much as a battlefield of petty territorial disputes. It was an exciting place and a difficult one.

I saw it as part of my job to encourage the students' sense of ownership and collective responsibility for what the School could be, so that having something to fight for and something to defend beyond their immediate individual concerns would inform how and what they learned. I tried to create an open environment where anything could be questioned even if only for the sake of debate and speculation. And the biggest question, which for some of the parties and observers concerned the very soul of the School, was how to reconcile the tradition of separate departments that correspond to the traditional concepts of the various visual and plastic arts with the common culture of art and the idea of teaching and learning art as a singular contemporary subject. How, in practical terms, do you teach and learn painting or photography as art while also respecting and preserving the different specialist competencies that are needed for the production of paintings or photographs? How do you make a school of art out of the various arts without either relegating the arts or reproducing an outdated model of art, or without merely adding some discussions about 'art' as an abstract concept to a standard range of 'artistic' skills-based learning?

There are no simple answers to this question, but the commitment and imagination it takes to address it in the concrete conditions of an institution, amongst the competing interests of its diverse constituencies, can make the debate productive in itself. You can learn a lot from scrutinising the values and principles of what and how you are teaching and learning. And I learned a lot from keeping the question in focus.

NT: *Your writings that appear soon after your professorial appointment at Manchester start upon a more diagnostic analysis of the pedagogy of fine art. How did your opinions about art education change in the wake of leaving Glasgow and relocating to Manchester?*

PB: My opinions did not change; my circumstances did. I left Glasgow School of Art after a protracted conflict with the management, the experience and frustration of which gave me little taste for working again in an academic institution in Britain. But the position I was offered Manchester seemed like an opportunity to pursue my interest in art teaching without compromising my values. It is true that the opportunity was slightly hypothetical – to profess, as it were, rather than to do – but that had its merits and suited me fine. Besides, to quote Terry Eagleton from his inaugural lecture at the University of Manchester, 'Let's face it, being a professor is nicer than having a job.'

NT: *One of the national changes that has marked the period through which you have taught fine art is a shift from art colleges to university departments. That shift signifies a different understanding of art's social role and the measures by which we judge art's value, built on a change, at the base, from technical training to academic knowledge production. A focus on the problems this engenders runs throughout many of your writings on art education. Could we, starting with the big conceptual question of knowledge or what it means to know, start to systematise your arguments?*

PB: The question of the effects of the assimilation of art education into universities is more complicated than your question implies. First of all, today's new universities that house most of the fine art programmes are not the same as their traditional counterparts, the old universities. Their aspirations are not the same, their prestige is not the same, their standards are not the same. Secondly, the demise of further education colleges and polytechnics has left a sizeable gap between secondary and tertiary provision. In our field, the tradition of foundation courses, some of which are among the best arenas for art education we have, has been preserved in some measure yet the provision is being broken up. What remains of it is struggling. Thirdly, there are the successive governments' policies on education, which on the one hand make higher education almost a matter of compulsion by cutting welfare support for young people in the hope of reducing or at least disguising unemployment, and on the other, for the same reasons, degrade and effectively discourage education in the arts. Fourthly, even though in this country the refashioning of further education into the generic university model is one specific legacy of Thatcherism, the trend is now pan-European and there is an increasing tendency to synchronise the various national models on the basis of their lowest common denominator, as instituted by the Bologna Process, which was formalised in 1999. Fifthly, the post-1992 transformation of tertiary education in Britain was only the first step toward higher education becoming a corporate industry, the implications of which are huge. I could keep going – this is not the end of the list by any means. There are also, among other things, the effects of new subjects and new qualifications. What does it say about art education when the PhD becomes the highest attainable qualification for artists? And what does it say about its future when the qualification, irrelevant to the profession, then becomes a pre-condition for employment in the same academic industry? Is the schooling that most of today's working artists have no longer sufficient to teach art? Does it not look like the education industry is trying to create a market for its own fancy product, to the detriment of future students?

The label 'students' is becoming an anachronism. They are now fee-paying customers. The effects of this change are perhaps even greater and further-reaching than any of the things I listed above, not least because it dramatically upsets the nature of the contract between the individual, educational institutions and society that is founded upon the right or privilege to study.

Against this background, such philosophical questions as 'what it means to know' can be translated into something more manageable, such as what it means to learn something, what it means to learn how to do something and what it means to learn how to be something. What follows from this are questions like: What can an academic education do for an aspiring artist? How relevant or necessary may it be to get such an education? What does the academic practice contribute to artistic discourse more broadly? And how do all of these changes to our educational complex help to maintain the continuity between the production and reception of art and its teaching?

It is useful to differentiate between knowledge, as something that can be acquired independently by an individual, and know-how, as practical knowledge which can only be passed on through direct human contact. These two concepts then mirror a related pair of concepts: expertise and experience. The relationship between these two pairs of concepts in the current academic environment is different from the relationship they used to be organised into by traditional art colleges. The reasons are cultural and ideological as well as simply technical. The modern university is typically a large corporate organisation and needs clear structures and systems to operate effectively. It has a tendency to impose uniform criteria and norms across generic groupings of disciplines and subjects – such as the sciences, humanities, arts, etc. – and across all qualifications. It prioritises what is quantifiable, comparable, and avoids what cannot be measured. The methods of experimentation, testing and evaluation, designed for and well established in academic subjects are then used, often with only crude modifications, in creative and vocational subjects. One of the misfortunes of fine art education may be that it has been shoehorned into the university system as part of the arts and humanities clusters. We might have been better off next to chemistry. Where the art colleges used to be dominated by empirical know-how, the universities are geared toward the obtaining of academic knowledge, by and large, by independent study and research. The dominant academic form is writing, the dominant mode is theory, the dominant product is information, and the reigning dogma is equivalence.

This new environment for art education promotes, in a new disguise, an obsolete art-educational paradigm. It is a return to an obsession with essential skills and methods and common standards of competence, except that these are no longer specifically artistic. The new methods are not the methods of production but of evaluation; and the new 'study skills', on the whole, serve no other purpose than to help the student through the obstacle course of their university degree.

It has become commonplace in the culture of our institutions to refer to learning as 'experience'. While the idea must have been born in the minds of marketing departments, it is worth thinking about what it may mean. Experience can be a companion term to education but the two are not synonyms. It can also be used to describe the opposite of what can be taught: an event that leaves an impression without necessarily having been understood. Two kinds of experience play a part in art education: Students learn from experience, where the word means a direct contact with the production of artworks, and teachers teach from experience, where it means their practical and pedagogical skills. This kind of experience is the way by which you learn how to do something in a manner that will, over time, make you an expert. But you also learn something just by being alert to what is around you, in a second sense of having an experience of something or somewhere.

Whatever it is that the marketing department means by 'student experience', this latter kind of experience is an anomaly in the academic hierarchy of knowledge and expertise. But in art education it should be as valid as the acquisition of skills or the development of techniques or any kind of instrumental knowledge. The best art education is anti-academic, idiosyncratic, eclectic and discursive. And since there is no longer an identifiable body of knowledge or a universal set of skills that every artist needs, the best pedagogical form is an open dialogue that grounds a way of doing something together without determining *a priori* what that 'something' should be.

NT: *You have vociferously nuanced some determined and counter-fashionable opinions about art education since the early to mid-1990s, introduced here by the 1994 conference paper 'No More '80s!' for example. Those opinions form a pretty coherent critique if not a* *plan. As an art teacher at the opposite point in my career, one of my motives for editing this book now was a want to air that critique and its insights because many of your predictions seem to have become sadly true. But I know that, day in, day out, you still question how and why we teach art like we do. Could you sketch out some of the questions on this subject that you are wrestling with at the moment?*

PB: You used to hear students talking about a piece of work as if that work were a conscious being and they had little choice in what it demanded from them. 'It wants to be bigger', 'it needs more work', 'the blue in that corner needs to be lighter' and so on. The way to work was discovered in the process of making by paying attention to the material in hand as it becomes a piece of work. This discovery also involved the reconciliation of the internal demands of the object you were working on – what it was willing to become – with the external demands posed by the precedents of art – what it has to become to be art. It involved reflection, which is a key component of all learning, as an act of looking back into the common past or history of art, as well as reflexivity.

Now it is more likely that a student will talk about his or her intentions. 'I wanted it big'; and as long as the thing is 'big', something has been achieved, independently, as if the student's will had freed the object from any external considerations. The process that connects the intention and the outcome may still give ample opportunity for speculation ('should it be even bigger?') and reflection ('is it what I wanted?'). You can change your mind at any stage, which then becomes a new departure point, or you may postpone your decisions until you have made up your mind ('I haven't yet decided how big it should be'). In any case, the work is an image of intentionality. The idea that we 'do' rather than 'make' art, that it is an activity rather than production, and the pedagogic changes that have come with this change of principle, have shifted the emphasis from the object to its presentation and then from the presentation of the object to the presentation of the artist's idea or intent. The focus now is on the student-artist-subject who stands beside the object.

There seems to be a widely held assumption that since artists do art, art is whatever artists do. But 'the artist' is not a self-determining identity. The question for education is how you become one; and one half of the answer probably rests in learning how to be a student of art, how you learn to look at art and learn from it, how you can do something that can exist in the world by and for itself. This is not simply a matter of 'placing your work in a theoretical or historical context', as per the current art school parlance, though theoretical understanding and an orientation in history are important. It also demands an instinctive understanding of the resources of art, of the space that your experience of art opens up for you. The other half of the answer may then rest upon learning how to forget about doing art while learning how to do art, how to free your thinking, your perceptions and the endless possibilities of your imagination. How do we teach that? I have no idea.

INDIVIDUATION

NT: *These changes are situated within broader trends of global capitalism. In fact, they are symptoms of those trends, toward ever more pervasive processes and kinds of individuation. High capitalism fosters an era of art production by individuals for individuals. I am going to stretch this point to play devil's advocate, but you have always upheld the idea that art is something that is socially constituted, and that the pressure toward individuation is a flow that some kinds of art working might work against because art can allow people to open up their world(s) in different ways. Can we talk about this?*

PB: Art is not going to cure the problems of global capitalism. It is entangled in it. The most art can do is to assert the autonomy of the artwork itself (and its promiscuity, and its irresponsibility) and resist any pressure on artworks to be enlisted for ideological ends, populism or political correctness. Individuation is the new socialisation. Art can articulate alternatives but it is not in art's power to renew any meaningful forms of social consensus and communal bond or give voice to freedom for the benefit of democracy. Art is non-democratic. A democratic art is a triumph of mediocrity.

Nor is it in the power of art to alter social reality or alter power relations themselves by reflecting or reproducing them. The social function of art as a catalyst of transformation and emancipation involves a paradox: in order to be recognised it needs to be differentiated and stand apart from the concerns of 'real' life, as a figure stands against a ground, yet it has to be integrated into lived experience and real-life relations in order to be realised. There are practices of art that strive to create conditions in which artistic freedom can be (temporarily) extended into social practice by improvising parallel models of educational work, self-organisation and self-sustaining networks or engaged social collaborations. There are others that try to disrupt social inertia and open up the space for imagination by tactical interventions or various forms of what could be called aesthetic disobedience. And there are yet others that, conversely, confront the audience of professional bystanders – curators, critics, theorists, fellow artists – who always surround art's every attempt to engage directly with the social world. But every work of art is an experiment with the purpose of creative freedom. This necessary attribute of every work of art appeals to our individual responsibility to think for ourselves while respecting those who think differently; which, in turn, is the best contribution artists as artists can bring to the debates about who we are or what we can be, what it is like to be human and what it is like to live together.

NT: *One distinctive feature in your writings and interviews, like the 2012 catalogue afterword 'But Is It Life?', is the idea that 'art', as something general that is continually being done and addressed, might be best understood as something like the cumulative value of lots of praxes – that it is, precisely, a collective production…*

PB: Art in the abstract is of course a cumulative historical concept and it is a shared collective construct. Every work of art confirms it, sometimes expands it a little, the greatest works of art challenge it. But the production of those objects is not the production of art. Rather, they are themselves the products of art. What we produce collectively as a culture are the conditions in which a certain kind of essentially solitary aesthetic production can have a certain purpose and meaning, and art is an ever-incomplete realisation of those conditions. Art is an ideal.

NT: *But the most shocking conclusion you draw from all this, in 'Somebody's Got to Do It' for example, simple though it sounds, is that high capitalist Western societies need artists more than they need their art objects – they need artists at work more than the material products made by artists. Could you expand on that?*

PB: As producers, artists are not too different from other leisure or knowledge workers. They follow similar routines and flexible work patterns, their labour fits the shape of deregulated neoliberal capitalism and the imperatives of initiative and 'creativity'; there is a market for the artworks they make and a demand for the entertainment or critique they provide. They use tools often developed for other purposes, their skills may no longer be specifically artistic, and the forms of the things they make may closely resemble other products; their content resembles information and is consumed as such. Seen from such a perspective, the society we live in needs artworks no more and no less than it needs all those other products that consumers have never known they wanted.

But precisely because the operative mode of artistic production parallels other types of enterprise while also being perceived as an activity which is culturally and psychologically exempt from the instrumental relations that bind individuals to society, the artist becomes something of a shadow, a phantom to the social body. This figure, 'the Artist', is not an actual person, the often unexceptional individual, but rather a persona that seems to be the product of a need felt by many to confront those aspects of life that are unaccountable and unrepresentative and that persist among the increasingly synchronised and coordinated interests and functions of the modern society.

Winter, 2014–15

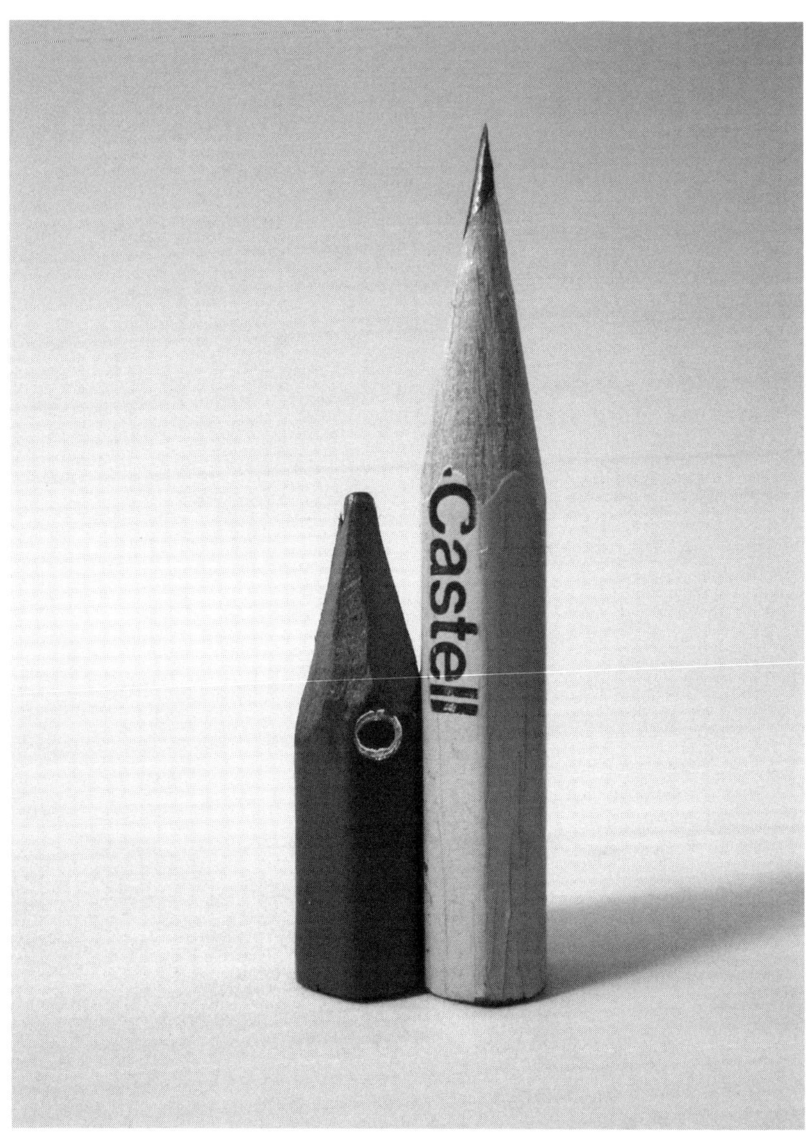

Il Castello, 2007, found pencils, 4.5 x 1 x 0.5 cm

In 2002, a builder working on the Büchlers' house in Manchester abandoned the stub of a blue pencil, not long enough to use anymore and chiselled to a rough blunt tip. A stray white embossed 'o' was the only sign left on the outside lacquer. Five years later, Pavel Büchler sharpened a yellow Faber-Castell pencil to a perfect conical point. The second pencil is just long enough, and plenty sharp enough, to still be put to some use – to be used to inscribe something, to produce an image. The descending, black embossed brand name on the outside lacquer of this tool (that is still a tool, or tool to be tooled, to somehow be put to work) has been shaved away to leave only the last word. The 'Castell' is capitalised as a proper noun yet relieved of its original context; it is nestled in the serrated collar edge between the yellow surface it has always been on (always spoken from) and the new point it has been given (its nearly-new articulacy).

Stood next to each other, read down from right to left, these two half signs montage the pose of a familiar whole: they declare themselves to be a 'Castello' or Castle. And standing together in isolation, elevated as an adjusted readymade, castellated by their shared lines (from their hexagonal shafts to the new image their joined outline creates), and charged by their title, they become a singular castle, *The Castle*. In Franz Kafka's famous novel of the same name, a town castle represents the singular and absolute centre of authority, as a lumpen mass and an allegorical shadow over the local townspeople. Kafka's castle is a castellation of all human power and authority, all human judgment, 'For everything comes from the castle'. It is a model – in bricks and whispers it remodels the concept of a castle as *the castle*, the castle that models those in the shadow of its jurisdiction with a 'clearer meaning than the muddle of everyday life'. It means what it says. And likewise Büchler's sculpture, disguised as a makeshift maquette or half-thought, is actually a reductivist architectural model – a building only in name, only because it clearly tells us so.

The scaling up of significative-ness from material to message performed by *Il Castello* is absurd. The castle is exactly what is in front of us and always infinitely more; indeed, it is too much, just as it is for Kafka's protagonist K. The Castle, in both cases, is a real thing built by men that is and is not exactly what it says, 'only a rambling pile consisting of innumerable small buildings closely packed together'. *Il Castello*'s self-declaration, its auto-authority, calls us in and pushes us away simultaneously, just like Kafka's model castle: 'The street he was in [...] did not lead up to the castle hill; it only made toward it and then, as if deliberately, turned aside'. Such is the paradox of all allegories.

When Franz Kafka died in 1924 he instructed his literary executor, Max Brod, to destroy all of his papers and unfinished manuscripts, including the beginnings of a novel that Brod heavily edited into *Das Schloss*, which was first published in Munich in 1926. In a letter written in September 1922, Kafka told Brod that he was abandoning the project and would never return to it. The published novel was recomposed from leftovers. Presumably Brod, like Büchler, wanted to see how *the* model castle might actually work.

BIBLIOGRAPHY

ARTICLES AND ESSAYS

'The Show', Le Grand Balcon, Sylvie Fortin and Philippe Pirotte (eds), La Biennale de Montréal, Montreal, 2016

'What Makes Art Contemporary', *Oslo Pilot Magazine*, no.1, December 2016

'Frames of Reference', *Luc Tuymans, Glasses*, MAS, Antwerp, 2016, pp.11–14

'Of Time And', *Evangelia Spiliopoulou: Of Time And* (exhibition leaflet), Bury Art Museum, 2013

'A Half-Finished Painting', *Rafal Topolewski* (exhibition leaflet), International 3, Manchester, 2013

'Afterword: But Is It Life?', *Cultural Hijack: Rethinking Intervention*, Ben Parry (ed), Liverpool University Press, 2012, pp.307–13

'Notes from the Bottom of a Bag', *Peep-Hole Sheet*, no.7, Mousse Publishing, Milan, 2011; translated into German as 'Notizen aus den Teifen eines Saks', *Wink*, Kunsthalle Bern, vol.4, no.14, 2011, pp.7–14

'Tenuous Notes: Jeremy Millar', *Exhibitions 2010*, Highland Institute for Contemporary Art, Dalcrombie, Inverness, 2011, pp.9–13

'What to Photograph?', *Source*, no.65, winter 2010, pp.28–29

'Dear Will', *F. R. David: With Love*, no.7, summer 2010, p.134

'Live View', *Philosophy of Photography*, vol.1, no.1, 2010, pp.14–17

'Where Nothing Makes Sense', *Voids*, John Armleder et al. (eds), JRP Ringier, Zurich, 2009, pp.442–45

'For MB', *Impossible Cinema*, Tanya Leighton (ed), Centro Cultural Montehermoso, Vitoria-Gasteiz, 2007, pp.22–23

'A True Story', *Lindsay Seers: Human Camera*, Article Press, UCE, Birmingham, 2007, pp.25–28

'Very Far Away: Vanessa Van Obberghen', *Monographic Projects, 2004–2007*, ed. Philippe Pirotte et al. (eds), objectif_ exhibitions, Antwerp, 2007, pp.38–43

'Between Words', *Breaking the Ice: Contemporary Art from Finland* (exhibition catalogue), Christoph Schreider et al. (eds), Kunstmuseum, Bonn, 2006, pp.156–63

'Whatever Happened to Social Democracy?' (with Charles Esche), *Framework: The Finish Art Review*. no.1, April 2004, pp.125–26; edited version reprinted as 'We Are Not There Yet', *Provisorium*, no.1, January 2005, p.5

'Some Notes on Art as Film As Art', *Saving the Image: Art after Film*, Tanya Leighton and Pavel Büchler (eds), CCA, Glasgow, 2003, pp.42–51

'Off the Peg', *Off the Peg* (exhibition leaflet), Mid Pennine Gallery, Burnley, 2003, n.p.

'Here's How It Works...', *Charles Sandison: Between Heaven and Earth* (exhibition catalogue), Larys Frogier (ed), La Criée centre d'art contemporain, Rennes, 2002; reprinted as 'Things for Words to Do' in *Framework: The Finish Art Review*, no.2, December 2004, pp.64–65

'Somebody's Got to Do It', *Art: What Is It Good For?*, Dolan Cummings (ed), Institute of Ideas and Hodder & Stoughton, London, 2002, pp.21–30

'Little Things in the Margins', *David Bellingham, ASP* (exhibition catalogue), Kunsthaus Nürnberg, 2001, pp.94–97

'The Nordic Sea', *Life Is Good in Manchester*, Simon Grennan (ed), Trice Publications, Manchester, 2001, pp.75–76

'Art School Galleries and Reading Lists: What Are They For?', *READ: Research for Education in Art and Design*, Amanda Wood (ed), Manchester Metropolitan University, no.1, November 2000, pp.27–32

'The Last Resting Place of an Anonymous Citizen', *Ian Rawlinson* (exhibition leaflet), CUBE, Manchester, 2000

'Bureauphilia: A Lost Case', *292: Essays in Visual Culture*, no.1, February 2000, pp.37–48

'Other People's Culture', *Curious: Artists' Research within Expert Culture*, Susan Brind (ed), Visual Arts Projects, Glasgow, 2000, pp.44–47

'Someone Else, Some Place Else, Some Other Time', *Douglas Gordon* (exhibition catalogue), Christine Van Assche (ed), Fundação das Descobertas, Lisbon, 1999, pp.98–108

'Blank Shots', *Ghost Stories: Stray Thoughts on Photography and Film*, Giles Lane and Brandon La Belle (eds), Proboscis, London, 1999, pp.113–17

'Shadow-Catchers', *ibid.*, pp.50–53

'Portrait of LI Brezhnev', *ibid.*, pp.54–56.

'The Freeze', *ibid.*, pp.61–63

'Institutions: Beyond Care', *Morning Star Evening Star* (exhibition catalogue), Max Delany et al. (eds), Australian Centre for Contemporary Art, Melbourne, 1998, pp.16–17

'Stalin's Shoes (Smashed to Pieces)', *DECADEnt*, David Harding and Pavel Büchler (eds), Foulis Press, Glasgow, 1998, pp.26–39; extracts reprinted in *Ghost Transmissions*, David Bussel and Nico Dockx (eds), Cubitt-co-curious, London, 2005, n.p.

'Seeing, Believing and the Matter of Taste', *(Re)visions of Sex*, Alice Angus (ed), Fotofeis, Edinburgh, 1997, pp.15–20

'The art school closes in 1997: imagine its reinvention', *Beck's New Contemporaries '97* (exhibition catalogue), Sacha Craddock et al. (eds), New Contemporaries, Manchester, 1997, p.50

'Bad News', *Variant*, vol.2, no.2, spring 1997, p.3; reprinted in *Generation: 25 Years of Contemporary Art in Scotland: Reader*, Moira Jeffrey (ed), National Galleries of Scotland, Edinburgh, 2014, pp.45–47

'Passing By and Being There', *Sugar Hiccup: Elisabeth Ballet, Sam Samore, Richard Wright* (exhibition catalogue), Charles Esche (ed), Tramway, Glasgow, 1997

'Books as Books', *Book Works: A Partial History and Sourcebook*, Jane Rolo and Ian Hunt (eds), Book Works, London, 1996, pp.13–22

'Fishbowl in the Library', *Patrick Bailey-Maître-Grand* (exhibition catalogue), Patricia Kruth (ed), Sainsbury Centre for Visual Arts, Norwich, 1996, n.p.

'Scotland v Europe, 0–0', *Circa*, no.77, September 1996, supplement, pp.15–16

'The One and the Many: An Introduction', *Random Access 2: Ambient Fears*, Pavel Büchler and Nikos Papastergiadis (eds), Rivers Oram Press, London, 1996, pp.1–8

'Shifting Sands: An essay in two parts', *Desert* (exhibition catalogue), Jim Harold (ed), John Hansard Gallery, Southampton, 1996, pp.11–40*

'Introduction', *Random Access: On Crisis and Its Metaphors*, Pavel Büchler and Nikos Papastergiadis (eds), Rivers Oram Press, London, 1995, pp.1–9

'My Passport with My Photograph', *Fotofeis* (exhibition catalogue), Alasdair Foster et al. (eds), Fotofeis, Edinburgh, 1995, n.p.*

'No More '80s!', *Drawing Fire: Journal of the NAFAE*, vol.1, no.1, December 1994, pp.25–29

'Three Artists from Glasgow', *Creative Camera*, no.325, December 1993, p.15

'A Double-Page Spread', *Creative Camera*, no.321, April/May 1993, pp.51–52

'Image: 1561', *Tim Brennan: Fortress Europe*, Mission Photographique Transmanche, Nord-Pas-de-Calais, 1992, n.p.*

'Framed', *Tracey Moffatt* (exhibition catalogue), Pavel Büchler (ed), Centre for Contemporary Art, Glasgow, May 1992, n.p.*

'Dear Jiří', *JH Kocman: Pure Experiences* (exhibition catalogue), Pavel Büchler (ed), Department of Typography, University of Reading, 1992, n.p.

'Mass of Figures', *Jim Harold: Mass of Figures* (exhibition catalogue), Cambridge Darkroom, Cambridge, 1992, n.p.*

'A "battle for the soul of art"', *Alba*, vol.1, no.3, June/July 1991, pp.18–19

'A Snapshot from Bohemia', *Creative Camera*, no.310, June/July 1991, pp.34–35; reprinted in *Creative Camera: 30 Years of Writing*, David Brittain (ed), Manchester University Press, 2000, pp.199–203

'The End of Words' (with James Lingwood), *Jiří Kolář: The End of Words* (exhibition catalogue), Pavel Büchler and James Lingwood (eds), ICA, London, 1990, pp.7–15

'Words Apart', *Jiří Kolář, Bela Kolářová, Jan Kotík: Three Artists of Czechoslovak Origin* (exhibition catalogue), James Hockey Gallery, Farnham, 1989, n.p.

'Corrected Writings: Not what photography is all about but about what all photography is not', *Creative Camera*, no.10, October 1989, pp.24–28

'Angled Mirrors', *Creative Camera*, no.8/9, August/September 1989, pp.9–11*

'Instead of an Introduction', *Figures* (exhibition catalogue), Pavel Büchler (ed), Cambridge Darkroom, 1987*

'The Pages', *Turning Over the Pages: Some Books in Contemporary Art* (exhibition catalogue), Pavel Büchler (ed), Kettle's Yard, Cambridge, 1986, n.p.

'Boundaries', *Boundaries* (exhibition catalogue), Pavel Büchler (ed), Cambridge Darkroom,1986, pp.4–10

'Multiple Vision', *Multiple Vision: Ron Haselden, Colin McArthur, John Stezaker, Paul Wombell* (exhibition leaflet), Cambridge Darkroom, 1986, n.p.

'Introduction', *Re-Visions: Fringe Interference in British Photography in the 1980s* (exhibition catalogue), Cambridge Darkroom, 1985, pp.3–6

'Night Works', *Night Works: Hannah Collins and Julia James* (exhibition leaflet), Cambridge Darkroom, 1985

EXHIBITION AND BOOK REVIEWS

'Until Death Do Us Part: Thomas Sauvin', *Source*, no.84, autumn 2015, p.64

'A Little Red Book: Cristina de Middel', *Source*, no.79, summer 2014, pp.70–71

'Vojtěch Preissig', *Print Quarterly*, vol.31, no.3, 2014, pp.338–40

'What's the Point?: Mishka Henner', *Source*, no.75, summer 2013, p.58

'That Life: Beat Streuli', *Source*, no.74, spring 2013, p.52

'The Unexplained Explained', *Source*, no.72, autumn 2012, p.72

'Two-Dimensional One-Liners: Rashid Rana', *Source*, no.69, winter 2011, p.66

'A Rebellion without Clues: Diane Bielik', *Source*, no.66, spring 2011, p.37

'Gabriel Orozco', *Source*, no.63, summer 2010, pp.76–77

'Dead Owl aka *Dead Owl*: Roni Horn', *Source*, summer 2009, p.46

'The Making of a Great Story: Miroslav Tichý', *Source*, no.57, winter 2008, pp.72–73

'Human Specimens: Pieter Hugo', *Source*, no.56, Autumn 2008, p.48

'Sian Bonnell: Out of Order', *Portfolio*, no.47, spring 2008, p.30

'All Together Now: Recent Photography from Colombia', *Source*, no.54, spring 2008, pp.52–53

'Dinu Li: Calling Home', *Portfolio*, no.46, winter 2007, p.58

'Out of Focus: The Painting of Modern Life', *Source*, no.53, winter 2007, p.53

'The Author Scavenger: Joachim Schmid', *Source*, no.52, autumn 2007, pp.76–77

'This Morning There Was No New Idea: Maeve Rendle', *Source*, no.51, summer 2007, p.40

'Double Happiness: Philippe Chancel', *Source*, no.50, spring 2007, p.45

'Towards a Philosophy of Photography by Vilém Flusser', *Dpict*, no.5, December 2000, pp.46–47

'Anne Zahalka: Theory Takes a Holiday', *Portfolio*, no.31, June 2000, pp.12–16

'Avoided Objects: Cornelia Parker', *Creative Camera*, February/March 1998, p.36

'The Lost Ark', *Artists Newsletter*, April 1997, n.p.

'John Stezaker: Garden', *Creative Camera*, no.340, June/July 1996, p.40*

'V-Topia: Visions of a Virtual World', *Portfolio Magazine*, no.20, December 1994, p.58*

'Digging It: Stan Douglas at Fotofeis', *Creative Camera*, no.324, October 1993, pp.48–49

'Lost (for) Words: Roger Palmer at Fotohoff, Salzburg', *Creative Camera*, no.317, August 1992, pp.47–48*

'Mass of Figures: Jim Harold at Cambridge Darkroom', *Creative Camera*, no.315, April/May 1992, pp.47–48

'On Reflection: David Ward in Cambridge', *Creative Camera*, no.314, February/March 1992, pp.47–48

'Experience of Recording: Craigie Horsfield at ICA, London', *Creative Camera*, no.313, December 1991, pp.48–49

'Photography Now?', *Creative Camera*, no.6, June 1989, p.39*

'Jannis Kounellis' in 'Personal Choice: A Book of the Year', *Creative Camera*, no.1, January 1988, p.38

'Edwina Fitzpatrick: Between the Lines', *Creative Camera*, no.3, March 1987, p.21*

LECTURES AND TRANSCRIPTS

(Untitled contribution), *Venice Agendas IV, 2005: Neighbours in Dialogure,* William Furlong and Mel Gooding (eds), Wimbledon School of Art, London, 2005, p.110

'Blank Page', *Transmission: Speaking & Listaning,* vol.4, Sharon Kivland, Jaspar Joseph-Lester and Emma Cocker (eds), Site Gallery, Sheffield, 2005, pp.180–94

'Making Nothing Happen: Notes for a Seminar', *Visualizing Anthropology,* Anna Grimshaw and Amanda Ravetz (eds), Intellect, Bristol, 2004, pp.152–67

'Responsibility', *Transmission: Speaking & Listening,* vol.3, Sharon Kivland, Lesley Sanderson and Emma Cocker (eds), Site Gallery, Sheffield, 2004, pp.114–23

(Untitled contribution), *On Communication,* David Osbaldeston (ed), Cornerhouse Publications, Manchester 2004, pp.46–48, 50–51, 57

(Untitled contribution), *International Venice Agendas 2003: A series of three breakfast meetings,* William Furlong and Mel Gooding (eds), Wimbledon School of Art, London, 2003, pp.20–21, 29, 47, 84

'The Blind Train-spotter: A Delirium of Doubt', *Where Is the Photograph?,* David Green (ed), Photoworks, Maidstone and Photoforum, Brighton, 2003, pp.81–91; translated into Spanish as 'El observator de trenes ciego: una duda delirante', *¿Qué Ha sido de la fotografía?,* Editorial Gustavo Gilli, Barcelona, 2007, pp.88–100

'Seeking a Compromise: The poster as alternative engagement in the public domain', *Signs of the Times: Culture, politics and Society in Central and Eastern Europe 1945-2000,* James Aulich and Marta Sylvestrová (eds), Moravian Gallery, Brno, 2003, pp.20–25

'New Academic Art', *Research and the Artist: Considering the Role of the Art School,* Antonia Payne (ed), University of Oxford, 2001, pp.18–26

'The Picture is the Territory', *Writing on Photography (and the Real),* John Leslie (ed), Light House, Wolverhampton, 1999, pp.53–58

(Untitled contribution), *Free Tutorials,* All Horizons Club, Glasgow, 1999, n.p.

'A Brave New World? Research and the future of art education', *Drawing Fire,* vol.2, no.4, summer 1999, pp.32–37

'War of Words', *Point: Journal of CHEAD,* no.7, spring/summer 1999, pp.7–9

'Studio Irrational', *Variant,* vol.2, no.6, supplement

'Can images have the last say?', *9th debate of the Group for Debates In Anthropological Theory,* Peter Wade (ed), University of Manchester, Manchester, 1998

'*Buster's Bedroom*: Rebecca Horn', *Tramline No.4,* Tramway, Glasgow, 1996, n.p.*

'Words in their Natural Setting', *Tramline No.1,* Tramway, Glasgow, 1994; reprinted in part as 'Virtual Confusion', *Conference Handbook: Conference for European Photographers,* Fotofeis 95, The Robert Gordon University, Aberdeen, 1995, n.p.*

'An Image of the Crowd', *The City: Interrogating the Polis,* Liam Kelly (ed), International Association of Art Critics, Dublin, 1995, pp.16–21; revised version reprinted in *Coil,* no.4, February 1997, pp.10–15; reprinted in *Tracing Architecture,* Nicos Giorgiadis (ed), *Architectural Design,* no.132, March 1998, pp.28–29*

INTERVIEWS AND CONVERSATIONS

'Art Is a Discovery: Pavel Büchler' (interview by Isabelle Malz), *The Problem of God* (exhibition catalogue), Isabelle Malz (ed), Kunstsammlung Nordhein-Westfalen, Dusseldorf, 2015, pp.399–401

'Honest Work: Pavel Büchler interviewed by David Briers', *Art Monthly*, no.387, June 2005, pp.1–4

'Doing Art Now: Pavel Büchler and Hester Reeve', *Transmission Annual, Volume IV: Labour, Work, Action*, Michael Corris et al. (eds), Artwords Press, London, 2013, pp.15–19

'Pavel Büchler' (interview by Mark Doyle), *Corridor8*, no.3, Part 4, September 2012, pp.32–41

'Generating New Meanings and New Understandings' (with Sally O'Reilly and Bob and Roberta Smith), *100 Years of Contemporary Art Society: What's Next? Inside Public Collections*, Lucy Byatt and Charlotte Troy (eds), Contemporary Art Society, London, 2011, pp.292–303

'An interview with Pavel Büchler' (by Patrick van Rossem), *Labour in Vain*, Jaroslav Andel (ed), DOX Centre For Contemporary Art, Prague, 2010, pp.96–100

'In Conversation: Pavel Büchler and Seth Sieglaub', *Art Monthly*, no.320, October 2008, pp.4–5

'Pavel Büchler' (interview by John Reardon), *Ch-ch-ch-changes: Artists talk about teaching*, David Molin and John Reardon (eds), Ridinghouse, London, 2009, pp.76–85

'Pavel Büchler in Conversation' (with Henry Meyrick Hughes), *International Triennale of Contemporary Art* (exhibition catalogue), National Gallery, Prague, 2008, pp.198–207

'Pavel Büchler', (interview by Neville Wakefield), *Frieze Art Fair Year Book 2008–9: Frieze Projects*, London, 2008, n.p.

'Conversation: Pavel Büchler, Charles Esche, Philippe Pirotte', *Absentminded-windowgazing* (exhibition catalogue), Esra Sarigedik Öktem (ed), Weenman Publishers, Rotterdam, 2007, pp.156–67

'Hanging Words on the Wall: Charles Sandison in conversation with Pavel Büchler', *Charles Sandison: The Reading Room* (exhibition catalogue), Koldo Mitxelena Kulturnea, San Sebastian, 2006, pp.47–78

'Red Flag on the Cathedral' (interview by Hester Reeve), *The Internationaler*, no.1, September 2005, pp.6–8; edited version reprinted in *Labour in Vain*, Jaroslav Andel (ed), DOX Centre For Contemporary Art, Prague, 2010, pp.30–36

'The Operations Necessary to Solve a Problem: Charles Sandison in an email conversation with Pavel Büchler', *Framework: The Finish Art Review*, no.2, December 2004, pp.66–69

'Word for Word' (with Nick Thurston), *Performance Research: On the Page*, vol.9, no.2, June 2004, pp.55–62

'The Manchester Pavilion' (interview by David Bellingham), *Matters*, no.17, Summer 2003, pp.18–19

'The Tyranny of the Subject: A Conversation with Oded Shimshon', *Oded Shimshon, Spirit Level* (exhibition catalogue), Impressions Gallery, York, 2000, n.p.

'Take it as read: Tristram Shandy' (interview by Ra Page), *City Life*, no.387, September 1999, p.73

'Picture of Nigeria in the Digital Age: A conversation with Owen Logan and Femi Folorunso', *Owen Logan: A Home of Signs and Wonders* (exhibition catalogue), British Council, London, 1998, n.p.

'Pavel Büchler: Interview' (by Mark Durden), *Pavel Büchler* (exhibition leaflet), Portfolio Gallery, Edinburgh, 1997, n.p.

'Signs and Wonders: Conversation with Owen Logan', *Portfolio Magazine*, no.26, December 1997, pp.54–56

'Conversation with Jan Fabre', *Transcript*, vol.3, no.1, Summer 1997, pp.30–37

'Filming Things: Conversation with Hannah Collins', *Portfolio Magazine*, no.25, June 1997, pp.64–66

'Near and Far: Another Conversation with Roger Palmer', *Portfolio Magazine*, no.21, June 1995, pp.51–53

'Interview: Pavel Büchler' (by Anne Barclay Morgan), *Art Papers*, vol.17, no.1, January/February 1993, pp.38–40

'An Epistolary Interview', *Jiří Kolář: The End of Words* (exhibition catalogue), Pavel Büchler and James Lingwood (eds), ICA, London, 1990, pp.65–70; reprinted in part in *The Rhetorical Image*, Milena Kalinovská (ed), New Museum of Contemporary Art, New York, 1991, n.p.

'On the Face of It: In Conversation with Roger Palmer', *Roger Palmer: Precious Metals* (exhibition catalogue), Serpentine Gallery, London and Cambridge Darkroom, Cambridge, 1986

'Talkback: Sharon Kivland and Pavel Büchler', *Creative Camera*, no.6, June 1986, pp.38–39

CZECH-LANGUAGE PUBLICATIONS

'Kroky do neznáma', *Ateliér papír a kniha* (exhibition catalogue), Gina Renotière (ed), Muzeum umění Olomouc, Olomouc, 2016

'Konceptuální paradox', *Kniha jako forma umění*, Julie Kačerovská (ed), FAVU, Brno, 2014, pp.263–82

'O půdě pod nohama' (interview by Karel Haloun), *Revolver Revue*, no.79, 2010, pp.117–132

'Krukám J. H. Kocmana', *Ateliér* , no.4, February 1997, p.4

'Aktuálni rozhovor s Pavlem Büchlerem' (interview by J. H. Kocman), *Ateliér*, no.20, September 1996, p.7

'Mono-Lisa a monetární mony', *Pepča Stejskal hlavou dolů* (exhibition catalogue), Galerie Městského divadla, Brno, 1996, pp.10–12

'Svižně a bez iluzí…' (interview by Karel Fabel), *Umění a řemesla*, no.4, 1990, pp.52–55

'Např.: poslouchejte očima', *Jazz*, vol.9, no.27/28, 1981, pp.100–01

'Psaní o knize', samizdat publication, Prague/Paris, 1980

'S Pavlem Büchlerem o knize jako projektu a knize jako interpretaci' (interview by Petr Rezek), samizdat publication, Prague, 1978

'Umění pro všední den', *Mladý Polygraf*, no.2, SPŠG, Prague, 1972

* Reprinted in *Ghost Stories: Stray Thoughts on Photography and Film*, Giles Lane and Brandon La Belle (eds), Proboscis, London, 1999

Published in 2017 by **Ridinghouse**

46 Lexington Street
London W1F 0LP
United Kingdom
ridinghouse.co.uk

Distributed in the UK and Europe by
Cornerhouse Publications
c/o Home
2 Tony Wilson Place
Manchester M15 4FN
United Kingdom
cornerhousepublications.org

Distributed in the US by
RAM Publications + Distribution, Inc.
2525 Michigan Avenue Building A2
Santa Monica, CA 90404
United States
rampub.com

Copyedited and proofread by Dorothy Feaver
Designed by Marit Münzberg
Printed in Latvia by Tallinna Raamatutrükikoda

ISBN 978 1 909932 31 9

British Library Cataloguing-in-Publication Data: A full catalogue record of this book is available from the British Library